WATERGATE EXPOSED

How the President of the United States and the Watergate Burglars Were Set-up

As told to Douglas Caddy
Original Attorney for the Watergate Seven

ROBERT MERRITT
Top Confidential Informant for the FBI and D.C. Police

Published by:
Trine Day LLC
PO Box 577
Walterville, OR 97489
1-800-556-2012
www.TrineDay.com
publisher@TrineDay.net

Library of Congress Control Number: 2010932354

Caddy, Douglas, and Merritt, Robert
Watergate Exposed: A Confidential Informant Reveals How the President of the United States and the Watergate Burglars Were Set-Up—1st ed.
p. cm. (acid-free paper)
Includes bibliography, references and index.
Epub (ISBN-13) 978-1-936296-35-4 (ISBN-10) 1-936296-35-7
Kindle (ISBN-13) 978-1-936296-36-1 (ISBN-10) 1-936296-36-5
Print (ISBN-13) 978-1-936296-11-8 (ISBN-10) 1-936296-11-X
1. United States—History. 2. United States—Watergate—History. 3. United States—Politics and government—History. 4. United States—Corruption—History. I. Title

FIRST EDITION
10 9 8 7 6 5 4 3 2 1

Printed in the USA
Distribution to the Trade by:
Independent Publishers Group (IPG)
814 North Franklin Street
Chicago, Illinois 60610
312.337.0747
www.ipgbook.com

Before Watergate and Viet Nam, the American public, as a whole, believed everything it was told, and since then it doesn't believe anything, and both of those extremes hurt us because they prevent us from recognizing the truth.

— Daniel Keys Moran

Even Napoleon had his Watergate.

— Yogi Berra

Until we have a better relationship between private performance and the public truth, as was demonstrated with Watergate, we as the public are absolutely right to remain suspicious, contemptuous even, of the secrecy and the misinformation which is the digest of our news.

— John Le Carre

You must pursue this investigation of Watergate even if it leads to the president. I'm innocent. You've got to believe I'm innocent. If you don't, take my job.

— Richard M. Nixon

PUBLISHER'S FOREWORD

An' here I sit so patiently
Waiting to find out what price
You have to pay to get out of
Going through all these things twice.
— Bob Dylan, *Memphis Blues Again*

Will we ever know our true history? What does it mean when our "republic" gets it strings pulled by unelected players? Do the people in the shadows really know better? Are they operating in our country's best interests? How would we know? Does it matter?

I was talking with a local newspaper editor, or more likely haranguing him about not covering TrineDay's books, when the subject of Watergate came up. You could feel the pride of his profession: the system had worked, the fourth estate had taken down the evildoer, the country was saved. I mentioned *Silent Coup* by Len Colodny and Robert Gettlin and Jim Hougan's *Secret Agenda*, and how those accounts of Watergate were different from the one told by Bob Woodward and Carl Bernstein. The alternative scenarios even included a local angle, since the serviceman caught with his hand in Henry Kissinger's briefcase was from Salem, Oregon. Yeoman Radford was spying for the Joint Chiefs ... at least as far as we know.

Cutting me short, the editor told me most reporters and news professionals wouldn't even look at a different view. I gathered this was because the "events" of Watergate were so ingrained in their psyche, their personas — celluloid reality heroes Robert Redford and Dustin Hoffman make great role models. Never mind the facts; feeling good about oneself and one's profession must be worth something.

With *Watergate Exposed*, we are again offered a different view of that historic scandal, and a very rare glimpse into the murky world of a confidential informant(CI). A domain of duress and duty, legality and illegality, pride and regret, tedium and excitement. Many times CIs don't even know whom they are truly working for, or the real objective of the activity they have been asked to perform. In their arena, the ends justify the means.

In the early 1970s, Robert "Butch" Merritt was profiled and then groomed as a CI by Carl Shoffler, the D.C. policeman who arrested the burglars at the Watergate complex on the night of June 17, 1972. Carl was no ordinary beat cop, but had special intelligence training. Before his D.C. police duties, he had worked at the National Security Agency's Vint Hill Farm Station in Virginia, a "listening post" that was generally staffed by members of the Army Security Agency.

Bob Woodward was no ordinary news reporter, As Russ Baker, author of *Family of Secrets* states at whowhatwhy.com: "Bob, top secret Naval officer, gets sent to work in the Nixon White House while still on military duty. Then, with no journalistic credentials to speak of, and with a boost from White House staffers, he lands a job at the *Washington Post*. Not long thereafter he starts to take down Richard Nixon. Meanwhile, Woodward's military bosses are running a spy ring inside the White House that is monitoring Nixon and Kissinger's secret negotiations with America's enemies (China, Soviet Union, etc), stealing documents and funneling them back to the Joint Chiefs of Staff."

A few short years later, had Charles Manson follower Lynette "Squeaky" Fromme or FBI informant Sarah J. Moore been better shots, President Leslie L. King, Jr. (aka Gerald R. Ford, Jr.), our country's first appointed president, might have been assassinated and Nelson Rockefeller then would have fulfilled his quest to become President of the United States. Ah, the vagaries of life.

I was not a political supporter of Richard Nixon, but I do support our Republic, and any attack upon Lady Liberty puts us all at risk Then there is something called "history." As George Santayana put it, "History is always written wrong, and so always needs to be rewritten."

With *Watergate Exposed,* history is being rewritten, or at least an account from a different vantage point is being told. Is it the truth? This may be difficult to judge. For the shadows are secretive and duplicitous, and memories get clouded with time.But you'll never find the truth if you don't look.

Here is direct testimony that challenges the official dogma, and *is* validated on many points in hundreds of pages at the National Archives. Will we listen? Does it matter? Time and history ... may tell.

Onward to the Utmost of Futures!

Peace,
Kris Millegan
Publisher
TrineDay
October 2, 2010

Robert Merritt is a Confidential Informant for the New York Police Department Intelligence Division. As a CI, he has also worked for the Washington, D.C. Metropolitan Police Department, FBI, U.S. Secret Service, U.S. Marshal Service, ATF, Manhattan District Attorney, and the U.S. Attorney for New York City.

Douglas Caddy, an attorney in Houston, is a member of the Texas and District of Columbia Bars and the author of five books. His biography appears in *Who's Who in American Law, Who's Who in America* and *Who's Who in the World.*

ACKNOWLEDGMENTS

Robert Merritt and Douglas Caddy wish to express their appreciation to the following persons, each of whom did something that made publication of our book possible:

Donald O. Graul, Jr., Executive Director, American Independent Writers, Inc.; Charles M. Klein; Will O'Bryan, Managing Editor, *Washington Metro Weekly*; Matthew Fulgham, Assistant Director, U.S. National Archives; William H. Davis, Archivist, U.S. National Archives; David Paynter, U.S. National Archives; Gregory Cumming, Supervisory Archivist, U.S. National Archives; John Simkin, Historian, United Kingdom; Brett Zongker, reporter, Associated Press; Frances D'Antuono, Esq.; Deacon MacCubbin, Lamba Rising; Antonio Williams, New York City; Ray Hill, Houston; Eben Rey with Los Angeles radio station KPFK 90.7 FM, Joyce Riley, The Power Hour.

The Daily Rag

vol 2 no 1
oct 5-12, 1973
washington, dc
circulation 35,000

free!

an exclusive interview

FBI Informer Confesses

With the disclosure of Robert Merritt's role as an FBI and Metropolitan Police informer, the reality of police surveillance of active community groups and illegal police activity in the District is confirmed. Such groups as the DC Statehood Party, RAP, Common Cause, Off Our Backs, the American Civil Liberties Union and the Gay Activists Alliance have been under surveillance. While the information Merritt provides on widespread police intelligence is substantial, it leaves open many questions as to what else is going on. For this reason, the open letter printed below is submitted to the local and congressional officials responsible for authorizing police actions. Citizens have a right to full disclosure of illegal police activity in the District of Columbia. Groups, organizations or individuals who may be interested in forming a coalition to deal with the issues raised here should contact the Daily Rag.

An open letter Mayor Washington, the DC Council, Sen. Bayh, Sen. Eagleton, Del. Fauntroy, Rep. Natcher, Rep. Diggs

1. Exactly how many community-active groups have been under surveillance? And what is the extent of recordkeeping on these groups?

2. What qualifies a group for surveillance?

3. Who authorizes such surveillance?

4. What regulations or departmental policies cover the use of surveillance, agents-provocateurs and the gathering of political intelligence.

5. How many tax dollars are allocated to the DC Police and their agents for gathering political intelligence.

6. How many members of the Metropolitan Police have been used for political intelligence work from 1969 to the present?

7. What are the formal and informal relationships between the Metropolitan Police, FBI, Justice Department, Internal Revenue Service, Secr... mission and other federal law enforcement and intelligence gathering agencies.

My real name is Earl Robert Merritt, Jr. I worked for the MPDC Intelligence, the AFTD [Alcohol, Firearms and Tobacco Division, Department of Treasury], and the local field office of the FBI from April 1971 until, officially, June 1972. Then I worked off and on, being used through friendship by Detective Dixie Gilden 'til April 1973.

Talk a little about your motivations on getting into this thing.

The day before Sgt. Schoffler came into my apartment to proposition me, I had just lost my job at Southern Drug Co, in which Schoffler was heavily involved. He had had several conversations with my boss at work prior to my being terminated. The day after I was terminated, he came to my apartment and asked if I would go to work for Police Department Intelligence.

He told me it was full time; that it would be something I could do for my country; that it would pull me out of the financial situation he knew I was in....He said that the only qualification he knew was that the person had to be gay.

Did they threaten you or did you have any reason to feel frightened at that time?

I don't recall any threats...except that I had met Schoffler in the spring, he was around Dupont Circle, undercover. I had come in contact with him almost daily. I had no idea that he was a tac officer or that he was a police officer-period.

There were several things which I had confided in him under what I assumed to be the trust of friendship, a matter of some checks in West Virginia. If he wanted to dig into those matters, it could perhaps have resulted in some type of an arrest.

Who is Dixie Gilden?

She is a detective in Intelligence, referred to as Officer Gilden. She picked up me as her source at my request in August or September 1971. Later she was transferred to uniform and later to scooter division, first district.

Were you close to her at that time?

Yes.

Who was Carl Schoffler?

Schoffler was a tac officer at the second precinct, later he was promoted to detective, and I understand he was transferred in March or April of this year to Intelligence, what he called criminal intelligence.

When did you first become disillusioned with the type of work that you were doing?

Not until I saw the mass arrests that were ordered by Jerry Wilson [Mayday, 1971], and the type of brutality that I had always heard about on the TV or radio. But it was the first time I witnessed it and knew that it actually existed. At this time I started feeling a disgust for what I was doing.

I started evaluating everybody around, not just the police, but the people, the different organizations, who they were representing, what they were representing, what they were. The more I did this, the more I became disgusted with the police.

I questioned the functioning of the metropolitan police intelligence division, period. They said their division existed because they handled local, and they tried to emphasize only local affairs.

Was this true in your experience?

No, because when the assignment for IPS [The Institute for Policy Studies, a radical think-tank] came on, and even before, I came up with different organizations that were in nothing but national, even international, affairs. The police showed an interest in all of these things.

.... you?

Yes, particularly with IPS. I asked them what they did with the stuff that did not concern them locally and they said that other people were very interested in it.

continued on page 6

Robert Merritt's first published public disclosure, October 5, 1973.

Author's Foreword

Why is Robert Merritt telling his complete story now? It is a natural question to ask. After all, it is 38 years after the Watergate scandal broke open, so why the long delay?

There is no single answer. There are many. First and foremost is that Merritt would have been killed if he attempted to reveal all he knew of the origins of Watergate while Washington, D.C. police detective Carl Shoffler, the officer who arrested the burglars, was alive. It is that simple. Shoffler, to whom Merritt confided his prior knowledge of the planned break-in at Watergate two weeks before it happened, also recognized his own life was on the line. As recounted by Jim Hougan in his 1984 best-seller, *Secret Agenda: Watergate, Deep Throat and the CIA*, Shoffler told Captain Edmund Chung, his former commanding officer at the National Security Agency's Vint Hill Farm Station, that if Shoffler "ever made the whole story public, 'his life wouldn't be worth a nickel.'"

After the Watergate arrests and ensuing controversy, Shoffler went to great lengths on many occasions to impress upon Merritt the necessity to remain quiet. In the two years before Watergate, Shoffler and the FBI had directed Merritt as a Confidential Informant to commit hundreds of crimes, all done in the name of "national security." Shoffler threatened Merritt that, on the basis these crimes alone, both of them could be prosecuted and imprisoned, as would certain FBI officials and agents.

Another factor was Merritt's open homosexuality. Watergate occurred only three years after the Stonewall riot, which marked the beginning of the gay rights movement. Homophobia still reigned supreme. Shoffler told Merritt that his homosexuality would be used to discredit him and to railroad him into incarceration. Indeed, as Merritt prepared to enter the building to testify in executive session before the Senate Watergate Committee, a Democratic committee staff member, Wayne Bishop, stopped and told him his credibility was zero because he was a homosexual and threatened that if he told what he knew about the origins of Watergate, he would be immediately thrown into the U.S. Capitol Building's jail.

Even the Republican in the White House, Richard Nixon, whose presidency could have been saved had Merritt disclosed what he knew, railed at the time against homosexuals. As revealed in a new book by Mark Feldstein, *Poisoning the Press*, Nixon wanted so badly to discredit, or even prosecute, newspaper columnist Jack Anderson that he contemplated an investigation to see if Anderson was a homosexual, even though Anderson was married and had nine children. Nixon Aide H.R. Haldeman is quoted on a tape of an Oval Office meeting with the president as asking, "Do we have anything on [Anderson aide Brit] Hume?... It'd be great if we could get him on a homosexual thing." In support of the witchhunt, another top aide, Charles Colson, ignorantly chimed in, "He sure looks it."

So the overt and widespread hatred of gays during this period was a key factor in Merritt's decision to keep quiet. He only had to look at what happened to me to see what fate might lay waiting for him. In the first month of the Watergate case, Chief Judge John Sirica falsely accused me of being a "principal" in the Watergate break-in crime. Sirica then held me, as attorney for the seven defendants, in contempt of court and ordered me jailed after I asserted the attorney-client privilege and Sixth Amendment right to counsel in behalf of my clients.

Sirica's vicious homophobia was matched only by the judges of the U.S. Court of Appeals for the District of Columbia Circuit, who upheld his contempt citation of me in a gratuitously insulting decision. This unreported segment of Watergate – how these prejudiced judges attempted to set me up and destroy my legal career because I was gay – is told in my Epilogue to this book. They ultimately failed because there was not one scintilla of evidence that I was involved, which is why I was never indicted, named an unindicted conspirator, disciplined by the bar or even interviewed by the Senate Watergate Committee.

Despite the pressure to keep him quiet, Merritt on a number of occasions came close to disclosing what he knew about the prior knowledge of Shoffler and certain agents of the intelligence community of the planned break-in. This is covered in Chapter 6, "A Series of Missed Opportunities: How Watergate Might Have Turned Out Differently." In each instance, for one justifiable reason or another, Merritt decided that the best strategy was to lie low about his total involvement: remain quiet about all that he knew.

From 1985 to 2000, Merritt was a "fugitive from justice," as he recounts in his story, even though during this period Shoffler continued to direct his activities from afar while the former worked closely as a Confidential Informant with law enforcement agencies in New York that were unaware of his wanted status. As a fugitive, Merritt's goal was not to get caught. Talking publicly about what he knew about Watergate was out of the question.

In 1996 Shoffler died. After 2000, when the Government dismissed the criminal case against him, Merritt could give his full attention to disclosing the untold story of Watergate's origins. He began to collect documents and information that would support his story, an effort that took years. Even so, the FBI has steadfastly refused to release over 300 documents from its files on Merritt requested under the Freedom of Information Act, documents that could contribute mightily to understanding what occurred.

In May 2008, Merritt contacted me to ask if I would help him write a book about what he knew. I agreed to do so. About the same time doctors who had been treating him for serious medical conditions told him that he had only three to four years to live. This knowledge spurred him to concentrate on getting his book finished. Even as I write this, I have learned that Merritt's doctors told him within the last week that he likely has three to four months to live due to advanced cancer of the spine. They set the outmost date as Valentine's Day 2011.

So this book is being rushed into print in order that Merritt can publicly answer questions that might arise while he is still capable of doing so. In a sense his story is a "deathbed confession," as his only desire at this point in time is that the historical truth about Watergate be told fully and accurately.

Douglas Caddy
Attorney
Houston, Texas
September 19, 2010

TABLE OF CONTENTS

SELECTED MEDIA COVERAGE OF ROBERT MERRITT

- **"Revelations of a Gay Informant"** by Sasha Gregory-Lewis, *The Advocate*, February 23, 1977 and March 9, 1977: "After Mayday [1971], police used Merritt for what appears to have been a crash course on homosexuality and gay liberation. 'The police were very disturbed,' Merritt says, 'about the fact that gay people weren't stereotyped anymore. They were mad about it. They said they couldn't recognize them any more.'"

- **"Informants for Police Exposed"** by Paul Valentine, *Washington Post*, October 7, 1973: "Merritt was quoted in The [Daily] Rag as saying he later did informant work for the FBI. FBI press spokesman Jack Herrington would not comment on that claim, but another source confirmed that Merritt performed 'voluntary' work for the agency and may have been paid for it."

- **"Informant Tried to Spy on Kennedy"** by Columnist Jack Anderson, *Washington Post*, October 23, 1973: "Washington police attempted to plant an informant in the household of Ethel Kennedy, widow of Sen. Robert Kennedy (D.-N.Y.) in 1971. The informant, E. Robert Merritt, Jr., committed burglaries and other dirty deeds for the police and the FBI. Confidential FBI files say of him: 'Nothing has developed ...to indicate that the informant has furnished other than reliable information.'"

- **"Informers Spied on D.C. Activists"** by Jarod Stout and Toni House, *Washington Star-News*, October 7, 1973: "Police confirmed that Robert E. Merritt, 28, and Ann Kolego, 20, have been police intelligence informants, but they and the FBI would not give details of the undercover work."

- **"FBI Informer Confesses,"** *The Daily Rag*, October 5-12, 1973: "With the disclosure of Robert Merritt's role as an FBI and Metropolitan Police informer, the reality of police surveillance of active community groups and illegal police activities in the District is confirmed. Such groups as the D.C. Statehood Party, RAP, Common Cause, Off Our Backs, the American Civil Liberties Union and the Gay Activists Alliance have been under surveillance. While the information Merritt provides on widespread police intelligence is substantial, it leaves open many questions as to what else is going on."

- *"Two Lift Curtain on Undercover Work"* by Paul W. Valentine, *Washington Post*, November 26, 1973: "Merritt said he also engaged in disruption and sabotage during street demonstrations. The actions included giving protesters false information about places and yanking the wires and tubes from two sound systems in West Potomac Park in early May 1971. Such is the varied life of the political informant."

- **"Behavior of Informers Employed by FBI, Other Agencies Disturbs Some Critics"** by Stanley Penn, *Wall Street Journal*, March 23, 1976: "Earl Robert Merritt stole mail from a prestigious Washington research institution. Robert Hardy taught anti-war activists how to burglarize buildings. Sara Jane Moore tried to kill the President of the United States. These people had similar sidelines. At one time or another each worked for the Federal Bureau of Investigation."

- *The American Police State* by David Wise, (Random House, 1976): "Some of the information had been provided [to Institute for Policy Studies attorney Mitchell Rogovin] by Robert Merritt, who told Rogovin that under the name of Robert Chandler he had worked for many months as an informant for the intelligence unit of the Metropolitan Police Department, and later for agents Terry O'Connor and William Tucker of the FBI."

- *Protectors of Privilege: Red Squads and Police Repression in Urban America* by Frank Donner, University of California Press (1990/1991):
"Merritt collected information relating to planned demonstrations at the Democratic and Republican conventions in Miami, and since he was a homosexual he was also assigned to spy on the gay community and cultivate radicals believed to be homosexuals. In June 1972, shortly after the Watergate break-in, MPD officers tried to induce Merritt to 'get close' to the lawyer for the Watergate burglars, a rumored homosexual 'associated with communist causes' and to develop a sexual relationship with him.... After Merritt surfaced in the fall of

1972, he gave extraordinary detailed accounts of his four-year career as a spy based on files he had kept."

- **"The User Who Got Used"** by J. A. Lobbia, *Village Voice*, September 9, 1999: "For years Tony Merritt did the dirty work for cops and landlords, helping them bust and evict drug dealers. So why is the Times Square Hotel, his latest home, showing him the door?"

- **"Inside Man Profile"** by Will O'Bryan, *Washington Metro Weekly*, March 13, 2008: "Butch Merritt was a leading spy in America's homegrown cold war against homosexuals."

- **"Watergate's Strange Bedfellows"** by Will O'Bryan, *Washington Metro Weekly*, April 15, 2010: "Community infiltrator Butch Merritt joins gay Watergate attorney Douglas Caddy for timely Watergate expose."

Special Note from Douglas Caddy

Readers of this book will find that there is redundancy in some sections with certain events being described a second time. This came about for several reasons. The first is that Robert Merritt told me his story over an eighteen month period and his repeating of some events was unavoidable. The second is that both Merritt and I during the writing of the book were targeted for abuse by powerful elements that did not want the book to see the light of day. On one occasion burglars broke into Merritt's apartment in the Bronx when he was away and destroyed his computer and printer, while not taking anything of value. Also, two persons with whom Merritt is acquainted told him on separate occasions that they had seen a letter from the U.S. Department of Justice to local agencies directing that steps be taken to hinder the publication of this book. Furthermore, both Merritt and I were regularly subjected to "spoofing" phone calls, a technique routinely engaged in by U.S. intelligence agencies.

To assure that Merritt's story would be told publicly in the event that publication of the book was prevented, I occasionally posted key parts of it on the Watergate Topic of the Education Forum, which operates under the direction of the noted historian John Simkin in the U.K. Some of what was posted, including two affidavits by Merritt, was subsequently incorporated directly into the book's final contents, resulting in some redundancy.

Both Merritt and I recognize that *Watergate Exposed* raises as many questions as it provides answers. It is our hope that historians and other interested parties will attempt to find the answers to these questions. Future disclosure of relevant files will go far towards clearing up the mystery. Two files that need to be disclosed fully are the U.S. Government and Washington, D.C. Metropolitan Police Department (MPD) files on Carl Shoffler and on Robert Merritt. Merritt obtained over 400 documents from the FBI under the Freedom of Information Act (FOIA) but almost everything in these was redacted. Persons and organizations who were targeted by the FBI and MPD, such as those named in third appendix in this book, are encouraged to use the FOIA to find out what is contained in their files. They may be surprised at what they learn, much as I was when I first read about myself in the Watergate Special Prosecution Force interviews of Merritt and Shoffler over three decades after they were written. *Watergate Exposed* is like a ticking time bomb in the sense that no one knows what documents and recollections will come flooding out in the wake of its publication.

February 1973: Watergate defendent G. Gordon Liddy and Douglas Caddy.
Photo: AP

PROLOGUE

By Douglas Caddy

Robert Merritt entered my life three days after the Watergate arrests of June 17, 1972, although I was not aware of this at the time. It was only in 1977 – five years later – when I read an interview with him in the national gay publication, *The Advocate*, that I first learned he had been recruited by the Washington, D.C. Police and the FBI to establish an intimate relationship with me. This effort occurred when I was the attorney for the Watergate defendants, although the defendants themselves and the general public were unaware at the time of my gay sexual orientation. On four occasions – twice in June 1972, an one in July 1972 and in March 1973 – law enforcement agents attempted to enlist Merritt in establishing a sexual liaison with me, offering him tens of thousands of dollars if he were to agree to do so. On one of the occasions in June 1972, a Washington, D.C. Metropolitan Police Officer accompanied by four intelligence agents asked Merritt to enter into a conspiracy to assassinate me because they feared I had obtained vital secrets of CIA activities and because I was a homosexual. As a gay person himself, Merritt was repulsed by these overtures to entice confidential legal information from me and rejected them outright on all occasions. Hence no relationship of any type was ever established, that is until May 2008 when Merritt telephoned to ask that I help him write the story of his life.

Merritt was the lowest man on the Watergate totem pole. Yet he is the most important in solving the mystery surrounding the circumstances that led to the arrests on June 17, 1972, primarily because of his unique relationship with Carl Shoffler, the Washington D.C. police detective who made the arrests. Dozens of books have been written about the scandal but only one author ever attempted to describe Merritt's role, and he deserves well-earned praise for doing so, even though he failed in his efforts to contact Merritt or interview him. He is Jim Hougan, author of the 1984 bestseller *Secret Agenda: Watergate, Deep Throat and the CIA.*

It would be exceedingly difficult to pass judgment on Merritt's revelations about Watergate as told in the chapters that follow without first reading what Hougan wrote over two and a half decades ago. The following excerpts can be found on pages 320-323 in his volume:

> Among those who are skeptical of the Ervin committee's investigation of the Watergate affair, there is a school of thought that holds that some Washington police knew in advance that the June 16-17 break-in was about to occur. In particular, skeptics as politically disparate as H.R. Haldeman and Carl Oglesby point the finger of suspicion at arresting officer, Carl Shoffler.
>
> The evidence cited by Oglesby and others is circumstantial, but not inconsiderable; and further investigation will yield even more information tending to bolster their suspicions. For example: the skeptics point out that Shoffler, injured on duty some months before, was assigned to desk work on the evening of June 16. They note that his shift ended at 10:00 P.M., and yet he voluntarily undertook a second shift, joining a plainclothes tactical unit cruising the streets in the early morning hours. The skeptics' suspicions are further aggravated by the fact that, contrary to police procedure, it was junior officer Shoffler (rather than Sergeant Paul Leeper) who responded to the dispatcher's call for assistance at the Watergate. Finally, the skeptics' theory is augmented by the fact that when the dispatcher's call came, Shoffler and his fellow officers were parked only a block or two from the Watergate, as if they were awaiting the dispatcher's summons.
>
> As evidence of a conspiracy involving Shoffler and the police, these facts are hardly conclusive. Further investigation, however, unearths even more reasons to wonder about Shoffer's role. For example, June 17 was Shoffler's birthday. The relevance of that coincidence has to do with the fact that Shoffler's wife and children had gone to Pennsylvania on the afternoon of June 16, intending to spend the weekend at Shoffler's parents' home. Shoffler himself was to join them on the seventeenth, driving up

from Washington to celebrate his birthday with Mom and Dad, the wife and kids. Given the long ride in front of him, it seems odd that he chose to work a second shift on that particular night.

Suspicion of Shoffler can only be heightened when we learn that the police officer deliberately changed Watergate guard Frank Will's statement to reflect a nonconspiratorial interpretation of events. As we have seen, Shoffler acknowledges his misquotation of the Watergate guard, saying that he changed Wills' statement because the timing 'did not make sense.' Which, indeed, it did not unless the break-in was sabotaged from within, in which case Wills' statement makes perfect sense.

Adding to the suspicions surrounding Shoffler is the fact that he is no ordinary cop. Prior to joining the police department in Washington, he had served for years at the Vint Hill Farm Station in Virginia. This is one of the NSA's most important domestic 'listening posts.' Staffed by personnel assigned to the Army Security Agency (ASA), Vint Hill Farm is thought to be responsible for intercepting communications traffic emanating from Washington's Embassy Row. By itself, this proves nothing, but it is ironic that the police officer responsible for making the most important IOC (Interception of Communications) bust in American history should himself have worked in the same area only a few years earlier.

Shoffler's work at Vint Hill Farm was mentioned in passing in the staff interviews of the Ervin Committee. This occurred as a result of an allegation against Shoffler that was made by his former commanding officer at Vint Hill Farm, Captain Edmund Chung. According to Captain Chung, he had occasion to dine with Shoffler in the aftermath of the Watergate arrests. Chung claimed that Shoffler told him the arrests were the result of a tip-off, that [Alfred] Baldwin and Shoffler had been in contact with each other prior to the last break-in, and that if Shoffler ever made the whole story public, 'his life wouldn't worth a nickel.'

****

The mysteries surrounding Shoffler are peculiar in the extreme, and none more so than the allegations made by one of Shoffler's former informants, Robert 'Butch' Merritt. A homosexual, Merritt was employed by the police and the FBI in spying on the New Left, a task that ultimately led to his infiltration of the Institute for Policy Studies (IPS), a bete noire of America's right wing. According to Merritt, Shoffler approached him sometime after

June 16, 1972, and asked him to undertake a bizarre assignment. If we are to believe the disaffected informant, Shoffler told him to establish a homosexual relationship with Douglas Caddy, stating falsely that Caddy was gay and a supporter of Communist causes. In fact, Caddy was about as conservative as they come, and there was no reason to suspect that he was anything but heterosexual. Indeed, testimony as to the conservatism of his politics was received by the Senate [in its Korean Influence Inquiry] during its 1978 questioning of Tong Sun Park, Caddy's former roommate at Georgetown University.

Sen. Weicker: "Who is Douglas Caddy?"

Tong Sun Park: "Douglas Caddy was... not only my roommate, but also treasurer of the class and, I believe, that he was Executive Director of Young Americans for Freedom... [He] was someone that I spent a lot of time with. So when I came to Georgetown, my exposure to the American politics was first to the conservative movement."

Predictably, perhaps, Shoffler ridicules Merritt's accusation, calling it absurd. One can only agree with the police detective, and yet, where Merritt is concerned there appears to have been more going on than met the eye. To begin with, Merritt's place of residence was above a pornography store at the corner of Columbia Road and Eighteenth Street. The proprietor of the store, whose tenant Merritt was, was a notorious Washington pimp named Buster Riggin. Riggin was credited by the police with having brokered the division-of-labor agreement (day shift/ night shift) between Columbia Plaza madam Lil Lori and Helen Henderson; reportedly, Riggin split a 40 percent commission on each trick.

In an apparent coincidence, *Washington Post* reporter Carl Bernstein was an acquaintance of Riggin's, and a sometime visitor to the pimp's porn parlor. Years later, word of Bernstein's friendship with Riggin would cause the *Washington Post* enough concern that the then metro editor Bob Woodward would assign *Post* reporter Tim Robinson to 'investigate Bernstein's sex life.' That, at least was Robinson's understanding of the unpleasant task, which he said was predicated upon fears that Riggin might somehow have compromised Bernstein in the past. Robinson says that he hated the investigation. Nevertheless, he confirmed Bernstein's friendship with Riggin, and found that Riggin had made presents of pornographic material to the Watergate hero. Robinson could not determine, however, whether Bernstein was burglars up in a form of entrapment. The Watergate scandal thus began and ultimately forced the resignation of President Nixon.

Shoffler came to my apartment in Washington, D.C. late in the morning of the day of the events at Watergate and exulted in having made the arrests. He told me that he had secretly telephoned the *Washington Post* soon after the arrests to tip the newspaper off to what had occurred. He then demanded his special birthday present from me, which I was only too happy to perform.

[*First meeting*] Three days later, on June 20, 1972, Shoffler showed up at my apartment with his supervisor, Police Sgt. Paul Leeper. They asked me if I knew someone by the name of Douglas Caddy, who lived at the Georgetown House, a high-rise apartment, at 2121 P St., N. W., which was directly across the street from my apartment. They told me Douglas Caddy was an attorney who was representing the Watergate burglars and that Douglas Caddy was a communist and pro-Cuban and was a leader of the Young Americans for Freedom.

They wanted me to establish a sexual relationship with Douglas Caddy to find out how Douglas Caddy knew to show up for the arraignment of the burglars after their arrest. They asserted that Douglas Caddy had to be in on the conspiracy with the burglars and that in the past he had been shadowed when he frequented a leather-Levi gay bar in Greenwich Village in Manhattan.

Shoffler and Leeper related that Douglas Caddy had been working as a White House attorney in a sensitive position. They claimed that I was butch enough to entice Douglas Caddy, a masculine gay guy, into a sexual affair to obtain the information they wanted. They told me that this was the most important thing that I could do for my country and that I would be well-paid if I undertook the assignment. Their initial offer was $10,000.

I asked Shoffler about who it was that so desperately wanted this information from Douglas Caddy and he said that it was from very high up sources in the Department of Justice and the U. S. Attorney's office.

I did not commit to doing the assignment.

Two days later, on June 22, 1972, which was my birthday, Shoffler came to my apartment to give me my birthday present. He spent the entire day with me. Afterwards, when we were relaxing in bed, he gently tried to persuade me to cooperate with him and Leeper regarding the Douglas Caddy assignment. I emphatically told him *"No."* I didn't know Douglas Caddy and I didn't know how to get to know him and I was bothered that undertaking the assignment could lead to the destruction of another gay person who apparently was still in the closet and merely attempting to represent his clients.

We talked about the break-in and Shoffler told me straight out that the burglars were hired indirectly by one of the 100 families of America, which Shoffler named as the Kennedy Family.

Shoffler said, "The intention of the Watergate break-in was to destroy the Nixon presidency. President Nixon was guilty of nothing in its planning."

Shoffler said that there were hidden motivations involved, such as the fear of law enforcement agencies that their turf would be reduced by President Nixon through a scheme known as the Houston Plan, the CIA's concern that President Nixon planned to reorganize the intelligence agencies and their operations, and the Defense Department's opposition to Nixon's new China policy.

I asked Shoffler if he was angry at me for refusing to take the Caddy assignment and he smiled at me and said he was glad that I didn't.

[*Third meeting*] In the March 1973, nine months after the initial overture and a month after the first Watergate trial ended, I met with Shoffler and Leeper, FBI agents Terry O'Connor and Bill Tucker and their FBI Agent-In-Charge, whose name escapes me. Leeper did most of the talking. He again tried to persuade me to take on the Douglas Caddy assignment, making an initial offer of $25,000. I refused outright. The group then said that I could be paid as much as $100,000 if I took the assignment but I still refused without providing any explanation. Once it was understood that I would not accept the offer, Leeper declared that the least I could do was to spread the rumor around Washington, D. C. that Douglas Caddy was gay in an effort to force him to come out of the closet. Their intention was to defame Douglas Caddy. This was the last attempt to persuade me to take the Douglas Caddy assignment. The group departed angrily, with the exception of Shoffler, who secretly winked at me as he went out the door.

DISCLOSURE OF SECOND MEETING

On June 17, 2009, 37 years after Watergate, I notified Douglas Caddy, now an attorney in Houston, Texas, of a well kept secret and informed him of a new Watergate revelation. (Previously I had disclosed to Douglas Caddy that there had been two meetings regarding the Caddy assignment as discussed above.)

I then informed Douglas Caddy that there had been another [*second*] meeting about the Caddy assignment. It took place on June 28, 1972, with Shoffler and four others agents who were never introduced to me. I am quite certain that these agents were from either Military Intelligence or the CIA. I know that they were not FBI agents from their manner and the special type of assignment they asked me to do regarding Douglas Caddy.

Shoffler and these agents met with me in my apartment at 2122 P Street, N.W. Douglas. Caddy did in fact live across the street from me in the Georgetown House at 2121 P St., N.W.

One of the agents, whom I will never forget, had two plastic bags, one containing two small blue pills and another that had a laboratory test tube with a small gelatin substance that was approximately ¼ inch in diameter. He referred to it as a suppository.

The assignment was to become intimately acquainted with Douglas Caddy as quickly as possible.

The exact description of the assignment was to engage in oral sex with Douglas Caddy and in doing so I was suppose to fondle his balls and ass, and at the same time insert the small gelatin-like suppository into his rectum, which would have caused death within minutes.

If there were any delay in the lethal process that would prevent me from leaving fast from his presence, then I was to take the small blue pills, which would have caused me nausea, providing me with an excuse to leave for home immediately.

The agents told me that Douglas Caddy had to be eliminated without fail.

My first reaction was that they were "nuts." But then Shoffler pulled me aside and whispered that this was a very real and serious situation and the decision was entirely up to me.

The agents were planning a pre-arranged way for me to meet Douglas Caddy, which they did not disclose at the time.

I asked the agents what the reason was that they wanted for me to go to this length and why they and the government were taking such a risk. I was told that this matter involved a high national security situation that they were not at liberty to disclose. The agents stated that their orders did not allow them to know the answers and that they were only following orders from their superiors who sometimes did not know the answers either and merely implemented instructions from those above. However, from the agents' comments I inferred that because Douglas Caddy was gay, that was reason enough.

The agents informed me that I would be well taken care of for this assignment. They also said that I would never have to worry about anything for the rest of my life.

I was totally repulsed by the entire assignment and proposition. After I emphatically refused, the agents swore me to secrecy and left.

Only in July of 1986 when I was subpoenaed by Shoffler to testify before the grand jury in the Lenny Bias case in Upper Marlboro, Maryland did he ever discuss this subject again. At that time he said, "Butch, I am glad that you did not go through with that Douglas Caddy assignment because I found out that those two little blue pills would have caused your instant death."

I regret that I never disclosed these facts until now. I suppressed this information out of fear for my life.

Some of the background information in this affidavit about my relationship with Shoffler as a Confidential Informant was disclosed by Jim Hougan in his 1984 best-selling book, *Secret Agenda: Watergate, Deep Throat and the CIA* (pages 320-323). Some was also disclosed in the Watergate Special Prosecution Force Memorandums of its two interviews of me and one of Officer Carl Shoffler in 1973.

This sworn statement is the truth, the whole truth and nothing but the truth, so help me God.

I, Robert Merritt, swear in this affidavit that the facts are true to the best of my knowledge under the penalty of perjury.

Robert Merritt

Subscribed and sworn to before me on the 28th of July, 2009, to certify which witness my hand and seal of office.

Notary Public in and for the State of New York
Ricardo S. Castro
Notary Public, State of New York
No. 01CA5041272
Qualified in Bronx County
Comm. Exp. 08/29/09
7/29/09

Although Merritt is not publicly recognized as a major figure in Watergate, he was well known to the Watergate Special Prosecutor. He was interviewed six times by the Watergate Special Prosecution

Force, one of the last interviews being on the day before the infamous Saturday Night Massacre in which the FBI stormed the office of the Special Prosecutor and seized dozens of boxes of documents. Special Prosecutor Archibald Cox was present at this interview of Merritt. The next day Cox was fired. No written memorandum of the key interview could be located in the National Archives, although memoranda of three of the prior Merritt interviews were stored there. Among these is the memorandum of July 24, 1973 to Terry Lenzer from Jim Moore, the opening sentence of which reads: "Lee Sheehy and I met on 7/20/73 with Mr. Merritt and his lawyer, David Isbell, at Mr. Isbell's office, 888 16th Street, N.W. (Covington & Burling)."

Moore's memorandum on page 3 states:

"On July 13, 1972, Merritt's one association with the Watergate affair began. Detective Schaffler[sic] and Sergeant Leeper of the DC police visited Merritt and asked him to find out all he could about Douglas Caddy, who was representing some of the Watergate defendants. Caddy lived at 2121 P Street, NW, across the street from Merritt's residence at that time. Merritt did not know Caddy. Schaffler and Leeper told Merritt that Caddy was homosexual and pro-Cuban. In response to Merritt's questions, Schaffler and Leeper said this assignment did not come from the police intelligence or the FBI or the Alcohol, Tobacco and Firearms Division or the CIA. They further denied the assignment involved the Justice Department in any way. They would not tell Merritt who had authorized their request, but Schaffler laughingly said that it could possibly come from sources higher than the Justice Department. They told Merritt that it could be his biggest job and that it was one of the best things he could do for his country. Merritt refused to carry out the assignment. He says that he was periodically asked during 1972 to find out about Caddy, these requests coming from Schaffler or Leeper. As recently as February 22 or 23, 1973 Schaffler asked him if he knew anything about Caddy or could find out anything about him. According to Merritt (I will check the transcript on this), on May 16 or 17, 1973 Leeper testified before the Senate Watergate Committee that there was no police involvement in Watergate in any way after the apprehension of the burglars on the night of the break-in. Merritt says that Leeper was personally involved in the effort to enlist him, Merritt, in the investigation of Caddy.

Consequently, Leeper committed perjury before the Committee. Isbell and Merritt are interested in pursuing possible perjury committed by Leeper and in pursuing the more general question of possible DC police involvement in post-break-in investigations and activities."

Of special significance is the Watergate Special Prosecution Force memorandum of December 20, 1973 prepared by staff attorney Frank Martin regarding an interview of Carl Shoffler. The first sentence of the documents states, "Sgt. Schoffler of the Metropolitan Police Department was interviewed on December 3, 1973, by Horwitz, Akerman and Martin."

The document further discloses,

> Schoffler was questioned concerning the incident involving [redacted]. Schoffler stated that at some time after the Watergate arrests, Shoffler and Leeper were in their car and met Merritt near his residence at 2121 P Street. Schoffler stated that he had first seen [redacted] the day after the Watergate arrests when [redacted] came to represent the Cubans. When Schoffler and Leeper met Merritt, Merritt stated that he might know [redacted] and Merritt had an article from the newspaper with a picture of [redacted] in it. Schoffler told Merritt to let him know if Merritt found out who [redacted] was and if he was 'funny', i.e., homosexual. Schoffler stated that this was an off-hand comment and he never expected Merritt to do anything, and Merritt never told Schoffler anything about Caddy.
>
> Schoffler stated that in the summer of 1973, after he had testified in the Watergate hearings, Schoffler met Merritt. Merritt stated that he had made all sorts of calls to Senators concerning Watergate and the Caddy incident with Schoffler. Schoffler stated that he told Merritt that if he, Merritt, reported a crime then that was one thing, but that if he reported something that was only in his head it was going to come back on him. Schoffler said that he did not in any way threaten Merritt.

It is interesting to note that the redacted document of the interview with Shoffler still mentions my name, Caddy, in two places.

When Robert Merritt informed me on June 17, 2009, of the 1972 conspiracy to assassinate me, I was both taken back and puzzled. I asked myself, why would these CIA intelligence agents want this

11

done? The reasons they gave Merritt were that I posed a national security threat and that I was a homosexual.

There is no way to know what was in their minds. However, to try to figure out their thinking, I decided to engage in role playing to see how I looked in their eyes. By doing this, I may have come up with a scenario as to why they were so concerned. This is as follows:

When I graduated from New York University Law School in 1966, I went to work for General Foods Corporation, then the world's largest food manufacturer. My assignment was to advise the corporate officers on government relations, legislation and regulation that might affect the company's operations. In 1969 General Foods transferred me to Washington, D.C. I was to open an office for the company after a year that would handle government relations, with the emphasis on lobbying.

General Foods told me that for the first year I would be working out of the offices of the public relations firm that had long handled its government relations. This firm was the Robert Mullen Company. What General Foods did not tell me was that the Mullen Company was a CIA front, having been incorporated in 1959 by the CIA and that General Foods was a partner in this arrangement.

So I started carrying out my General Foods assignment, which consisted primarily of close coordination with the Grocery Manufacturers Association, the national trade organization that represented food manufacturers.

In mid-1970 Robert Mullen informed me that Howard Hunt was joining the staff of his company. Hunt and I quickly found we had something in common: I had worked closely with William F. Buckley, Jr. in founding the modern conservative movement in the late 1950's and early 1960's and Buckley not only was godfather to Hunt's children but had served under Hunt years previously in the CIA's office in Mexico City.

Howard Hunt and his wife, Dorothy, herself a former CIA agent, became my closest friends in Washington. Howard and I conversed daily on any number of topics.

At one point Robert Mullen told Hunt and me that he was making plans to retire and asked if we were interested in buying his company, and making payments on the purchase price from the profits over the future years. In the end Robert Mullen sold his company to Robert Bennett, a key associate of the Howard Hughes operation and of the CIA. Today Robert Bennett, Senator from Utah, is known as the tool and operative of the CIA. It is not known if this was a factor in Utah primary voters rejecting Bennett's bid for being the the Republican Party's senatorial candidate in 2010.

I left General Foods in late 1970 and joined Washington law firm Gall, Lane and Kilcullen as an attorney. Hunt immediately became a client and I handled his personal and business matters.

In early 1972, the law firm assigned me to do volunteer presidential campaign legal work out of the office of John Dean, then White House Counsel to President Nixon. Hunt was pleased to learn of this assignment.

Around April 1972, two months before the Watergate break-in, Hunt invited me to join him and the CIA's General Counsel in what turned out to be a meeting about whether I would be interested in working for the CIA. If I were interested, the General Counsel told me that my CIA assignment would be to construct and open a luxurious hotel on the seashore in Nicaragua, then dominated by the Sandinistas. I told them I would think about it but in my heart knew that I could not accept CIA employment because the vetting process would inevitably reveal that I was homosexual. The CIA did not employ anyone who was homosexual. As with other federal agencies, there was an unrelenting witch hunt against homosexuals, who were driven out, blackballed and had their careers destroyed.

On June 17, 1972, the Watergate case broke with the arrests of the five burglars inside the offices of the Democratic National Committee. Later that same day Hunt and Gordon Liddy retained me as their attorney to represent them and the five other arrested individuals.

On June 28, eleven days later, Washington, D.C. Metropolitan Police Officer Carl Shoffler showed up with four intelligence agents at the apartment of Robert Merritt where they attempted to enlist Merritt in assassinating me, as disclosed in Merritt's affidavit.

Why did they want me eliminated? One must look at it through their eyes:

1. I was one of Howard Hunt's closest friends and his attorney in the Watergate case. What had Hunt told me about the CIA operations during the period of

our friendship? Did I know some of the CIA's darkest secrets? After all, Hunt was a protégé of Richard Helms, the Director of the CIA, and had worked for the agency his entire life.

2. What had I learned while working inside the Robert Mullen Company as an employee of General Foods Corporation? Had I gained access to the CIA files and documents inside the Mullen Company and acquired knowledge of its world-wide operations? [For example, Robert Mullen had once spoken to me on the telephone when he was sent by the CIA to Chile to organize the media campaign to overthrow President Allende.]

3. Could I have recorded the conversation that I had with Hunt and the CIA's General Counsel about the Nicaragua plan?

4. Could Hunt have told me in my capacity as his Watergate attorney about the technical assistance that the CIA had provided Hunt in the months prior to the arrests on June 17, 1972?

5. Had Hunt told me about the role played by key CIA officers and agents in the assassination of President John Kennedy? In his deathbed confession that was audio-recorded in January 2004, Hunt fingered CIA officers Cord Meyer, David Philips, Frank Sturgis and David Morales as being part of the assassination plan that originated with Vice President Lyndon Johnson (see appendix J).

In summary, it appeared to these intelligence agents on June 28, 1972, that I had somehow worked myself into a position of knowing too much about the CIA, and thus of being a potential national security threat and a hated homosexual to boot. They feared that the mushrooming Watergate case could lead to my opening a Pandora's Box that threatened to expose some of the darkest secrets of the CIA. So the easiest solution would be to make me an early casualty of a domestic Operation Condor.

In reality, these agents' fears were unfounded. Hunt was always circumspect in what he told me, I never even thought of examining the files and documents housed inside the Mullen Company, I did not record the conversation between the CIA's General Counsel, Hunt and me about Nicaragua, and I knew nothing about the CIA agents' role in the JFK Assassination as later described by Hunt.

Actually, I did not know for certain that the Robert Mullen Company was a CIA front until Senator Howard Baker disclosed this in his separate report released as part of the final report of the Senate Watergate Committee.

But the agents on June 28, 1972, feared the worst and concocted a plan to remedy the situation.

What probably made them later change their course of action was that also on June 28, 1972, I was served in the courthouse with a subpoena to appear "Forthwith" before the Grand Jury investigating the Watergate scandal and this event made national headlines. In short, I became too hot to be offed.

Merritt's mind-boggling revelations about the Watergate Scandal and the controlling roles played by "Military Intelligence" and the CIA in causing it to happen constitute only about a third of the incredible story of his life as told to me in the pages that follow. Brace yourself because you are about to be introduced into a world that most persons cannot imagine exists.

A young Earl Robert "Butch" Merritt, Jr.
Photo: Author's archives

— Chapter One —

In The Beginning

I was born on June 22, 1944 in Charleston, West Virginia and was controversial even before my birth. I am the great-grandson of slave masters and also the grandson of slaves. I was born and raised as a white man, but at the age of 28 years found out that I was also a Black man, or more aptly a zebra. I am the great-grandson of gentiles but also the great grandson of a Jewish maternal grandmother. So by some accounts, I am also a Jew.

On the day that I was born the nurse handed me to my 16 year-old mother and said, "Here's Butch." Little did she realize the truth of her words: later I became known as being both gay and butch.

I was raised by my material grandparents because my mother and the white man whom I thought was my father quarreled constantly and got married and divorced several times. So my younger brother, Danny, and I were products of a broken home. I witnessed my so-called father on many an occasion cruelly abuse my mother both physically and mentally. Eventually I came to despise him. No one will ever know how happy I was on the day that I found out that the white man was not my father, and that my real father was a Black man. His name was Joseph Booker. He was light-skinned, with green eyes and light brown curly hair. He was killed in the Korean War. Later I received his Purple Heart when what I wanted most was to be with him, my real father.

I was raised by my maternal grandparents in an overly strict, old-fashioned Presbyterian home. I was baptized at the age of twelve with water brought from the River Jordan, the same river that Jesus was baptized in. As a child I was considered mischievous and while I never got into serious trouble, I loved to play the role of a menacing figure. I belonged to the usual community youth organizations, such as the Cub Scouts, 4-H and Jr. Deputy Sheriff's

Clubs. Little did I realize at the time that the latter organization was, in effect, a crystal ball that foretold my future.

I loved going to school and had plenty of friends. I was always considered to be the most popular kid on the block. It seemed like everybody wanted to be around Butch. Our family owned a farm that we visited every summer. I found happiness there, and being the outdoors type, loved animals and nature and climbing mountains and going fishing.

My family had a strong cultural and historical background that sprang out of its migration from a plantation in Virginia. I remember hearing the stories of the slaves being freed and the plantation mansion and fields being burned. I also remember the stories of cutting down trees and crossing over mountains, making a trail that later became the famous Midland Trail.

My mother had two brothers and two sisters. I loved my Uncle William and Aunt Anne, but detested her youngest sister, Tiny, who was a real bitch. Oscar, my mother's other brother, was a real wimp, totally useless and never worked a day in his life. I remember my grandmother dreading his presence and wishing that he would leave and make a life for himself. My mother's oldest brother, William, became a professor at the University of North Carolina.

To spite my family, especially my uncles who were ardent Presbyterians, I became a convert to the Catholic faith. This sudden action on my part turned out to be a big mistake. At the age of 16 years, I was abused and raped by two Catholic priests, the first being from my parish at St. John's Catholic Church in Belle, West Virginia.

When I was seventeen I volunteered to work on John F. Kennedy's presidential campaign in West Virginia, which was deemed a key state in the 1960 election. I worked at the Presidential primary campaign headquarters in Charleston with Judge James Melon. This was my first taste of politics.

My mother had become an alcoholic because of her failed marriages. This affected my life terribly. It was difficult for me to continue to attend my nearby public high school out of shame and embarrassment. So I switched from Dupont High School to Charleston Catholic High School, also known as Sacred Heart High School. Like my conversion to Catholism, this switch was also a big mistake. I was again sexually molested, this time by a Franciscan priest. This occurred almost every day. I found it increasingly difficult to concentrate on my studies with this priest genuflecting on his knees before me and telling me that he was blessing St. Peter.

All this took place when I was still 17 years old. I was becoming acquainted with the ways of the world at an early age. Although under age I started going to Charleston's only gay bar, The Regency, which was owned by two lesbian lovers. Soon, as my life became wilder, I was introduced to moonshine and to a commercial liquor called "Rebel Yell." However, getting drunk a couple of times with the boys proved to be more than enough for me. I never developed a thirst for alcohol again.

I started hanging out in the red light district of Charleston called Court Street, which was only three or four blocks long. This was my first experience with whores, pimps and every vice of life.

I became fed up with my mother's alcoholism, my two bigoted uncles, my lying and conniving Aunt Tiny and, most of all, being sexually abused by Catholic priests. I found it increasingly difficult even to face my friends. So I dropped out of high school just two months short of being graduated in 1962. Hurt, humiliated and ashamed, I ran away from West Virginia to begin a new and hopefully more peaceful life with a new identity, in the nation's capital, Washington, D.C.

CHAPTER TWO

PRE-WATERGATE WASHINGTON

I arrived in Washington, D.C. after hitch-hiking rides from my home in West Virginia. I had little money, not enough to rent a room or even buy three meals for a day. Like many runaways, even though I was 18 years of age, I ended up at the Trailways bus terminal. I went into the terminal's restaurant to get something to eat. While sitting there the terminal's restaurant manager approached me. His name was Eddie and ethnically he was an Eskimo (don't ask.) He inquired if I were new in town and looking for a job. Of course, I grabbed the opportunity, which included moving in with Eddie in his Capitol Hill apartment. Yes, I knew that Eddie was a classic closet case and trying to put the make on me but I had no other choice but to go along until I managed to get a few paychecks under my belt. I did not want to contact my grandfather for the money that I desperately needed, as I desired to be independent at long last.

After a month or so I managed to save enough money from the job to get my own room on the 1800 block Columbia Road, N.W. from an old lesbian landlady by the name of Miss Crim. I used to call her Miss Grim because she was somewhat weird. She only rented rooms to men. Everyday she would ask me to have lunch with her, which invariably consisted solely of a cup of tea and a small sandwich of cream cheese spread lightly on pumpernickel bread. Even though she was a lesbian, I came to suspect that her secret desire was to have a sexual experience with a young man.

Soon I managed to change jobs at the bus terminal from working in the restaurant to a baggage agent. My immediate supervisor was gay and he quickly promoted me to baggage manager. This did not last long as the terminal manager soon fired me: he was homophobic and constantly made anti-gay remarks; this led me to send about 12 bus loads of passengers' luggage to the wrong destinations around the country as a means of getting even with him for his smart-ass anti-gay remarks. It really didn't bother me that I got fired because by then I had enough money saved up to live for a few weeks without a job.

In the spring of 1965, I moved to 19th Street, N.W. to share an apartment with a young lady about my age whose name was Sarah. Sarah was from Macon, Georgia and had boyfriend by the name of Robert. Sarah was a modern interpretive dancer, while Robert was a manager in the credit department at the prestigious Woodward & Lothrop department store, locally known as Woody's. Robert was head over heels in love with Sarah, which presented a problem because while Sarah was strikingly beautiful, Robert was the classic nerd. Sarah eventually ruined him after she persuaded him to make dozens of false Woody's credit cards using various female names, which Sarah used to charge over $150,000 in merchandise in about three weeks time.

Then in 1966, I met a man who was the property manager of the Envoy Towers. He became very aggressive towards me and offered a free apartment in the Envoy Towers for one year in exchange for sex. The Envoy Towers was a first-class apartment building. I accepted his offer and soon found myself living for the first time in my life in luxury surroundings.

I got a job at a hospital in N.W. Washinton. My job title was post mortem technician or deiner. My task was to remove the hearts and aortas from children up to the age of 21 years. This was for government research on children's heart diseases under the auspices of the National Institutes of Health in Bethesda, Maryland, so essentially my job was under a subcontract from the government. For some reason I found that I had no problem in doing this type of work. I viewed it as a dead-end job, but one that continually offered up unusual experiences.

One of these that stands out in my memory was discovering that a female pathology intern, who was from India and had a painted star on her forehead and wore a sari, was a necrophiliac. Before performing an autopsy she would cover the face of the small cadaver with a wet brown paper towel and run her fingers over the body from head to toe, always spending too much time with fingertips touching the sexual organ. The first time I caught her doing this she tried to explain that this was a custom and ritual in India conducted on the dead. Naturally, I did not believe her because every time she performed an autopsy on a child who was 12 years or older, she made moaning noises and sounds as if she were reaching a sexual climax.

On another occasion during autopsy I opened up the head of a dead but healthy looking six month old child to remove the brain but there was no brain, just red liquid water. I even turned the baby upside down and drained the water through a huge tea strainer and could not find one microplasm of brain tissue.

I had the opportunity to perform another autopsy on a healthy-looking nine month old child but when I opened the chest cavity with the normal "Y" incision to get the abdominal organs, I was shocked to see the heart hit two beats and stop. I was by myself and immediately called for help. By the time doctors had rushed into the morgue, there was no heartbeat. To this day I often wonder if the child was alive or dead when it was brought to the morgue. I remember that when I started the autopsy its little body was still warm. Was the baby alive – did I kill it or did the doctors? The thought of this today often leaves me shaken.

My assistant technician, James, would sometimes work with me. During autopsies he would on occasion eat a sandwich with one hand and use the scalpel with the other hand. He would also smoke a cigarette and use the cadaver's toes as a cigarette holder.

After doing over a thousand autopsies in less than two years at the hospital it seemed to me that the doctors there were experimenting on children from poor families that had no money or insurance. I soon left, but sadly not before contracting hepatitis B, after accidentally pricking my hand with the point of the scalpel during an autopsy. I became extremely ill. My skin turned a golden brown and my hair turned silver.

When I went to the emergency room at a different hospital, the Washington Medical Center, for the hepatitis, the staff there had to ask me if I were white or Black. I was isolated for three months.

When the hospital finally released me, I no longer had my apartment or any of my belongings. I was forced to go to Saints Paul and Augustine Catholic Church to beg for help. There I met a kind priest, Father Andre, who rented an apartment for me and gave me enough money for food and clothing. He even helped me find a new job. I certainly did not want to return to employment at the hospital morgue. I'd had enough of working with the dead.

The hospital, where I had contracted hepatitis B in its employ, refused to pay for my hospitalization at the Washington Medical Center. I was presented with a medical bill of over $100,000 and had no medical insurance. I attempted on several occasions to telephone the Center's billing office to work out some type of arrangement to pay the bill as I did not want to ruin my credit for something that was caused by a work-related accident. But the credit manager refused to even discuss the matter with me. He was a former detective with the Washington, D.C. Metropolitan Police Department and relished his new role as a gang-busting debt collector. Since there seemed no way to deal with him with principled integrity, I dealt with him another way.

I simply changed my name to Robert Antoine Chevalier and got a job at the Washington Medical Center in the billing department as an insurance adjuster. In no time at all I managed to misplace permanently all of the billing records for Robert Merritt, right under the nose of my immediate boss.

Then in January 1968 I got a new job as payroll clerk for Merkel Press, located right across the street from where I lived on Bryant St., N.W. I soon quit because my boss, Jerry, took up the annoying habit of wanting to work too close to me, and I mean really too close. So I accepted a position at Judd & Detweiller Publishing Company in the color productions departments. The pay was decent but the work was so boring that I soon decided to quit.

In April of the same year I went to work as a skip tracer for a collection agency in Mt. Rainer, Maryland. I found the work extremely stressful as I daily had to deal with countless persons who were suffering financial difficulties. On April 4, the office telephones started going crazy all of a sudden. We soon found out that Martin Luther King, Jr. had been assassinated. I lived about 10 miles from the office and no buses or cabs were running. I ever involved with prostitutes working for Riggin, and found no evidence that Bernstein had ever provided Riggin with police information in return for sexual materials or favors. Which is not to say that the investigation was a dead end. Aside from confirming Riggin's gifts to Bernstein, Robinson uncovered a matter of fact that he found tantalizing. This was that Bernstein was a participant in the frolics of an informally organized 'social club' whose membership seemed to be dominated by CIA officers, their girlfriends and wives. Among those who participated in the club's affairs, Robinson said, was John Paisley, who at that time was the CIA's liaison with the [White House] Plumbers.

All of which may be more than a chain of coincidences, though Shoffler himself, considering the information, shakes his head and says, "If I was a jury, I'd convict me." Of what? "I don't know. Setting up Watergate, or something. Prior knowledge." Would the jury be right? "Hell no! I'm innocent."

And, really, in spite of all appearances, Shoffler would indeed seem to be innocent of everything but making the Watergate arrests.

It is not my intention in this preface to overshadow Merritt's startling disclosures that appear later in this volume. However, it is appropriate at this time to reproduce verbatim an affidavit that Merritt executed on July 29, 2009:

AFFADAVIT

1972 CONSPIRACY TO ASSASSINATE DOUGLAS CADDY, Original Attorney for the Watergate Seven

I, Robert Merritt, attest to the following facts regarding my involvement with the Watergate attorney Douglas Caddy, who represented the burglars known as the Watergate Seven. On Saturday, June 17, 1972, five burglars broke into the Democratic National Committee offices in Watergate and were arrested at 2:30 A. M. by Washington, D.C. Police Officer Carl Shoffler. At the time the Washington, D.C. Metropolitan Police Department employed me as a Confidential Informant and assigned me to work directly with Officer Shoffler. Two weeks before the arrests at Watergate I provided information to Shoffler about the planned break-in of the DNC that I had obtained as a Confidential Informant from a highly unusual source. By using this advance information, Shoffler developed a successful triangulation strategy that in effect set the got home by riding in the rear of a National Guard truck, one of many that were pouring into Washington, D.C. While I lived in a Black neighborhood, I had no fear as everyone there loved me. I had only a small amount of money on me and wasn't even certain where I could purchase food as stores were being burned down. I reluctantly phoned my grandfather and asked him to wire me some funds so that I could survive until the crisis abated. He agreed to help and I set out to find a taxi that would take me to the Western Union office. I found one but on the way we had to pass through an area of the city where the rioters were still looting. One of the rioters apparently thought the taxi driver was white, when in reality he was Black but light skinned, and threw a brick through the windshield. The brick struck the driver's three year old son in the head. I jumped out to avoid other problems for the driver so that he could race his son to the nearest hospital emergency room. I never found out if his son lived or died. I was forced to walk through the rioting area by myself but got through unharmed and found my way to the Western Union office.

In May 1968 I moved to 1818 Riggs Place, N.W. While living there I had a series of jobs. I was one of the first males to work for Kelly Girls, Inc. I broke the sex equality barrier before females started breaking into jobs held only by males. I later worked part-time as a soda jerk for Trio's Restaurant at 17th and Q Streets, N.W. and subsequently as a soda jerk for Schwartz' Drug Store at Connecticut Avenue and R Street, N.W.

I took a job as an orderly at Doctors Hospital located just two blocks from the White House at 1815 I St., N.W. I would run from there to pull a double shift at the George Washington University Hospital where I worked as a clerk in the accounting department. (Years later I returned to work in the hospital's dermatology department, as a histopathology technician making slides for the famous Dr. Braun, a specialist in skin cancer and basil cell carcinoma. The only exciting thing that happened to me there was meeting George Meany, the powerful head of the AFL-CIO. Meany had cancer of the nose.)

I later worked for the Columbia Hospital for Women as a delivery ward technician. I have forgotten the name of the hospital's director at that time but remember her as a beautiful lady in every respect.

The head nurse of the delivery ward was Mildred Turner. For some reason I loved that job. I guess it was because I just loved hospital and medical work in general.

While at Columbia Hospital for Women, I had several interesting experiences. I vividly remember one woman who climbed out of her labor bed and had her baby in the commode. Another lady who was in labor was screaming Peter, Paul, Tom, Harry, George and a host of other male names. The staff was wondering who the father was.

One day the delivery ward had a VIP (Very Important Patient). She was the personal confidential secretary to President Lyndon Johnson. I do not remember her name, it being too long ago. She had a caesarean section, her body being draped off with a spinal block. She was laughing and talking to the attending physicians all the while her belly was being opened. There were all sorts of whispering and rumors flying around the hallways as to who was the father since she was not married.

From February 1969 to January 1970, I began hanging out at Dupont Circle, and I worked other various jobs: as part-time cashier for the Whelan Drug Company at Connecticut Avenue and Rhode Island Avenue, N.W., and as a cashier for Safeway Supermarket in the Watergate complex. I also worked part-time as a cashier for the Southern Drug Company at 15th & H Sts., N.W., located a two-minute walk from the White House, until I abruptly lost that job.

Unknown to anyone in the world at the time, my losing that job was the first step in a long chain of events and actions involving a large number of people and ultimately resulted in the resignation of President Richard Nixon four years later. From being a soda jerk and part-time cashier I was to be transformed into a Confidential Informant and intelligence gatherer for the U.S. Government. Having arrived in Washington, D.C. eight years earlier, fleeing West Virginia, I was about to embark on a new career. Little did I dream that I would be presented with the unique opportunity of changing the course of history in two ways: either by telling what I had learned as a Confidential Informant or by keeping my mouth shut. At the time I chose the latter and today question whether I made a mistake.

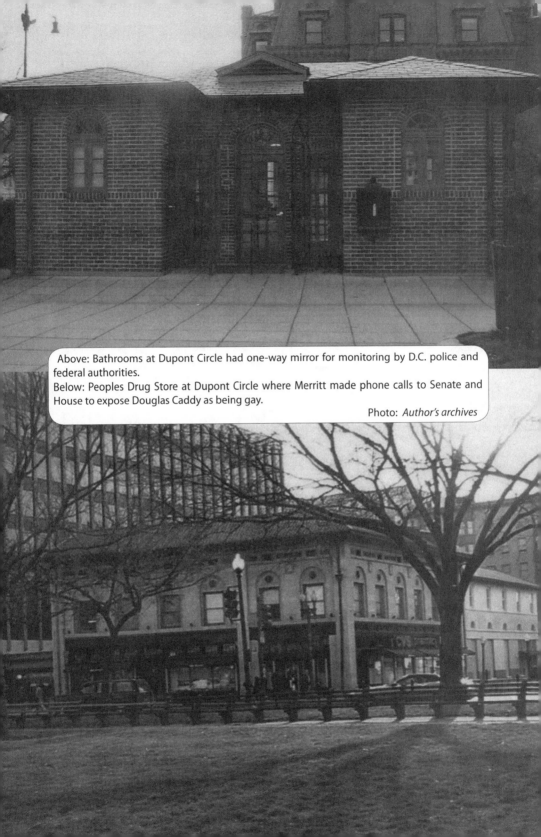

Above: Bathrooms at Dupont Circle had one-way mirror for monitoring by D.C. police and federal authorities.
Below: Peoples Drug Store at Dupont Circle where Merritt made phone calls to Senate and House to expose Douglas Caddy as being gay.

Photo: *Author's archives*

May 1971: Anti-war demonstrators sit on the steps of the Capital building during the 1971 May Day Protest in Washington D.C.

Photo: *University of California, Los Angeles. Library. Department of Special Collections.*

May 1971: Dupont Circle ringed with police, troops, buses and military vehicles. The center of the circle was later used as a holding pen until those arrested could be transported to jail.

Photo: *Washington Star*

1972: The Wategate Complex

— CHAPTER THREE —

THE WATEGATE BREAK-IN

For the purposes of disclosing what I know about Watergate, I shall begin when I first met Carl Shoffler, which was in January 1970. In the preceding month I had noticed Carl in Dupont Circle, where I used to hang out and socialize daily. Dupont Circle is about eight blocks from the White House. At the time it was a gathering place for hippies, gays and radicals of all persuasions. I thought Carl, because of his appearance and actions, was just another hippie.

The second time I noticed Carl was when I was working at the Southern Drug Company at 15th and H Streets, N.W., not far from Dupont Circle. Carl started coming into the store while I was on duty and talking to the owner, who was also the pharmacist. Carl visited the store regularly for about a week when suddenly, without any explanation, the owner fired me. This came as a shock as my employment at the store was my only source of income, which was $70 per week. I lived at 2122 P Street, N.W., also near Dupont Circle, where my rent was $35 per week, which left me with a small amount to live on.

My little abode was a small one bedroom apartment with a door at the side of the building in the alley. There was a small white painted brick by the door that had been placed there by a prior tenant who was drug dealer. I had a second door around the corner and at the end of the building that led into my kitchen. It was through this door for the next two years that cops and FBI agents came to visit me without being noticed by anyone.

An evening after I was fired there was a knock on one of the doors to my apartment. When I opened it, not so much to my surprise for some reason, there was Carl. He promptly invited himself inside by flashing a police badge in my face.

Carl then admitted that he was responsible for making me lose my job at the drug company. At that point he thrust in my hand an envelope that contained $1000 in cash, explaining that it was compensation for the loss of my employment.

Carl told me that for several months he, the Washington, D.C. Metropolitan Police Department (MPD) and federal agents had been profiling me as a prelude to requesting my enrollment as a confidential informant (CI) for the U.S. Government. Carl said my profile revealed that I was well known and popular to the persons who constituted the Dupont Circle community. He said that on the basis of my profile it had been concluded that I did not have any political ambitions or affiliations with any of the persons in the Dupont Circle community. This was true because I was then, and am today, apolitical. He did not ask but bluntly told me he knew I was gay.

He said he was authorized to state that he was representing the police, the District of Columbia, and the U.S. Government in informing me that they were looking for a patriotic white gay male who would work for them as an undercover intelligence agent in the capacity of a confidential informant, and that I fitted the bill. Carl described my undercover role as gathering vital intelligence on many of the people I associated with at Dupont Circle, most of whom I considered to be friends, and that if I were to take the assignment it would be the most important and patriotic thing I could do for my country.

Carl told me that because I was gay I could not join our military forces but I could serve and be more valuable to our country and the government as an undercover intelligence agent for the police. He said that most of the people I thought were my friends and who appeared to be happy-go-lucky or hippies were instead engaged in a subterfuge to commit serious and evil acts against our government and our free society. Carl appeared to be sincere and I believed him. I accepted his offer, which, as things turned out, was the biggest mistake of my life! My intelligence work with Carl was to last more than two decades, from 1970 to 1994.

Carl told me that his primary assignment at the time was working undercover in Dupont Circle in an attempt to apprehend a bank robber by the name of Mike. By chance I knew Mike and his wife, Judy, and their little boy, Mikey, Jr. Mike and Judy were an integrated couple. Mike in fact had robbed a bank and escaped with quite of bit of money. With Carl on his tail Mike was forced to abandon his wife and child. His wife owned a hippie head shop that sold beads, jewelry and drug paraphernalia. She soon lost her business and was forced to go on welfare.

When Mike's trail went cold, Carl was ordered to concentrate only on intelligence gathering and to train me in my capacity as an undercover agent. We hung out at the Hubbard House and Buffalo Bill's, two restaurants located near Dupont Circle.

Carl was one year younger than me, he being 25 and I being 26 years old. From the beginning we hit it off well. In a momentary lapse of caution Carl told me that he was a military intelligence agent who had been assigned clandestinely to work within the Washington, D.C. Metropolitan Police Department and that he was a graduate of Vint Hill Farm Station in Virginia, where intelligence agents are trained in their craft, especially in wiretapping and electronic eavesdropping. After he related this he adamantly told me that he would never discuss the subject again.

At the beginning of my agreement to work as a confidential informant, I had to be signed up. So Carl publicly handcuffed me at Dupont Circle, placed me in the back of a police car and took me to the Second District substation where I was placed in a cell. When the coast was clear, I was escorted to the second floor Tactical Unit. There Carl's boss, Sergeant Paul Leeper, gave me code number SE-003. SE was shorthand for Special Employee or Source Entry and 003 was my assigned confidential informant number. Strange as it may seem, I was never fingerprinted or photographed or even asked for identification. The technicians in the tactical unit who carried out the task of enrolling me as a CI assumed, as had Carl, that my name was Robert Chandler, which was the name that appeared on my apartment's mail box. On a past occasion, someone named Robert Chandler lived at the same address until I threw him out of the apartment. It was stupid and presumptuous for the police, and later the federal agents, to think that Robert Chandler was me. After all, Chandler was Black by skin complexion and I was white by skin complexion. At least I thought I was white at the time, but

I was in for a surprise a few months later. Chandler had a District of Columbia driver's license that showed his picture, while I had no such photo identification.

One day Carl got a bag of weed and said that he wanted to go to my apartment to smoke it. I had never smoked pot before that night and when I did I found it made me horny.

Once Carl was at my apartment the first thing he did was remove his badge and gun. He took a shower and jumped into my bed after which he rolled up a joint. He took out his handcuffs and cuffed my hands behind my back. He then sucked my dick and kissed me from head to toe! After he finished with me, he asked me to handcuff him and return the favor. This was the beginning of a sexual routine between us steeped in lust that went on for a couple of years. Nobody knew anything about Carl being my secret lover except a few others, two of whom were cops.

Carl stayed with me at my apartment at least four days of the week. It was convenient for him as he worked out of the MPD Second District substation about four blocks away. Also it fit into his image as a hippie, as he always wore shabby clothes and had a goatee, mustache and long hair. Underneath Carl's outward appearance was the body of a Greek god. He lived a double sex life, having a wife, Helene, back home in Pennsylvania whose time was consumed in raising their children. I always joked with Carl that he was not bisexual but trisexual, meaning that he would try anything.

Carl told me that my task as a CI was to get information on criminal activities in the Dupont Circle community, such as drugs, robberies, burglaries, fencing [selling stolen property], prostitution and anything else that he might find of interest.

Soon thereafter Carl expanded my duties to intelligence gathering, which became paramount to the police because of the mobilization of anti-Vietnam war sentiment. Carl explained that the White House, under what later became known as the Houston Plan, was pressuring government intelligence agencies to monitor and build files on various groups that were planning to overthrow the U.S. Government and that the Communist Party was providing the financing to these groups.

Carl noted that Dupont Circle was a heavily diversified community with many activists of all types, including the far left, far right, pro-American and un-American, Nazi and Communist, Black Panthers and to the Gay movement – you name it, it was there.

Because my nickname was "Butch" and I was known in the Dupont Circle community as being gay, I could swing in all the groups, no matter what the political affiliation. Everyone loved Butch.

Three of my best gay friends in Dupont Circle were drag queens. Of these, the closest was James Reed, also know as Rita Reed. We were just friends with nothing sexual between us. Two of Rita's friends were drag queens by the names of Gregory Sewell, also known as Christine Keeler, and Jerry Smith, also known as Sherry or Jerry the fairy. One butch gay hanging out with two effeminate drag queens made for an intriguing sight, especially during the time when the gay revolution was in its formative stage.

Carl trained me quickly in intelligence gathering and eventually I infiltrated hundreds of organizations. He directed me to have my name and address placed on the mailing lists of these groups. I even used the female name of Martina Morgan when I infiltrated women's and feminist's groups. I used my home address and also a box at the main city post office on North Capitol Street. Carl would pick up the unopened mail from these organizations and deliver it to the appropriate law enforcement agencies.

Carl took delight in teaching me the tricks of intelligence gathering, such as the use of eavesdropping equipment. He gave me a hundred 18-carat gold Cross pens that had the capacity of being eavesdropping bugs. The pens housed a transmitter with two little wires in the heads. Each pen was in a cellophane wrapper that bore a number. Carl would tell me to take a specifically numbered pen and leave it on a targeted person's desk when I visited them. On many occasions these unwitting targets picked up the pen and placed it on their person. Unbeknownst to them they were carrying a live bug. These targets were usually lawyers, politicians and organizers of radical groups.

Carl also provided me with bugs that were magnetized so I could stick them almost anywhere. They were small and unnoticeable. I placed many of these in the vehicles of targeted individuals. He gave me a small spy camera to use for taking pictures of documents and floor plans. Because I could not carry a gun or a badge, Carl gave me a hat-pin about three inches long that I wore in the collar of my shirt or jacket for use as a weapon in self-defense.

Carl loved to deliberately liken the gay revolution to the Black civil rights movement. This was an attempt by him to cause trouble for gays. He thought that he could inflame Blacks by this comparison. Carl loved to refer to the gay revolutionaries as terrorists, even though he was a closeted gay guy who was married with children. It seemed that his homophobia stemmed from his macho military and intelligence training. I came to believe that Carl had been brainwashed by the same governmental agencies and personnel that were also trying to brainwash me.

Carl was outspoken in his contempt for Blacks and Hispanics, referring to them as niggers and spics. This was typical language used by the police and federal agents with whom I worked. A special target of Carl's contempt was Louis Farrakhan, whom he said was a false prophet of Islam and a Jew hater.

In October of 1970 Carl extended my CI services to the Washington, D.C. MPD Intelligence Division. I worked there under Sergeants Chris Scrapper, Charles Robinson and Dixie Gildon. The Intelligence Division was located in the main police headquarters at 300 Indiana Avenue, N.W. I found it difficult to get along with Sergeants Scrapper and Robinson because they were vociferously homophobic. So I had to regularly report verbally to Connie Fredericks, a secretary in the Intelligence Division. If I had to meet with anyone in the Division it was with Sergeant Gildon and such meetings were always concerned with the actions of anti-Vietnam War groups and related political activities.

From the spring of 1970 until October 1971, I worked both for Carl and the MPD Intelligence Division. While in the employ of the latter I received many orders from Sgt. Scrapper and Sgt. Robinson, although most were from Sgt. Scrapper, who sometimes issued them through Connie Fredericks. These instructions included engaging in multiple criminal acts, such as planting drugs (they gave me about 500 "dime" bags of pot valued at $10 each and 5 or more ounces of cocaine) to clandestinely place upon unsuspecting protesters against the Vietnam War or radical political foes of the Nixon White House, bugging, instigating violence at demonstrations by throwing the first rocks at the police, cutting wires to sound equipment at left-wing public events and protests, giving misinformation to protesters, spreading lies and rumors, creating racial friction, causing thousands of protestors to be arrested, engaging in theft, burglary, mail fraud, filing false police reports against individuals, and many other crimes against citizens who were merely exercising their First Amendment rights.

Sgt. Scrapper specifically ordered me to break into the Community Bookstore, the Third Day Book Store and various offices at 1029 Vermont Avenue, N.W. in order to remove anti-Vietnam war petitions, plant drugs, steal files, photograph documents and destroy office equipment. He also instructed me to steal thousands of names, addresses and phone numbers of citizens who were supporting and financing these left-wing organizations.

On one occasion Sgt. Scrapper ordered me to break into the Red House Book Store. This was actually to test my prowess in carrying out an intelligence operation because the radical book store was in reality a police front operation. The test was whether I could break in and steal records under the very eyes of the police. I passed it with flying colors.

Because I was gay I was ordered to seduce and engage in sexual acts, including sodomy, with over 70 targeted individuals. The MPD Intelligence Division was especially interested in my being able to establish sexual contact with Senator William Proxmire, a Democrat from Wisconsin, whom they said was bisexual. While I was able to worm my way into jogging with the Senator on one morning, nothing more came of this.

The MPD Intelligence Division also ordered me to break into the embassies of two foreign countries, which I successfully did. My attempt at one embassy, which was timed to occur during its Christmas party, was made easier when I was invited inside by the daughter of the ambassador, who asked me to smoke pot with her in the library.

In October 1971, after working with the MPD Intelligence Division for about a year, Carl arranged for me to be transferred to the Washington, D.C. Field Office of the Federal Bureau of Investigation. I was delegated to work with Special Agents Terry O'Connor and Bill Tucker. The FBI assignment primarily dealt with targeting the Institute for Policy Studies and the Weather Underground, two organizations deemed radical and dangerous under the government's COINTELPRO program, although no organization in the country was immune from investigation. COINTELPRO stood for: co=counter, intel=intelligence and pro=program. The FBI assigned me the code names of the Reverend, then Eric and eventually Top Cat.

Under the FBI's expert training I became an even more proficient CI. I was trained to be a spy, eaves-dropper, saboteur, infiltrator, provocateur, instigator, male prostitute, thief and burglar. Activities that normally would be considered illegal became routine – any means to an end. I could become your confidante and cut your throat at the same time. My task was to demoralize, dehumanize and deprive my targets and ordinary American citizens of their lives, freedom and liberty. I had no gun or badge but I literally had the power to destroy anyone whom I targeted or got in my way. I was your best friend or your worst enemy.

All this time Carl was interacting with any number of federal law enforcement and intelligence agencies, such as the FBI, Department of Justice, Central Intelligence Agency, National Security Agency and military intelligence. One time I chose to resurrect the forbidden topic between us, joking with Carl about his being a federal agent himself, and not merely a lowly police detective, to which he replied, "How do you know that I am not?" My suspicion that this might be so was heightened by Carl always having large wads of cash, and I mean really large wads, on his person for use in his intelligence gathering activities.

One of my FBI assignments as a CI was to accept a job as chauffeur and gardener at the Virginia home of Ethel Kennedy. I was recruited for this task by another CI named Banwar, who had turned down the assignment. Banwar was an Indian Sikh. He was a handsome man in his early twenties who wore a white turban and loin cloth when I visited him at his apartment. He always went through a ritual of burning incense and praying to Buddha before performing fellatio on me.

I went so far as calling up and speaking with Ethel Kennedy by telephone, who confirmed the position. All I had to do was show up and the job would have been mine, despite the fact that at the time I did not have a driver's license. However, that was not a problem because the FBI said it would furnish me with one under an assumed name, which I found amusing because at the time I was already operating under the assumed name of Robert Chandler without the agency even knowing it. I decided not to pursue the position at Ethel Kennedy's residence, where my task would have been to spy on what happened there.

I was slowly becoming exasperated with being passed around among different agencies, even though I was free lancing as was Carl. So I decided after a few months to tell FBI agents O'Connor and Tucker of my true identity, of not being Robert Chandler. This revelation made them look stupid. Their stupidity was enhanced even further when I told them that I was a fugitive from justice and was so listed in the files of the FBI under my real name. This was because a few years previously I had passed a bad check for $200 at a bank in Charleston, West Virginia, drawn on my account at the Riggs National Bank in Washington, D.C. This constituted an interstate transaction and came under the FBI's jurisdiction. I wrote the check because I was short on funds after being summoned suddenly to see my mother at a hospital in Charleston, whose poor health had taken a turn for the worse. My plan, which ultimately failed, was to cover the bad check upon my return to Washington, D.C. before it was presented for payment by the Charleston bank. After I recounted this to the FBI agents, they contacted the U.S. Attorney in Charleston, who declined to prosecute me. The FBI agents did admit that I had been clever in having worked for them as a fugitive under the name of another person and that they were dumb in not checking out my background before employing me as a CI. With this revelation behind me, I nevertheless continued to work for the FBI, but with growing animosity towards me from Agents O'Connor and Tucker, whose reputation for professionalism within the agency had been tarnished.

Meanwhile, I also labored for Carl and the Washington, D.C. MPD, all the time without the knowledge of the FBI. This was a special arrangement insisted upon by Carl, who was orchestrating my career as an undercover intelligence operative. At one point Carl even had me working for the Secret Service on a counterfeiting assignment.

It was about this time that Carl again transferred me to work for yet another agency, without the knowledge of the FBI. This was the Alcohol, Tobacco and Firearms Division of the U.S. Department of the Treasury. I was introduced to ATF agent Bill Seals. Agent Seals was only interested in the Weather Underground, which had attempted to bomb the Capitol Building, and in other organizations that were prone to violence and explosives. My relationship with Agent Seals was a pleasant and professional one. He never once crossed me or treated me underhandedly as had the MPD and the FBI due to my being a gay person.

In the latter part of 1971 and early 1972 the FBI and the MPD instructed me to break into the buildings of a number of groups in the nation's capital, including the Institute for Policy Studies and the Hebrew Congregation. I never broke into the latter because it was impossible but did manage to steal a box of hundreds of envelopes of unopened mail.

Despite the fact that my work was illegal and immoral, I was constantly reminded by the FBI and MPD that it was being done in the best interests of the national security of the country. I was led to believe that I was above the law, that I was beyond reproach.

In carrying out my CI work, besides the intelligence gathering, I purchased illegal drugs, guns, hand grenades and even a bazooka rocket. I remember carrying a three-foot bazooka rocket, wrapped in a towel, while walking 12 blocks down Massachusetts Avenue in the heart of Washington, where I surrendered it to Sgt. Dixie Gildon. She was waiting for me in a police vehicle at a gas station, not the safest place to facilitate transfer of an explosive weapon. When I placed the rocket in the back seat of the car, Officer Gildon jumped out and ran a safe distance away while awaiting the arrival of the MPD bomb squad. Meantime, I remained in the back seat and slowly disarmed the rocket by unscrewing and detaching its detonator head from the body of the bomb.

The most important case in which I was involved in purchasing explosives – and which was destined to play a crucial role in the making of the Watergate scandal – was my purchase of two small incendiary devices from a member of the American Nazi Party at the Columbia Plaza Apartments in Washington on October 29, 1971. As I have already recounted, one of my best and closest friends was James Reed, also known as Rita Reed. Rita was a handsome man about 25 years old. "She" was also a beautiful drag queen, who when dressed up looked exactly like Marlo Thomas from the hit TV show, *That Girl*. Rita was from Parkersburg, West Virginia. She lived in an apartment on Massachusetts Avenue, N.W., not far from where I resided. I used to accompany Rita when went to the doctor. to get female hormone shots.

Rita worked at the Columbia Plaza Apartments as a telephone operator on the PBX switchboard. She facilitated my purchasing the two small incendiary devices from the American Nazi Party, which secretly operated out of an apartment there. To my knowledge no arrest was ever made of the Party member who sold the devices because his father had a high position in a munitions manufacturer that had contracts with the U.S. Army. The two devices that I bought were sterile and had no markings where they were made, although the FBI told me they were manufactured by the CIA.

On April 9, 1972 I received the message from my grandparents that my mother Rebecca was dying. My grandfather sent me $500 for travel money. When I told the FBI I had to go home, they became very adamant and even threatened me about going to see my mother. Carl Shoffler contributed money out of his pocket to help me go home even though I didn't really need it. I took the plane the next morning and arrived in Charleston in the early afternoon. I told no one in my family that I was in Charleston. I remember walking from the Kanawha airport to the hospital, which was bout 7 miles. I remember walking across the old Kanawha City Bridge and peering through holes in the sidewalk big enough for a small pony to drop through. I remember it being a frightful and scary event for me since I was afraid of heights and water.

Later on, when my mother did die, I made plans to attend her funeral. I boarded my plane at Washington National Airport and as the plane began to descend over the Kanawha airport I could see from my plane window the funeral procession beginning to ascend to the grave site. I jumped in a cab and went to Spring Hill Cemetery, which was on top of small hill right beside the mountain top that Kanawha airport was on. When I arrived at her grave site my mother's casket was already being lowered into the ground. The funeral director asked me if I wanted to see my mother for the last time and I said yes. He said was against the law for him to use the key to reopen the casket, but said he would since I was a member of the family. He ordered the casket to be raised and he placed his key in the seal to reopen the lid. I heard the key turn and a clicking sound of the reopening and the lid began to rise about 3 inches. I stopped the director's hand and told him that I wished a moment to be alone with my mother. So, he and other people who were present walked away from me with their backs turned to give me respect and privacy.

At this point, I reached in my jacket with my right hand and still holding the casket lid open with my left hand, placed a small package inside the casket. Not once did I raise the lid any further than 3 or 4 inches because I did to wish to see or remember my mother dead. I wanted to keep the thoughts and memories of her being alive. I placed inside my mother's casket a small bible, a lock of my hair, a small photo of me, two cassette tapes, several photos of agents Tucker and O'Connor with me in the elephant room in the Smithsonian Museum and my 100 days diary. I called the diary my first 100 days as a CI because it was a hand written diary from January 1, 1970. The diary contained personal notes regarding criminal activities and instructions from the police and FBI. The two tape recordings contained secret telephone recordings of illegal instructions from the police and the FBI to me.

No one present at the graveside saw what I did.

My mother died young at the age of 42 from drinking herself to death. Beside her gravesite someone had left a can of Budweiser. I remember picking it up and throwing it as far as I could.

I stayed that evening with my grandparents and other close relatives. That night I went next door to sleep at my mother's home and slept in her bed, which was unmade from the time she last slept in it. It gave me great comfort being there that night in her bed. The next morning I got up and started to look through my mother's personal belongs, which I noticed had already been ransacked. However, I found a letter and some other personal papers in a small plastic bag hidden in her bottom dress drawer. Inside I found a package of envelopes that turned out to be old love letters between my mother and my real father Joseph Booker, a Black man who had died in the Korean War.

When I returned from West Virginia, FBI agents O'Connor and Tucker came to my apartment on P Street, N.W. and said that in a job evaluation of me, their supervisor, Special Agent Kunkel, had given me the highest grade – excellent. The two agents also carried an unusual message to me from J. Edgar Hoover, who expressed his personal appreciation and complimented me on my work in obtaining the two small explosive devises from the Nazi Party.

Little did the FBI suspect that I was slowly becoming disillusioned with the agency and was sick of targeting friends and innocent people and getting some of these arrested on trumped up charges. I felt I was losing my religious background and morality. I came to believe that the FBI was brainwashing me, believing that I was merely a malleable hillbilly from West Virginia who never finished high school, even though I had received a score of 138 plus on an IQ test. I realized that I had committed so many crimes at the direction of the FBI that had I been indicted, the list of felony counts would have set a world record and, if convicted, I could have received one of the longest sentences in history.

May Day of 1972, although smaller than the 1971 demonstrations, began a week of chaos, with over 100 organizations mobilizing their members and sympathizers to march on Washington. Their intent was to shut down the government as a way of protesting the Vietnam War. Even though I no longer was locked in step with the MPD and the FBI, I kept my promise to do everything in my power to cause harm to the May Day protestors and assisted in the arrests of many of them. In the midst of the demonstrations J. Edgar Hoover died on May 2. Ironically, at the time of his death I was sitting in an FBI vehicle with Agents O'Connor and Tucker just a few feet away from Hoover's home when they received word over the FBI radio that Hoover's housekeeper had discovered his dead body. O'Connor promptly gave me $20 to catch a cab home.

It was about this time that my good friend Rita Reed told me that ever since she had arranged for me to purchase, in October 1971, the two small incendiary bombs from an American Nazi Party leader, there had been daily chaos on her job as the PBX operator at the Columbia Plaza Apartments. Rita said the police, FBI, and other federal agents were tripping all over each other in monitoring telephone calls going in and out of the apartment from which the bombs had been purchased and also in investigating a prostitution ring with a VIP call girl service that was run out of another Columbia Plaza apartment. She admitted that she had listened in on some of the calls going in and out of the unit from which the prostitution ring operated but she dismissed the affair as unimportant, merely terming it as one where boys will be boys. Carl told me that a pimp named Buster Riggin was involved and that he wanted to bust him because Riggin was associated with a low-life mafia figure named Joe Nesline. He told me that they also dealt in pornography, including several infamous snuff films.

Rita knew that I worked with Carl as a CI because I had told her and she had seen him at my apartment on many occasions. She also knew him as an undercover cop from his visits to Columbia Plaza Apartments where he participated in monitoring from a trunk room adjacent to the PBX switchboard the phone calls that went in and out of the apartments of the American Nazi Party and a prostitution ring. Rita was one of my closest friends and we shared intimate details of our lives with each other. I trusted her without hesitation. She had already helped me purchase munitions from the Nazi Party.

Rita, like most drag queens, was curious by nature. She loved to listen in on telephone conversations that went in and out through her PBX switchboard when she was on duty from 4 P.M. until Midnight. Over the months from October 29, 1971, which was when I purchased the two incendiary devices, until June 1, 1972, Rita and I would see each other almost daily and she invariably shared what she had heard over the lines of the Columbia Plaza switchboard.

Starting sometime during the 1972 May Day week she told me that she had heard telephone conversations about a planned break-in at a nearby building. She said that her switchboard had three holes that, in contrast to the others holes that were for apartments in the building, were merely numbered lines 1, 2 and 3, and that her supervisor had told her these were extra lines kept in reserve for possible use. She told me that the calls dealing with the planned break-in all went out through line number 2. She was not able to figure out the location in the building of the phone that used line number 2. She did determine from the conversations on line 2 that the party using that line had been instructed to make only outgoing calls and not to expect any incoming calls. Since no calls came in to be connected to line 2, she surmised that perhaps a two-way radio was being used to contact the party within the Columbia Plaza Apartments.

On May 31, 1972 Rita began intently to listen in on telephone conversations on line 2 because on this day she received an outside call that asked to be connected to hole 2. This was the first time such a call had occurred.

The next day, on June 1, 1972 Rita came by my apartment on P St., N.W. around noon. I had never seen him so scared and upset. He asked me to go for a walk with him. He said that he did not want to talk to me in my apartment for fear that it was bugged and did not want to talk while we walked on the street for fear that our conversation could be picked up by long-range audio means. Rita suggested that we enter an area that would make it difficult to monitor our conversation. We chose P Street Beach, which was about half a block from my apartment. It was a favorite location for persons who liked to lay on a hill's sloping grass to get some sun or to socialize. At the bottom of the hill was a wooded area with a trail. Once we reached the woods and began walking south on the trail, Rita visibly relaxed, having previously been in a pretend-playful mood and at the same time extremely nervous. I knew something was amiss because Rita rarely had serious moments in her life. As we continued walking though the wooded area, Rita started to recite a short poem that he had composed.

The poem went like this:

> Down by the bridge
> Through the trees
> Onto the green
> Back into the forest
> With the trees in full bloom
> With their beautiful green leaves
> By the water
> We walked down the path
> Along the creek
> And we came upon an old gate
> That was in the middle of the water

We had walked to the end of the trail and suddenly there in front of us was the complex of buildings known as the Watergate.

Rita raised his right arm and with his hand pointing to Watergate, said "Butch, this will be the fate of the President of the United States."

Rita went on to comment that even though he did not know what apartment or room line 2 was plugged into, he thought it was foolish that those talking on it would do so on a telephone line that went thought a PBX switchboard, which allowed an operator to listen in on the conversation. On the other hand, he pointed out that calls coming into a PBX switchboard could not be traced except though the building itself. She said that those talking on line 2, the calls she had monitored the evening before (May 31), specifically spoke with confidence and authority about breaking into the Democratic National Committee offices at Watergate on Sunday, June 18, 1972 at 2 A.M. She overhead them say that the plan was complete. She said those talking on the line spoke harshly of President Nixon. They referred to a "Crimson Rose" coming to a full bloom. Rita said to me, "Butch, I think this rose stinks."

Rita had never lied to me about anything during the four years that I had known him/her. At the end of our conversation within the view of Watergate, Rita implored me never to tell anyone what he had learned. I promised that I would not.

Nevertheless, in accordance with my training as a CI, the next day, on June 2, 1972, I called Sgt. Dixie Gildon at MPD and started to tell her about what Rita had told me. Sgt. Gildon cut my recitation short by stating that she could not talk then because she was late for a meeting. I pressed on, telling her about Rita's poem and its significance to Watergate. Sgt. Gildon immediately expressed concern and said that she would get back in touch with me soon. She did not, however.

In the afternoon of the next day, Saturday, June 3, 1972, Carl came by my apartment and I told him everything that Rita had told me. Carl became overly excited at hearing about this. He instructed me not to call Sgt. Gildon back or speak to anyone else about what Rita had said. I told to Carl that Rita had asked that I not talk to anyone about what she had learned and Carl assured me that he would never mention Rita's name. He pointed out that no action had been taken against Rita in her helping me with the purchase of the explosive devises from the Nazi Party.

Carl left but came back about 8 P.M., the same day. He was accompanied by two men, a military intelligence agent whose name I cannot remember, and another man whom Carl introduced as retired CIA agent William Sullivan. Sullivan produced a CIA identification card that had holes punched in it. They asked me to repeat in detail what Rita had told me. After I did this Sullivan proclaimed that Carl was about to become the most famous cop in American history. After further interrogation of me by Carl and his two friends, they made me promise not to talk to anyone else about the matter, including law enforcement officials or even Rita.

I never saw Rita after our walk in the woods on June 1, 1972. I tried for days to reach her at her home and at work. But she had disappeared. To this day I fear that my breaking my vow was somehow connected to her disappearance, and have been haunted by the thought that I may have put her life in danger.

Carl had been my roommate and part-time lover for almost two-and-half years. In my heart I knew him to be a stone cold freak, capable of anything and everything. Little did I suspect how Rita's information would ultimately pan out or that my intimate relationship with Carl was about to come to an end.

On June 4, Sunday, I had told the FBI I was going that very same day with Jack Davis of the Weather Underground to New York City and Philadelphia to meet possibly with William Ayers and Bernadine Dorhn, two key leaders of the group. This was a lie. I was fed up with the FBI, of the many crimes that I had committed at their direction, and especially their treatment of me at the time of my mother's death. I was entering a state of open rebellion against the agency.

On June 5, Monday, FBI Agents O'Connor and Tucker picked me up at my apartment and started driving into nearby Rock Creek Park. We drove to a clearing and stopped. They began to interrogate me about my claim of having traveled the prior day with Jack Davis. They said that the FBI had tailed Jack Davis and that I was not telling them the truth. I persisted in lying to them about the trip. At this point Agent Tucker threatened to kill me by putting my feet in cement galoshes and tossing me into the Potomac River. Upon hearing this threat I suddenly bolted from the FBI vehicle. I ran to a picnic table not far way where some people were having a meal and told them that I was in fear for my life. Agents O'Connor and Tucker then hastily departed. To this day I believe that I would have been killed if I had remained in their vehicle. I would have disappeared off the face of the earth, just as Rita had. I knew too much about the shady and corrupt activities of the FBI, so much that I posed a threat to the agency's invincible aura of credibility that had been built up during Hoover's reign, which had ended with his death a month earlier.

On June 8, 1972, Carl informed me that the FBI had terminated me as a Confidential Informant. I was swept by a feeling of relief and then of joy. Unfortunately, as things worked out, this was not the end of my relationship with the FBI.

From June 3 until the Watergate arrests on June 17, 1972, Carl spent two to three hours with me every day. He told me that Rita's information about the planned break-in at the Democratic National Committee offices in the Watergate was one hundred percent accurate.

We always celebrated each other's birthdays with one another by having sex and I knew that June 17 was Carl's birthday. I remarked to him that it was a shame that the break-in was going to happen on Sunday, June 18, 1972, one day after his birthday. Carl said that he had already taken care of that. I asked him how he had done this. He said that he had used a method of triangulation to put a message on the telephone line that the burglars were wire-tapping at the Democratic National Committee office, which had been monitored by the burglars from the time of their first break-in in May. Carl said his message was that an extremely important envelope containing vital information had been left by accident at the Democratic National Committee offices and that it was going to be picked up by noon on Saturday, June 17, 1972. Carl said that he had a hunch that this tantalizing message left on the wire-tapped line would cause the burglars to move the date of the break-in forward from June 18 to June 17, 1972. I knew Carl was a graduate of the NSA's Vint Hill Farm Station, where wire-tapping was taught, and so I was not surprised that he had been able to locate the telephone line being wire-tapped by the burglars at the Democratic National Committee offices.

Carl told me that he had made special arrangements with a security guard at Watergate, who turned out to be Frank Wills. I asked why he didn't use an undercover cop to replace the security guard and Carl said they were concerned that the burglars might notice the difference. I didn't inquire who "they" were but assumed that this included Sullivan and maybe others. Carl told me that this was not a matter of small-time burglars, reinforcing what Rita had said about the voices talking on line 2 spoke with confidence and authority.

On Saturday, June 17, 1972, five burglars broke into the Democratic National Committee offices in Watergate and were arrested at 2:30 A.M. by Carl. His strategy had worked – in effect, setting the burglars up in a trap. The Watergate Scandal had begun.

Carl came to my apartment late in the morning of the day of the arrests and exulted in having made the arrests. He told me that he had secretly telephoned the *Washington Post* soon after the arrests to tip the newspaper off to what had occurred. He then demanded his special birthday present from me, which I was only too happy to perform.

Three days later, on June 20, 1972, Carl showed up at my apartment with Sgt. Leeper. They asked me if I knew someone by the name of Douglas Caddy, who lived at the Georgetown House, a high-rise apartment building, at 2121 P St., N.W., which was directly across the street from my apartment. They told me Caddy was an attorney who was representing the Watergate burglars and that Caddy was a communist and pro-Cuban and was a leader of Young Americans for Freedom. They wanted me to establish a sexual relationship with Caddy to find out how he knew to show up for the arraignment of the burglars after their arrest. They asserted that Caddy had to be in on the conspiracy with the burglars and that in the past he had been shadowed when he frequented a leather-Levi gay bar in Greenwich Village in Manhattan.

Carl and Leeper related that Caddy had been working as a White House attorney in a sensitive position. They claimed that I was butch enough to entice Caddy, a masculine gay guy, into a sexual affair to obtain the information they wanted. They told me that this was the most important thing that I could do for my country and that I would be well-paid if I undertook the assignment. Their initial offer was $10,000.

I asked Carl about who it was that so desperately wanted this information from Caddy and he said that it was from very high up sources in the Department of Justice and the U.S. Attorney's office.

I did not commit to doing the assignment.

Two days later, on June 22, 1972, which was my birthday, Carl came to my apartment to give me my birthday present. He spent the entire day with me. Afterwards, when we were relaxing in bed, he gently tried to persuade me to cooperate with him and Sgt. Leeper regarding the Caddy assignment. I emphatically told him no. I didn't know Caddy, didn't know how to get to know him, and I was bothered that undertaking the assignment could lead to the destruction of another gay person who apparently was still in the closet.

We talked about the break-in and Carl told me straight out that Watergate would destroy the presidency but that President Nixon was guilty of nothing in its planning.

Carl said that there were hidden motivations involved, such the fear of law enforcement agencies that their turf would be reduced by Nixon through a scheme that later became known as the Houston Plan, the CIA's concern that Nixon planned to reorganize it, and the Defense Department's opposition to Nixon's trip to China and his new China policy. Carl intimated that military intelligence and the CIA, having gained prior knowledge of the planned break-in through the information that I had provided, were orchestrating the fallout from the arrests. The fate of President Nixon, unbeknownst to him, was in the hands of these agencies. When I asked Carl about his prior claim that one of the One Hundred Families was behind the break-in, that being the Kennedy family, he became agitated, leaving me with the impression that this prior claim was to throw me off-guard as to the real roles played by military intelligence and the CIA.

I asked Carl if he was angry at me for refusing to take on the Caddy assignment and he smiled at me and said he was glad that I didn't.

On June 28, 1972, Carl showed up at my apartment with four other men who I was led to believe were CIA agents. They wanted me to enter into a conspiracy to assassinate Douglas Caddy because he knew too much about the CIA and because he was a homosexual. This effort is described in my affidavit of July 29, 2009, which appears in the prologue of this book.

In the March of 1973 – nine months after the initial overture and a month after the first Watergate trial ended – I met with Carl, Sgt. Leeper, FBI agents O'Connor and Tucker and their FBI agent-in-charge, whose name escapes me. Sgt. Leeper did most of the talking. He again tried to persuade me to take on the Caddy assignment, making an initial offer of $25,000. I refused outright. The group then said that I could be paid as much as $100,000 if I took the assignment but I still refused without providing any explanation. Once it was understood that I would not accept the offer, Sgt. Leeper declared that the least I could do would be to spread the rumor around Washington that Caddy was gay in an effort to force him to come out of the closet. (This I did later through telephone calls to the offices of U.S. Senators, being guided in doing so by Shoffler at my side. We used a pay phone at People's Drug Store on Dupont Circle. By dropping a lousy dime for each call, Shoffler orchestrated an effective campaign to destroy Caddy, with me serving as his pawn and secret weapon.)

The March 1973 meeting was the last attempt to persuade me to take the Caddy assignment. The group departed angrily, with the exception of Carl, who secretly winked at me as he went out the door.

Carl Shoeffler Testifying before Senate Wategate Hearings
Photo: AP

Chapter Four

WHO REALLY WAS CARL SHOFFLER?

Affidavit of Robert Merritt regarding Carl Shoffler

I, Robert Merritt, attest to the following information regarding Carl Shoffler, the Washington, D.C. police detective who arrested the burglars at Watergate on June 17, 1972. The information that I am providing is derived from personal knowledge as I knew Shoffler for over 20 years, from 1970 until 1994, two years before his death at age 51.

There exists a great deal of information on the public record about Shoffler. I shall not repeat it here as it can easily be accessed merely by typing "Carl Shoffler" in the Google search engine.

I first laid eyes on Shoffler in December 1969 when he became part of the freak scene of a large group of persons who regularly gathered around Dupont Circle in Washington, D.C. Dupont Circle was within walking distance of the White House, about eight blocks away. The group of diverse persons who regularly gathered there cut across all strata of American society. There were Nazis, Communists, conservatives, liberals, straights, gays, drug dealers, drug users – you name it, they were there. Shoffler blended into the mixture easily because he was young (25 years old), had a scruffy beard and was shabbily dressed. At the time I was the most popular guy in the Dupont Circle freak scene. Everybody liked "Butch."

I had a job at a nearby drug store earning just enough above subsistence level. Early in January 1970, shortly after Shoffler had begun hanging around Dupont Circle, he showed up at the drug store. He did so twice, each time conferring privately with the store's owner.

To my dismay one day early in January the owner fired me, letting me go without explanation. I was crushed and retreated to my small apartment at 2122 P St, N.W., about two blocks from Dupont Circle. My monthly rent was $35 and I feared that I would be unable to pay it. On the evening of the same day that I was fired, as I sat in my apartment and attempted to gather my wits, there was a knock on the door. When I opened it, there stood Shoffler. For some reason, and I don't know why, I was not overly surprised at seeing him.

Shoffler pushed his way into my apartment and started talking. The first thing he said was that he was responsible for my being fired from the job at the drug store. The next thing he said was to take an envelope from him and open it. When I did so, there was $1000 in cash. Shoffler then informed me that he was an undercover detective with the Washington, D.C. Metropolitan Police Department (MPD) and that I had been the object of profiling by several law enforcement agencies. These agencies had concluded that I was an ideal candidate for being recruited as a Confidential Informant (CI). I met the criteria: young, good looking, non-political and hailed from the hills of West Virginia where I had grown up. The big plus was that I was popular with the crowd that hung out at Dupont Circle, which was the initial purpose of my being recruited. Law enforcement viewed the members of the crowd as being dangerous radicals who posed a serious threat to the American way of life.

Shoffler explained to me that because I was gay, I could not serve in the U.S. military. He asserted, however, that I could best serve my country and help defeat its enemies by agreeing to become a Confidential Informant and report to him on everything that was going on with the Dupont Circle scene. I accepted without hesitation, taking at face value Shoffler's enticement without questioning it in any way.

With the CI agreement then being verbally concluded, Shoffler asked if he could move into my apartment. He said that living there would facilitate his police undercover work. I was 26 years old, a year older than him. I readily agreed and we sealed the arrangement by downing a few beers. When it became late, Shoffler lay down on the couch and I climbed into my bed. I had hardly closed my eyes before I felt Shoffler sliding into bed beside me. He lost no time in performing oral sex, thus initiating our homosexual relationship that lasted for several years.

The next day, to give me cover, Shoffler arranged for two of his fellow officers to "arrest", hand-cuff, and place me in a police vehicle right in front of the Dupont Circle crowd, which stood agape as what they were seeing. I was then taken to a nearby police substation where I signed the necessary papers, was photographed and assigned a CI number, which was SE3.

My duties quickly expanded beyond informing on the Dupont Circle crowd. Shoffler arranged for me to do CI work for the FBI, working under the direction of FBI agents William Tucker and Terence O'Connor. After being taught CI techniques, I was assigned to target individuals and organizations that were considered politically Left. Pursuant to instructions, I planted illegal drugs on individuals, causing them to be arrested. I put wire-tap and eaves-dropping devices on the desks of "Leftist" lawyers and leaders and also on their vehicles. I broke into the offices of "Leftist" organizations and stole documents for MPD and the FBI. I attended rallies and cut the cords leading to the loud-speakers. On an occasion I stole 5000 addressed envelopes from the Hebrew Congregation in Washington as Shoffler and the FBI wanted the names and addresses on the envelopes as the recipients were deemed to be vocal opponents of the Vietnam War Another target was the Institute for Policy Studies, which I broke into and stole documents. Other targeted organizations included any considered to be active in protesting the Vietnam War and those that were gay. When the American Psychiatric Association voted to remove homosexuality from its list of mental disorders, Shoffler and other MPD officers ordered me to devise a means of targeting the association in retaliation. Shoffler also ordered me to engage in homosexual sex with about 70 targeted men, which I did. Once this was done their names were added to the government's database. I also, upon Shoffler's instructions, had homosexual sex with five MPD officers on different occasions whose names were provided to me. Later I identified each targeted individual through a two-mirror in MPD's Internal Affairs Division.

Shoffler acknowledged to me on two occasions that he was a military intelligence agent and had been assigned to MPD to monitor radical groups. Shoffler and I were considered to be above the law. We could do no wrong.

The above described events took place in the years and months leading up to the Watergate case. In an affidavit that I executed on July 29, 2009, I described my role in informing Shoffler on June 3, 1972 of the planned break-in at the Democratic National Committee scheduled for June 18, 1972. A highly unusual source provided me with this information. Rather than repeat this again, I incorporate my prior affidavit of July 29, 2009 into this affidavit.

My forthcoming book, *Watergate Exposed: A Confidential Informant Reveals How the President of the United States and the Watergate Burglars Were Set-Up, by Robert Merrit, as told to Douglas Caddy, Original Attorney for the Watergate Seven*, provides further details of my CI work for Shoffler in Washington, D.C. in the years after the Watergate case to 1985 and my CI work for him in New York City, after I moved there in 1986 and until two years before Shoffler's death in 1996.

It is important to note that in 1973 I met with the Special Watergate Prosecutor, with the staff of the Senate Watergate Committee and even testified in Executive Session before the Committee. While I provided much information to these, I did not disclose what I knew about the origins of Watergate. I did not do so because I was threatened by Shoffler, who told me that I would be 'hung publicly" for being a homosexual and would be prosecuted for the illegal acts that I had committed as a CI, even though these were done under the direction of Shoffler, the MPD and the FBI.

There are many secrets yet to be told about Watergate. Once these are revealed, the perception of the public as to what actually occurred will be radically altered. To give only one example: Shoffler told me of a secret dinner he had with Chief Judge John Sirica at the latter's invitation after the Watergate case broke. It was Judge Sirica who assigned the case to himself and presided over the grand jury investigation into the break-in and the trial of those arrested and later of those indicted for the cover-up. Judge Sirica's longtime mentor was Edward Bennett Williams, who served as legal counsel to the Democratic National Committee during the Watergate case.

This sworn statement is the truth, the whole truth and nothing but the truth, so help me God. I, Robert Merritt, swear in this affidavit that the facts are true to the best of my knowledge under the penalty of perjury.

/S/ROBERT MERRITT

Subscribed and sworn before me on the December 31, 2009 to certify my hand and seal of office:

Ricardo S. Castro

Notary Public State of NY

No. 01CA5041272

Qualified Bronx County

Comm. Exp. 03/22/2011

• • •

Carl Shoffler and I became roommates in 1970 after Shoffler recruited me to become a Confidential Informant. In 1972, before Watergate broke, Shoffler accidently left a card from his wallet on a table in the apartment that we shared. I picked it up and looked at it. Shoffler immediately grabbed it from my hand and told me that I had no right to do so. I responded that since we were lovers and worked and lived together I did not see what the big deal about the card was.

The card was from the Riggs National Bank in Washington, D.C. The name on it was Karl Maurice Schaffer.

Shoffler subsequently told me that in addition to being a detective for the Washington, D.C. Metropolitan Police (and a military intelligence agent) he also worked for Interpol. His assignment for Interpol was to monitor the intelligence agencies of Israel and the United Arab Emirates. This work included not only gathering information about the agencies' activities but also disseminating true and false information to those same agencies in a form of cointelpro.

On a number of occasions I accompanied Shoffler to the Riggs Bank where he withdrew large sums of cash using the card bearing the name of Karl Maurice Schaffer.

About ten days after the Watergate case broke, Shoffler told me that if it ever became known what he and I had done in the previous two years while living and working together, our lives would be

ART & FRAM

OPEN

OPEN
SUNDAYS
12-4

8
3
0
0

SAKAN
JAPANESE RESTA

2010 view of Merritt's apartment at 2122 P St. NW.
Photo: Author's Archives

worth nothing and that there was no place in the world we could hide and not be found. I interpreted this to encompass our pre-Watergate illegal efforts to infiltrate and destroy New Left and Peace groups, and also our knowledge of the planned Watergate break-in gained two weeks before the event took place and Shoffler's secret relationship with Interpol.

In light of Shoffler's claim that he worked for Interpol, excerpts from the article below are of special interest:

Missing American feared a victim of 'dirty war'

By Guy Dinmore in Washington and Najmeh Bozorgmehr in Tehran
Financial Times (U.K.)

April 13, 2007

Just why Robert Levinson, a former Federal Bureau of Investigation agent and now private investigator, should venture into Iran to meet an American fugitive wanted for murder in the U.S. remains a mystery that the highest Bush administration authorities are trying to unravel.

As the *Financial Times* revealed this week, Mr Levinson disappeared on March 8 after a six-hour meeting on the Iranian island of Kish with Dawud Salahuddin, an American who converted to Islam and was recruited by revolutionaries to assassinate an Iranian opposition activist near Washington in 1980.

Friends of Mr Levinson are mystified that he took the risk of travelling for such a meeting. They fear he is the victim of a sting operation by Iranian secret services engaged in an escalating "dirty war" between the U.S. and Iran, involving hostage-taking and covert cross-border operations.

Mr Salahuddin, who fled to Iran after the 1980 murder and has at times expressed interest in returning to the U.S. to face justice, told the FT in Tehran that he, too, feared Mr. Levinson was an "innocent victim" of the clash between what he calls Iran's paranoia about the U.S. and Washington's misguided foreign policy....

Over the years, Mr Salahuddin – who goes by the name of Hassan Abdulrahman in Iran, where he is married to an Iranian and works as an editor – developed an intense relationship over the telephone with Carl Shoffler, a legendary Washington, D.C. police detective.

Mr Shoffler, who died in 1996, followed the 1980 murder file and tried to persuade Mr Salahuddin to return to the U.S.. M. Salahuddin says he nearly did. In the meantime he helped Mr Shoffler liaise with an Iranian criminal investigator on tracking down drug smugglers bringing heroin from Afghanistan through Iran and on to the west. Mr Levinson shared those same interests.

******

Jim Hougan, in his best-selling 1984 book, *Secret Agenda*, wrote that at the time the Watergate case broke, Carl Shoffler "had assisted the CIA in the past and was personally acquainted with General Paul Gaynor." Gaynor was head of the CIA's Security Research Staff, a cadre within the Office of Security. He was burglar James McCord's "immediate superior for many years."

In preparation for telling my story in this book, I spoke on the telephone with a member of the Shoffler family. She told me that all members of the family were forbidden to discuss publicly the life of Carl Shoffler because the U.S. Government had required them to sign a confidentiality, non-disclosure agreement after his death in 1996. The implications of this action by the Government are self-evident.

Mark Felt

— CHAPTER FIVE —

THE MYSTERIOUS ROLE OF MARK FELT

T he role of Mark Felt in the origins of Watergate has never fully been revealed. That story will be told here in two parts. The first consists of biographical material on Felt that appears in Wikipedia. The second consists of my revelations about Felt's role in Watergate.

EXCERPTS FROM WIKIPEDIA:

William Mark Felt, Sr. (August 17, 1913-December 18, 2008).

On July 1, 1971, Felt was promoted by [J. Edgar] Hoover to Deputy Associate Director, assisting Associate Director Clyde A. Tolson. Hoover's right-hand man for decades, Tolson was in failing health and no longer able to attend to his duties.

Hoover died in his sleep and was found on the morning of May 2, 1972. Tolson was nominally in charge until the next day when Nixon appointed L. Patrick Gray III as acting FBI director. Tolson submitted his resignation, which Gray accepted. Felt took Tolson's post as Associate Director, the number-two job in the bureau.

In his memoir, Felt expressed mixed feelings about Gray.... His frequent absences, combined with Gray's hospitalization and recuperation from November 20, 1972 to January 2, 1973, meant that Felt was effectively in charge for much of his final year at the Bureau. Bob Woodward wrote "Gray got to be director of the FBI and Felt did the work." Felt wrote in his memoir: "The record amply demonstrates that President Nixon made Pat Gray the Acting Director of the FBI because he wanted a politician in J. Edgar Hoover's position who would convert the Bureau into an adjunct of the White House machine."

As Associate Director, Felt saw everything compiled on Watergate before it went to Gray. The agent in charge, Charles Nuzum, sent his findings to Investigative Division head Robert Gebhardt, who then passed the information on to Felt. From the day of the break-in, June 17, 1972, until the FBI investigation was mostly completed in June 1973, Felt was the key control point for FBI information. He had been among the first to learn of the investigation, being informed at 7:00 on the morning of June 17. Robert Kessler, who had spoken to former Bureau agents, reported that throughout the investigation they "were amazed to see material in Woodward and Bernstein's stories lifted almost verbatim from their reports of interviews a few days or weeks earlier."

Despite initial suspicions that other agents, including Angelo Lano, had been speaking to the *Post*, in a taped conversation on October 19, 1972, [H.R.] Haldeman told the President that he had sources, which he declined to name, confirming Felt was speaking to the press. "You can't say anything about this because it will screw up our source but there's a real concern. Mitchell is the only one who knows about this and he feels strongly that we better not do anything because...if we move on him, he'll go out and unload everything. He knows everything that's to be known in the FBI. He has access to absolutely everything."

On another White House tape, from May 11, 1973, Nixon and White House Chief of Staff Alexander M. Haig spoke of Felt leaking material to the *New York Times*. Nixon said, "he's a bad guy, you see," and that William Sullivan had told him Felt's ambition was to be director of the Bureau.

Felt retired from the Bureau on June 22, 1973, ending a thirty-one-year career.

In the early 1970's, Felt oversaw Operation COINTELPRO during the turbulent period in the FBI's history. The FBI was pursuing radicals in the Weather Underground who had planted bombs at the Capitol and the Pentagon and the State Department. Felt, along with Edward S. Miller, authorized FBI agents to break into homes secretly in 1972 and 1973, without a search warrant, on nine separate occasions. These kinds of FBI burglaries were known as "black bag jobs." The break-ins occurred at five addresses in New York and New Jersey, at the homes of relatives and acquaintances of Weather Underground members, and did not lead to the capture of any fugitives. The use of "black bag jobs" by the FBI was declared unconstitutional by the United States Supreme Court in the Plamondon case, 407 U.S. 297 (1972).

The Attorney General in the new Carter administration, Griffin B. Bell, investigated, and on April 10, 1978, a federal grand jury charged Felt, Miller and Gray with conspiracy to violate the constitutional rights of American citizens by searching their homes without warrants, though Gray's case did not go to trial and was dropped by the government for lack of evidence on December 11, 1980.

After eight postponements, the case against Felt and Miller went to trial in the United States District Court for the District of Columbia on September 18, 1980. On October 29, former President Nixon appeared as a rebuttal witness for the defense, and testified that presidents since Franklin D. Roosevelt had authorized the bureau to engage in break-ins while conducting foreign intelligence and counterespionage investigations. It was Nixon's first courtroom appearance since his resignation in 1974.

The jury returned guilty verdicts on November 6, 1980. Although the charge carried a maximum sentence of 10 years, Felt was fined $5,000. (Miller was fined $3,500).

Felt and Miller appealed the verdict.

In a phone call on January 30, 1981, Edwin Meese encouraged President Ronald Reagan to issue a pardon, and after encouragement from law enforcement officials and former bureau agents, he did so. The pardon was given on March 26, but was not announced to the public until April 15. (The delay was partly because Reagan was shot on March 30).

Vanity Fair magazine revealed Felt was Deep Throat on May 31, 2005 when it published an article (eventually appearing in the July issue of the magazine) on its website by John D. O'Connor, an attorney acting on Felt's behalf, in which Felt said, "I'm the guy they used to call Deep Throat."

Speculation about Felt's motives at the time of the scandal has varied widely.... Some suggested it was revenge for Nixon choosing Gray to replace Hoover as FBI Director. Others suggest Felt acted out of institutional loyalty to the FBI. Political scientist George Friedman argued that, "The *Washington Post* created a morality play about an out-of-control government brought to heel by two young, enterprising journalists and a courageous newspaper. That simply wasn't what happened. Instead, it was the FBI using The *Washington Post* to leak information to destroy the president, and the *Washington Post* willingly serving as the conduit for that information while withholding an essential dimension of the story by concealing Deep Throat's identity."

[End of excerpt from Wikipedia]

As previously recounted, I first learned from Rita, a highly unlikely source, on June 1, 1972, of the Watergate break-in planned for Sunday, June 18.

I told Carl Shoffler the evening of June 3 around 6 P.M. when the latter returned to the apartment that we shared about what Rita had related to me. Shoffler promptly ordered me not to inform anyone else about the matter. Shoffler's edict troubled me, but he was adamant. He intoned, "Butch, leave it alone. Stay out of it. This is my police assignment." Shoffler then left. That same night he returned to the apartment with two men and had me recount in detail to them what I had learned about the planned break-in. One of the two men was a retired CIA agent.

On June 4, 1972, one day after I told Shoffler of what I had learned, FBI Agents Bill Tucker and Terry O'Connor appeared at the door of my apartment. They told me that they had picked up a rumor of a meeting that had been held in my apartment during which I disclosed information about a planned break-in. They wanted more information. I remembered Shoffler's edict and refused to answer their questions. I was still mad at the agents for forbidding me to attend my mother's funeral two months earlier and for their subsequent physical threats against me in Rock Creek Park.

About two weeks later, two days after the arrests at Watergate on June 17, 1972, Agents Tucker and O'Connor again appeared at my front door and this time vociferously demanded that I tell them anything I knew about the break-in. When I refused to cooperate, Agent Tucker warned me that I "should remember what happened to someone whom I knew," and that "we'd hate to find you in the Potomac with cement over-shoes." I immediately interpreted this as an overt threat, especially in light of the recent disappearance from the face of the earth of Rita, the highly unlikely source who had told me of the planned break-in. From having worked with Tucker I had reason to be deathly afraid of him. This was not true of O'Connor and had he shown up at the apartment alone or with a different agent I would have told him everything that I knew about the origins of Watergate.

The same day of the FBI agents' visit Shoffler moved out of our apartment and never stayed there again. He was now in the public limelight. After two years our intimate relationship was over.

Who sent FBI agents Tucker and O'Connor to see me about the planned break-in, the first visit being on June 4, 1972 (13 days before Watergate broke) and the second being on June 19, 1972 (two days after the case broke)?

From comments made to me by Shoffler, I determined that it was Mark Felt. Shoffler and Felt shared common qualities. I remembered that the day after Hoover died, Shoffler remarked to me that "Hoover was felled by Felt." On a later occasion he told me that Felt was "the most evil, powerful person I have ever met." He also described Felt as being "an extremely angry man," referring to Felt's being upset for not being named as FBI Director by President Nixon after Hoover's death.

So did Mark Felt know in advance of the planned break-in at Watergate? Let's see.

Shoffler enlisted me as a Confidential Informant in early 1970. In 1971, impressed with my performance, the FBI enrolled me as one of its Confidential Informants. As described in a Watergate Special Prosecution Force memorandum of November 20, 1973: "Later in September [1971], Special Agents of the FBI Terry O'Conner or Bill Tucker came to Merritt's apartment with Officer Shoffler. At this time they were trying to locate the residence of [redacted.] At this time Merritt mentioned his financial problem and O'Connor suggested that he come to work for the FBI. Shortly thereafter, Merritt was informed by Dixon Gildon that he had been terminated due to lack of funds [from the Washington, D.C. Metropolitan Police] and the next day he received a call from O'Connor asking Merritt to work for the FBI. Merritt's assignment was to be the Institute for Policy Studies[IPS]."

In another Watergate Special Prosecution Force memorandum dated November 27, 1973, a burglary at the Institute for Policy Studies is described as follows, "After startling the girl at IPS, Merritt picked up one of the bags of mail and left with it... Merritt then called the Washington Field Office of the FBI to attempt to contact Tucker to see what he wanted to do with the mail. Tucker was not there and finally called Merritt back and asked Merritt to describe the mail and to open an envelope with a plane ticket in it. Merritt did this and xeroxed the ticket and envelope. Later Tucker picked up the mail and returned it to Merritt approximately two days later, telling him to return it to IPS...Merritt stated that from his examination of the material when it was returned to him by Tucker, he knew that at least the following material had been opened: the airline ticket of Arthur Waskow, the manuscript that had been delivered to Waskow had been unstapled and apparently xeroxed and restapled, there was a personal letter from Mexico to Waskow which Merritt later learned from Tucker the contents of the letter since Waskow was referred to as 'comrad" in the letter..."

Subsequently my work for the FBI was expanded beyond IPS. In a FBI memorandum dated 11/1/71 released to me under the Freedom of Information Act, it is stated:

> On 10/29/71, [redacted, referring to me] telephonically contacted the writer. Source stated that a friend [redacted] has offered to sell him some incendiary devices...The source described the devices as tubular in shape and about 21/2 inches to 3 inches in length. [Redacted] told the source that he could obtain dynamite, dynamite caps, fragmentation and smoke grenades, stink bombs, and another small type of incendiary device...The source was told by [redacted] that the incendiary devices and explosives are obtained from a [redacted] (LNU), who works with [redacted] at [redacted.] According to [redacted] obtained these items from [redacted] former member of NSWPP, who operates [redacted] in WDC. [Redacted] has told the source that [redacted] is a former member of NSWPP who quit the party because he believed that its members were not true Nazis.

A short time later I purchased the incendiary devices and delivered them to the FBI. Later O'Connor and Tucker made a special visit to me, stating that they carried a commendation directly from FBI Director Hoover for my work in obtaining the explosives.

Not long thereafter the FBI expanded my CI work to include attempting to infiltrate the Weather Underground. Again I found myself working closely with Agents Tucker and O'Conner.

Mark Felt directed the campaign against the Weather Underground, whose leaders were fugitives. He was later indicted for authorizing warrantless break-ins at the homes of relatives of the fugitives. Jennifer Dohrn, appearing on Amy Goodman's Democracy Now on June 2, 2005, related that,

I remember when I was pregnant with my first born feeling extremely vulnerable because I was followed a great deal of the time, and then it was revealed when I received my Freedom of Information Act papers, over 200,000 documents, that there actually had been developed by Felt a plan to kidnap my son after I birthed in hopes of getting my sister to surrender...I was not asked to testify [at Felt's trial in 1980], and it's interesting that the concrete thing that he could be convicted of were burglaries against me and several other people, break-ins, which were documented and recorded."

I began to become disenchanted with the FBI in April 1972. The occasion that triggered my disillusionment was when O'Connor and Tucker forbade me to attend my mother's funeral in West Virginia that month. They told me that my work in monitoring the Weather Underground superseded everything. I finally was able to scrape enough funds together to defy the FBI ban and arrived just as my mother's casket was about to be lowered into the ground. Upon my return from West Virginia, Agent Tucker remarked sarcastically to me, "How long did you think the stupid, drunken bitch would live?"

Thereafter, my resentment against the Bureau grew and festered.

On May 2, 1972, Hoover died. At the moment of his death I was sitting in a FBI vehicle with O'Connor and Tucker at the bottom of the hill on which Hoover's residence sat. When it came over the FBI radio that Hoover had died, the agents hurriedly gave me some money to catch a taxi home. Then they raced up to Hoover's home.

After Hoover died, Nixon appointed Patrick Gray as the Acting Director of the FBI with Felt next in command. In reality, Felt actually ran the FBI. He continued to direct COINTELPRO against the Weather Underground. He steadfastly employed Agents O'Connor and Tucker and me in this cause. As previously recounted, O'Connor and Tucker visited me on June 4, 1972, one day after I had told Shoffler about the Watergate break-in scheduled for June 18, 1972. O'Connor and Tucker wanted me to tell them what I knew about a planned break-in. It was Felt who sent O'Connor and Tucker to visit me. So Felt knew of a planned break-in two weeks before it occurred. And after it took place, *he* directed the FBI investigation into the scandal.

As Gordon Liddy once observed regarding Felt, "He's certainly not a hero, because the law enforcement official who obtains knowledge of the commission of a crime and has evidence of it, and who did it and so forth, is ethically obliged to go to the grand jury and bring his evidence in there so an indictment can be obtained and justice can be done. He didn't do that. Instead, he selectively leaked it to a single news source."

William F. Buckley, Jr. in his column of June 3, 2005, after Felt disclosed that he was Deep Throat, wrote:

> Now Mr. Felt steps forward and says that it was he who in effect staged the end of the Nixon Administration. What he did, over a period of months, was to report to two industrious journalists at the *Washington Post*, Bob Woodward and Carl Bernstein, everything that came to his attention through the fish-eye lens. Mr. Felt wanted to know everything about the traffic of dollars to and from the Committee to Reelect the President, and everything about the background and the activities of everyone associated with the White House, from the Attorney General down to the plumbers.
>
> As evidence accumulated of wrongdoing and crime, he reported not to the director of the FBI (his immediate superior), not to the Justice Department, but to two journalists. Bob Woodward was thoughtful enough to have recorded, the day after the news about Felt broke, his first meeting with Deep Throat back in 1970, two years before the Watergate break-in. There they both were, waiting, in the West Wing of the White House, Woodward to deliver a message from the Chief of Naval Operations, the Assistant Director of the FBI on a mission of his own. 'I could tell he was watching the situation very carefully. There was nothing overbearing about his attentiveness, but his eyes were darting about in a kind of gentlemanly surveillance. After a few minutes I introduced myself. 'Lieutenant Bob Woodward,' I said, carefully appending a deferential 'sir.'
>
> Mark Felt,' he said.
>
> Mark Antony, meeting Brutus, deserved no greater headline in history.

Ironically, it may well be that my testimony in 1973 before the Senate Watergate Committee and the Watergate Special Prosecution Force about my illegal CI activities, including those against the Weather Underground, carried out under the direction of the FBI, had the effect of opening up the criminal case that subsequently led to the indictment of Felt and Miller in 1978, five years later.

August 1974: Nixon leaving the Whitehouse

A Series Of Missed Opportunities: How Watergate Might Have Turned Out Differently

The first opportunity occurred the day after Rita told me of the planned break-in. On June 2, 1972, I attempted to alert MPD Sergeant Dixon Gildon. I telephoned her from a pay phone and said, "Dixie, I have a matter of national security that I need to talk to you about as soon as possible." She responded, "I'm rushing to a meeting. I'll see you later." Dixie and I had a working arrangement to meet at a set time during the day to exchange intelligence information. But for some reason Dixie failed to show up later that day at our pre-arranged meeting place.

I was also deeply upset at Rita's disappearance, which occurred the same evening that I told Carl about what Rita had learned. When I later complained aloud to Carl that "I haven't seen Rita," Carl's response was curt and blunt. He said, "Forget about that fucking drag queen. She's not in your life anymore and stay away from the other drag queens."

In August 1972 Sergeant Gildon came to my apartment at 1705 R St., N.W. where I had relocated upon Shoffler's direction, who feared that the media or someone would stumble upon our relationship. I had worked closely with Gildon for over two years. On one occasion she even had me as a dinner guest in her spacious home in Maryland where she resided with her husband, a successful contractor, and their daughter and son. Because she was in MPD Intelligence and worked undercover, she normally wore street clothes. But on her visit to me that August Gildon was dressed in her police uniform. Instead of giving me a friendly hug as she usually did, she begged off, saying she had a cold. She then crossed the room and turned off the television. When she did so, I spotted a bulge in her back and realized that she was wearing a wire to record their conversation.

Gildon then bluntly asked me, "Have you ever had sex with Carl Shoffler?" Aware that I was being recorded, I merely gave her a non-committal smile. Gildon then said, "Butch, have you run across something that Intelligence should know about, maybe even something that Carl has told you? Are you hiding something and not telling us? Did you tell something to Carl that we don't know about?" She paused for a second and then declared, "It's possible that you learned something on your own that is so volatile and sensitive that it could destroy the presidency. We know you are good at what you do but we also know that you are not politically astute."

I merely shrugged my shoulders and did not verbally respond. Gildon continued, "You should know that eyebrows are being raised about Carl. Some people think he knows more about the Watergate arrests than he is letting on." I responded, "If you think so, why doesn't MPD question him directly?" Gildon replied, "There are difficulties in doing that. He has reached celebrity status. Plus he is very clever." I then asked, "What about giving him a polygraph test?" Gildon rejected the idea outright, saying "If it ever came out that we asked him to a take lie-detector test, it would make us look bad." Gildon's response triggered my memory that Shoffler had once boasted that he had been taught how to beat a polygraph test at NSA's Vint Hill Farm Station.

Gildon then cut to the chase. She told me that "you have been involved in too many undercover activities that if disclosed would be very controversial," clearly referring to the numerous illegal activities that I had engaged in under Shoffler's and MPD's direction and that of FBI Agents Tucker and O'Connor, such as the theft of documents from the Institute for Policy Studies and sundry break-ins at other organizations. Gildon continued, "I realize now that I made a mistake when I told you that you were being paid for doing these things by White House funds from the Houston Plan." She had previously informed me that an undisclosed official high in the White House was dispensing the funds for the illegal activities that I had been directed to carry out.

Gildon then asked me to name a sum of money that it would take for me to remain quiet and to relocate far from the nation's capital. I responded emphatically, knowing that my words were being recorded, "I don't want any money and I'm not leaving Washington." Gildon recognized by the tone of my voice that the conversation had reached a dead end. She asked me to escort her to her car. When we exited the apartment building, Gildon mentioned she had parked a block away and began walking slowly. I then spotted a photographer at the northeast corner of New Hampshire and R Streets who was taking our picture. I exclaimed to Gildon, "That man is photographing us" to which she replied, "What man? I don't see anyone."

Once Gildon had driven away and I had returned to my apartment, I realized that the MPD had attempted to set me up to keep me quiet about the illegal activities funded by the White House under the Houston Plan and that if I had accepted the offer of money, I would have been arrested on the spot. MPD obviously believed that I knew too much. I strongly suspected that had I agreed to their plan it was quite likely that I would have been quickly transported to some distant location, such as Alaska, and secretly incarcerated there or, more likely, committed to St. Elizabeth's Hospital and kept in a state of permanent sedation. I was also scared because I had learned that the three drag queens with whom Rita and I had been friends before her disappearance had in recent weeks each died under mysterious circumstances.

But I also realized that Dixie's visit represented a missed chance to tell her about the origins of Watergate. Had I done so, Gildon, an ardent law-and-order Republican, might have whisked me directly to police headquarters where I would have been given protection. If that happened, the Watergate case could have taken a drastic change of direction. But then the thought came to me that because my highly unlikely source of information, a drag queen, about the planned break-in was so shocking, the homophobic MPD probably would choose to cover this up rather than disclose it, even if it meant saving the Nixon Presidency.

The next opportunity that arose to disclose what I knew was in 1973 when I testified before the Senate Watergate Committee in Executive Session. On the day that I was scheduled to testify, I spoke to Wayne Bishop, who was on the staff of the Senate Watergate Committee, and attempted to tell him the full story about the origins of Watergate. I had been referred to Bishop by a member of the staff of Senator Edward Kennedy. Bishop response was to threaten me. This incident took place as I was entering the Senate Building to testify before the Senate Watergate Committee, having been previously served with a subpoena. Bishop warned me that if I attempted to tell what I knew about the origins of Watergate that I would be arrested and charged with perjury and obstruction of justice. He made a point of telling me that I would be incarcerated in a jail located inside the U.S. Capitol Building. Bishop said that I was a known homosexual and thus "had no credibility." Bishop told me that I should leave the Senate Building immediately and that he would inform the Committee that I would not be able to testify because I had suddenly been taken ill. Bishop's overt threats and belligerent attitude instilled fear in me as I felt I was but a single individual against whom were aligned the most powerful forces in the land. It left me with the impression that the Senate Watergate Committee was not interested in finding out what really happened in Watergate. I soon learned that this impression was not far from the mark as I took my seat to testify before the Committee.

After I was administered the oath to tell the truth, virtually the first question from one of the Senators was, "Are you a homosexual?" I responded, "Yes", to which there was an audible gasp by the Committee's members. Still another Senator virtuously proclaimed that "homosexuals have no credibility." At that point I realized that what Shoffler had warned me about was true – that if I told what I knew I would be "publicly hung" as a despised homosexual and my knowledge of the origins of Watergate curtly dismissed as lacking credibility.

Nevertheless I pressed forward with my testimony about the sundry illegal activities that Carl Shoffler, the MPD and FBI had ordered me to carry out. Afterwards, Senator Sam Ervin, chairman of the Committee, told me, "Mr. Merritt, I believe your testimony but I am not quite certain that the American people are prepared to hear the shocking revelations that you have made." Later John Dean would testified before the Committee about the cover-up and as a consequence the Committee's primary agenda shifted to removing Nixon from office. However, the Committee continued to express interest in learning more information from me about the illegal activities. At this point, my attorney, David Isbell of Covington & Burling, refused to let me testify further unless I was granted immunity from prosecution. Such a grant was not forthcoming.

The next opportunity that arose was when I met with the Watergate Special Prosecution Force in late 1973 and repeated again what I had told the Senate Watergate Committee about the pre-Watergate illegal activities I had engaged in under the direction of Shoffler, MPD and FBI. Prosecutor Archibald Cox was present at one of these meetings. At my second meeting with the Force I began to feel that I could trust Cox and those who worked with him. I mentally decided to tell Cox at our next meeting what I knew about the origins in defiance of Shoffler's prior threats. But the very next day Cox was fired in the Saturday Night Massacre and I became afraid to spill what I knew.

The Watergate Special Prosecution Force interviewed me in depth on three occasions before it conducted a single, short interview of Carl Shoffler. A ten-page, single-spaced memorandum prepared by the Force dated November 20, 1973 opens as follows:

> Earl Robert Merritt, accompanied by his attorney, David Isbell, was interviewed on three occasions. On October 18 and 19, 1973, Merritt was interviewed by Martin and Hecht; on November 1, 1973, Merritt was interviewed by Martin and Akerman. Merritt is a former informer for the Metropolitan Police Department, the FBI, and on one occasion, the Alcohol, Tobacco and Firearms Division of the Treasury Department.

Shoffler in his subsequent interview on December 20, 1973, told the Force that he "introduced Merritt to FBI Agents O'Connor and Tucker and it took about a week for them to find that he was a liar." However, in preparation for writing this book I obtained hundreds of documents from the FBI under the Freedom of Information Act (FOIA). One of these documents is dated March 22, 1972, and addressed to "Director, FBI" and states in regard to me that "During the period the informant has been contacted, he has shown no signs of emotional instability or unreliability. He has maintained very regular contact and there has been no indication that he has furnished any false information." Another FBI document obtained under FOIA dated April 4, 1972, and addressed to FBI SAC R.C Kunkel, states:

> The file pertaining to the above-captioned informant has been reviewed by the Inspection Staff, and the informant has been rated as Excellent.

Ultimately it must be recorded for posterity that the greatest missed opportunity occurred in 1973, when both the Senate Watergate Committee and the Watergate Special Prosecution Force refused to give me a grant of immunity so that I could tell what I knew about the origins of Watergate. My attorney, David Isbell of Covington & Burling, repeatedly attempted to obtain the grant of immunity, stating that he would not let me testify without first getting it. Attorney Isbell, a powerhouse in the legal community, maintained if I told what I knew without first obtaining immunity that inevitably the FBI and other entities would retaliate by having me indicted and tried for whatever crimes they might dream up.

Had either the Senate Watergate Committee or the Watergate Special Prosecutor given me immunity in 1973, the full story of the Watergate Scandal could have come out then instead of 37 years later in this book. Given my knowledge of the break-in and the role played in it by Carl Shoffler, which I would have revealed, it is unlikely that President Nixon subsequently would have been targeted for impeachment or forced to resign from office. In short, the history of Watergate would have turned out vastly different.

The next opportunity was in 1985 when I wrote Chief Judge Carl Moultrie of the District of Columbia Superior Court and asked that I be allowed to testify under oath before a grand jury as to what I knew about the origins of Watergate. I received no response to my letter, so one day I showed up in the courthouse and attempted to enter the room where the grand jury was sitting to ask that I be allowed to testify. The prosecutor in the room promptly ordered armed guards to escort me out of the building.

After 1985, my life drastically changed and I never again felt I was free to disclose what I knew – until the death of Carl Shoffler in

1996. After he died from an extremely rare blood disease, I began a search for a co-author who could assist me in writing a book about the untold origins of Watergate. By chance I read on the Watergate Topic of the Education Forum, a web site in the United Kingdom, a posting by Douglas Caddy in which he stated that he suspected I had a vital story to tell about the scandal. I decided to write him and it was not long before we reached an agreement on co-writing the book. I felt comfortable with this arrangement as he was the author of five published books. Since he was present at the beginning of the Watergate case, he could readily grasp what had happened to me once I gained knowledge from Rita as to its origins. As our work progressed, both he and I were to find it ironic that we were working together on a book manuscript in which I was to disclose for the first time that I had been approached by Carl Shoffler and four other government agents in the days following the burglars' arrests to assassinate him.

"All the News That's Fit to Print"

The New York Times

VOL. CXXIII...No. 42,234

NEW YORK, SUNDAY, OCTOBER 21, 1973

LATE CITY EDITION

SECTION ONE

NIXON DISCHARGES COX FOR DEFIANCE; ABOLISHES WATERGATE TASK FORCE; RICHARDSON AND RUCKELSHAUS OUT

Kissinger Meets Brezhnev on Mideast Cease-Fire Plan

Secretary of State Kissinger with Leonid I. Brezhnev yesterday in Moscow

TALKS BEING SPED

U.S. Responds Quickly to Personal Appeal by Soviet Leader

By BEDRICK SMITH

MOSCOW, Oct. 20 — Secretary of State Kissinger arrived in Moscow today and quickly entered into talks with Leonid I. Brezhnev on the outbreak of Middle East war.

Israel Reports Enlarging Of Foothold on West Bank

By TERENCE SMITH

TEL AVIV, Oct. 20 — Israeli forces to the west bank of the Suez Canal pushed out to clear-cut and attack.

Saudi Oil Is Cut Off

OUTCRY IN HOUSE

Impeaching Nixon Is Openly Discussed by Leadership

By RICHARD L. MADDEN

WASHINGTON, Oct. 20 — For the first time tonight, members of the Democratic and Republican leadership of the House of Representatives began talking publicly and seriously about impeaching President Nixon.

BORK TAKES OVER

Duties of Prosecutor Are Shifted Back to Justice Dept.

By DOUGLAS E. KNEELAND

WASHINGTON, Oct. 20 — President Nixon, moving swiftly tonight to rebuke those who defy his orders, discharged Archibald Cox, special Watergate prosecutor.

Ex-Deputy Attorney General William D. Ruckelshaus

Attorney General Elliot L. Richardson introducing Archibald Cox, left, as special Watergate prosecutor last May.

Ervin at First Renounces, Then Accepts Tapes Plan

By the New York Times

WASHINGTON, Oct. 20 — Senator Sam J. Ervin Jr. at first renounced today and then accepted President Nixon's proposal to release a partial summary of the White House tapes.

RICHARDSON QUITS OVER ORDER ON COX

Attorney General Says He Couldn't Deal Prosecutor — Cites Autonomy Vow

By JOHN M. CREWDSON

WASHINGTON, Oct. 20 — Elliot L. Richardson resigned as Attorney General tonight rather than carry out President Nixon's order to discharge Archibald Cox, the special Watergate prosecutor.

Oakland Defeats Mets, 3-1, to Even World Series; Final Game Is Today

The Quality of Life Here Is Rated High in Survey

By PETER KIHSS

WATERGATE SPECIAL PROSECUTION FORCE INTERVIEWS OF ROBERT MERRITT AND CARL SHOFFLER

- MEMORANDUM OF JULY 24, 1973 TO TERRY LENZER FROM JIM MOORE REGARDING INTERVIEW WITH ROBERT MERRITT.

- MEMORANDUM OF NOVEMBER 20, 1973 REGARDING INTERVIEW WITH ROBERT MERRITT

- MEMORANDUM OF NOVEMBER 27, 1973 REGARDING INTERVIEW WITH ROBERT MERRITT

- MEMORANDUM OF DECEMBER 20, 1973 REGARDING INTERVIEW WITH CARL SHOFFLER

Senate Select Committee on
Presidential Campaign Activities
Staff files — James C. Moore
Box B186
Bob merritt

MEMORANDUM

TO: Terry Lenzner

FROM: Jim Moore

SUBJECT: Interview with Earl Robert Merritt, Jr.

DATE: July 24, 1973

Lee Sheehy and I met on 7/20/73, with Mr. Merritt and his lawyer, David Isbell, at Mr. Isbell's law office, 888 16th Street, NW (Covington & Burling). Mr. Isbell would like the committee to put Merritt under an investigative subpoena as soon as possible, a course of action that -- based upon what Merritt told us--seems questionable for our purposes. Isbell wants the subpoena as a shield against pressure that Merritt has allegedly been receiving from former associates not to testify.

Merritt has not talked with any other governmental agencies about his activities. Isbell and Jerry Norton of Covington know his story, as does Mitch Rogovin, who represents the Institute for Policy Studies, one of the places Merritt has been involved with. Bob Hertstein of Arnold & Porter also knows at least some of Merritt's story; Merritt initially went to Hertstein, who is on the Board of the Institute for Policy Studies, and Hertstein referred him to Isbell because of a possible conflict of interest between the IPS and Merritt. Merritt will not speak with the Metropolitan Police Department in the District because of his association with them, and he will not speak with Archibald Cox's office because of his wariness about the FBI's association with that office.

83

MEMORANDUM
Page 2

Merritt is 29 years old and lives at 1703 R Street, NW, phone 265-2051
(unlisted, presently disconnected). He is now cashier at Whelan Drug,
1201 Connecticut Avenue, NW. Merritt is a homosexual, and he has often
been used in undercover work with suspected homosexuals. Prior to the
1971 May Day demonstrations Merritt was involved in regular undercover
work for the DC police. From May Day until the latter part of 1972 he
was involved in political intelligence work for the DC police, the FBI, and,
for a brief time, for the Alcohol, Tobacco, and Firearms Division of the
Treasury Department. Almost all his work has been unrelated to Watergate
At the time of May Day he was asked by Detective Schaffler of the DC police
to get to know Rennie Davis and Jack Davis and to find out through them
everything he could about the May Day demonstration. He reported
directly to Detective Charles Robinson and Sergeant Chris Scrapper.
On July 15, 1971, Merritt was asked to begin infiltrating the Institute for
Policy Studies (IPS). Since then Merritt has been associated with IPS off
and on. In late September or early October, 1971, he was hired by the
FBI when the Metropolitan Police said they had run out of funds to pay him.
Merritt says he never saw anything subversive about IPS. He also says
that he never provided much information to the police or the FBI about IPS.
His biggest success was stealing a bag of mail from IPS one night and
giving it to the FBI and later to the Police Department. He has no idea
what was in the mail or how, if at all, it was used by the police or the FBI.
According to Merritt, both the FBI and the police, but particularly the
police, have a fixation about the subversiveness of IPS.

MEMORANDUM
Page 3

From January to June, 1972, Bob alternated between reporting on IPS and reporting on the Weathermen to the FBI. His heart was not in either task, and in fact he told Rennie Davis about his job. He also attended meetings and received mail from about a dozen DC area peace groups, social action groups, and gay organizations.

Shortly before the Berrigan trial began, he was asked by FBI agents Tucker and O'Conner to travel with a group of demonstrators from Washington to the trial. The agents told him that IPS had initiated pro-Berrigan demonstrations in the District. He did not make the trip because of a death in the family.

Merritt says he tried to break with the FBI around the time of a bombing at the Pentagon (5/19/72). Agent O'Conner told Bob that if he told his stories publicly he would be sorry. Specifically, O'Conner threatened to revive a dormant West Virginia bad check case that the FBI had long held over Merritt's head. Merritt told them that he was breaking his association no matter what they might threaten. It was his contention throughout the interview that, almost from the start, he was less than enthusiastic about his work and grew progressively more disenchanted.

On July 13, 1972, Merritt's one association with the Watergate affair began. Detective Schaffler and Sergeant Leper of the DC police visited Merritt and asked him to find out all he could about Douglas Caddy, who was representing some of the Watergate defendants. Caddy lived at

MEMORANDUM
Page 4

2121 P Street, NW, across the street from Merritt's residence at that
time. Merritt did not know Caddy. Schaffler and Leper told Merritt
that Caddy was homosexual and pro-Cuban. In response to Merritt's
questions, Schaffler and Leper said this assignment did not come from
the police intelligence unit or the FBI or the Alcohol, Tobacco, and
Firearms Division or the CIA. They further denied that the assignment
was involved with the Justice Department in any way. They would not
tell Merritt who had authorized their request, but Schaffler laughingly
said that it could possibly have come from sources higher than the Justice
Department. They told Merritt that it would be his biggest job and that
it was one of the best things he could do for his country. Merritt refused
to carry out the assignment. He says that he was periodically asked
during 1972 to find out about Caddy, these requests coming from Schaffler
or Leper. As recently as February 22 or 23, 1973, Schaffler asked him
if he knew anything about Caddy or would find out anything about him.
According to Merritt (I will check the transcript on this), on May 16 or 17,
1973, Leper testified before the Senate Watergate Committee that there
was no DC police involvement in Watergate in any way after the apprehension
of the burglars on the night of the break-in. Merritt says Leper was
personally involved in the effort to enlist him, Merritt, in the investigation
of Caddy. Consequently, Leper committed perjury before the Committee.
Isbell and Merritt are interested in pursuing possible perjury committed
by Leper and in pursuing the more general question/possible DC police

MEMORANDUM
Page 5

involvement in post-break-in investigations and activities.

Merritt's most recent association with IPS was in the early morning
hours on or about May 24, 1973. He was walking in DuPont Circle near
IPS when he saw lights on and shadows through a window. He place an
anonymous call to Barbara Raskin (the way to contact Marcus Raskin,
who has an unlisted number). Shortly thereafter two men rushed out of
the side of the Institute and jumped into what Merritt thought was an
unmarked DC police or FBI car. The car drove around the circle past
where Merritt stood. The men inside, whom he could not recognize,
saw him and sped away. Merritt got the license number, which he and
Isbell now have. Rogovin wrote the FBI and the police to complain about
the break-in, moves that Merritt sees as futile in light of what he thinks
is the involvement of one or both of those agencies in the break-in itself.

It is Merritt's feeling, and it seems to be shared by Isbell, that a
number of phones are probably tapped by the police or the FBI, including
Merritt's home phone and perhaps the Arnold & Porter phone. Merritt
once called Rogovin at Rogovin's office from a pay phone to arrange a
meeting. An undercover agent (he can't remember whether FBI or police)
shortly thereafter told Merritt that he knew about the planned meeting.
Shortly after making other calls from his home phone Merritt was contacted
by undercover agents who told him not to attend the meetings he had set
up. On June 12, 1972, Merritt called the Watergate Committee from his
home phone and was connected to Wayne Bishop. He told Bishop (he thinks

87

MEMORANDUM
Page 6

anonymously) that Leper had perjured himself. Following the call and before he spoke with anyone else, an old undercover friend of his from the Metropolitan Police, Dixie Gildan, called and said she understood that Merritt was planning to testify before the Ervin committee. He later got a call from Schaffler, who said the same thing. Merritt views such calls as part of a pattern of harassment intended to keep him from telling his story. (Merritt is still officially associated with the DC police in an undercover role. His job is to keep a tab on gay organizations in the DC area. He was given this task in the spring of 1973, but he says that he provided them with little relevant information.)

If all that he says is true, Merritt has quite an interesting story. However, most of it is unrelated to Watergate. The alleged Caddy investigation request after the break-in seems worth pursuing. What Isbell understandably wants is an investigative subpoena from this committee as protection for his client for all the activity he has been involved in, including the non-Watergate activity. I question whether that is a proper use of a Watergate Committee subpoena. Merritt is more than willing to go into much greater detail about his political undercover work with Rennie Davis, May Day, etc. He says that he has told us everything in this first interview that he knows about his involvement with Watergate. He also says that he was never contacted about any other Watergate investigation and never heard about any other Watergate activity involving the Police Department or the FBI.

WATERGATE SPECIAL PROSECUTION FORCE

Hornwitz

DEPARTMENT OF JUS

Memorandum

TO : Files

DATE: November 20,

FROM : Frank Martin ꟼM

SUBJECT: Interview of Earl Robert Merritt (AKA Robert Chandler

Earl Robert Merritt, accompanied by his attorney, David Isbell, was interviewed on three separate occasions. On October 18 and October 19, 1973, Merritt was interviewed by Martin and Hecht; on November 1, 1973, Merritt was interviewed by Martin and Akerman. Merritt is a former informer for the Metropolitan Police Department, the FBI, and on one occasion, the Alcohol, Tobacco and Firearms Division of the Treasury Department.

October 18, 1973 Interview:

Background

Merritt stated that his first contact leading to his informant work was with Carl Schoffler of the MPD. In the spring of 1970 Merritt met Schoffler but did not know until the fall of 1970 that Schoffler was an undercover policeman. In the fall of 1970, Schoffler introduced Merritt to agents of the ATF, including Bill Seals, Richard Campbell, and Dick Caldan. Merritt was told that Seals was interested in making contacts to set up buys of firearms, explosives, and narcotics. Approximately two or three weeks later in October Merritt introduced Seals to people he knew in the Washington area as someone interested in getting into organized crime an interested in buying firearms, explosives, and narcotics. From October 1970 to April 1971, Merritt worked as an informe on narcotics and street crimes cases for the Metropolitan Police Department.

Intelligence Assignments

On April 5, 1971, Merritt lost his job at a drug stor at 15th and H Streets. Merritt blamed the loss of his job on Schoffler who looked like a hippie and often contacted hir at the drug store leading his boss to think that Merritt was dealing in narcotics. The next day Schoffler came to Merritt

89

2

apartment and offered him a full-time job in intelligence
work stating that they needed a gay, white male for "our own
little spy department."   Schoffler then introduced Merritt
to Sgt. Rice who was waiting in the car, and he was taken to
the Second District Headquarters at 23rd and L.   At the stat:
he met narcotics officers Light, Blackburn, and Det. Linda
Sanker, as well as Sgt. Carl Maddox of Intelligence and
Christopher Scrapper who was a friend of Rice's.   Schoffler
then took Merritt to the Washington Monument to meet two
intelligence officers, Dets. Scrapper and Charles Robinson.
The officers told Merritt that his assignment would be with
regard to May Day and that he was to try to get close to
Jack Davis and to Rennie Davis.   Merritt stated that he had
once met Jack Davis at a Gay Liberation Front meeting.   The
officers also wanted him to get close to Raymond Twohig
who was Jack and Rennie Davis' lawyer and who worked at the
Georgetown Legal Interns.   Merritt also knew Twohig.   Merritt
called Scrapper the following day and told him that he would
accept the assignment and that he had been in the Vermont
Building (a building on Vermont Avenue where many of the
demonstrators' headquarters were located).   Merritt was to
call him twice a day and was given the code number 16.   Merri·
stated that it got closer to May Day he was calling in
once every hour.   Merritt stated that he spoke to various
people at the main MPD number and was later given other
numbers in the MPD offices.

        At this time Seals also told him that his assignment i
ATF was to infiltrate the May Day demonstration.   As part of
his assignment Merritt arranged for Seals to go through
training to be a Marshal for the May Day demonstrators.   Scrap
and Robinson also asked Merritt to get a floor plan for some
of the buildings which housed the demonstrators.   Merritt
stated that he may have a note from Scrapper and Robinson
asking him to do this and that the offices he was to get the
floor plans for included the Vermont Building, an office in
the 2100 block of M Street, the office of Georgetown Legal
Interns, the Quicksilver Times, the Gay Liberation Front,
Raymond Twohig's home, and the D.C. Statehood Party offices.
Merritt stated that he felt the assignment of drawing the floo:
plans was more as a check to insure that Merritt had actually
been there since he assumed that Scrapper and Robinson
could get the floor plans in detail from other sources if
they wanted them.

        Merritt was instructed by Scrapper to be a "saboteur"
at the May Day demonstration.   Merritt described this role as
giving misinformation to demonstrators and stated that he
was told by Scrapper that there was no limitation on his action

3

that he was to use his own judgment and do whatever was necessary to discourage or stop May Day. Scrapper also told him that there were others doing this type of work. Scrapper stated that the information going to the counter-intelligence desk or the Council of Governments (COG) and what Scrapper referred to as the Sabotage Department.

Concerning sabotage, Merritt stated that Scrapper suggested to him that he sabotage the public address system cutting wires and pulling tubes. Scrapper also told Merritt to take any petitions with names and addresses and to get the automobile license plate numbers of any cars that were involved with the people who were working on the May Day demonstration. Scrapper also told Merritt to locate the communications system in the Vermont Building which would be used for May Day and to find out what codes were being used so that someone would then be able to jam the communications Merritt was told by Seals that this was going to be done.

Merritt stated that he performed only one job for AT[That involved going to New York City for two days to follow Jack Davis. Merritt stated that he received a $100 check and $50 in cash as part of this assignment and that he did in fac go to New York but did not do any work in connection with following Jack Davis.

Merritt stated that he was told by Bill Seals that al agencies, local and federal, had been given instructions to become intelligence agencies with regard to May Day. With regard to information being given to Seals and being passed on through ATF, Seals stated that the information went into one central location near Washington (Falls Church) and then was sent to Richmond, Virginia for analysis, and the: was sent back to Washington to the Justice Department. Merri stated that he was also aware that there was a room in the ba: ment of IRS for counter-intelligence information which would (to IRS about demonstrations. Merritt stated that he believed that this information went also to the Justice Department. Isbell stated that the reason that Merritt was asked to get petitions seems to be two-fold. One, to get names of those who had signed petitions, and two, to disrupt the petitioning process. Merritt stated that Seals had told him that the Government liked to keep a list of those he termed "enemies of America."

With regard to May Day itself, Merritt stated that he
reporting approximately every half hour on crowd size and
movements. Merritt stated that he also had been instructed
to pull tubes and cut wires on PA systems. Merritt stated
that the MPD officials with whom he had contact during this
time were Lt. Acree, his secretary Connie Fredericks, and
Lt. Crook. Merritt stated that he was also told to become
"a provocateur" which instructions included rock throwing
and breaking windows either by himself or provoking others to
do so. At one point, it was suggested that he say something t
the demonstrators like "I'll tell you where the President
lives if you'd like to kill him." During this period, Officer
Light and Blackburn asked Merritt
                                           At the time of this
request, which was by phone, Light and Blackburn were with
Ann Kolago in MPD headquarters. Merritt stated that shortly
after he was instructed to do this,
                                     The next day Merritt called
the Second District Narcotics Squad and

The next day Merritt called Scrapper and Scrapper was
apparently angered that Light and Blackburn were interfering
in intelligence operations. Scrapper stated that he would
talk to their Sergeant which apparently he did since Light
and Blackburn became hostile to Merritt over the incident.

October 19, 1973 Interview:

Merritt added to his description of his May Day activi
Merritt stated that he was told that if he were arrested
he was not to say who he was working for but was to call intel
ligence offices after he was in the police station.

Post-May Day

After the May Day operation, Merritt stated that he
was in a sort of limbo status, still being paid but not doing
much work. In late May 1971, Merritt was contacted by phone
by Scrapper asking him to break into the Georgetown Legal
Interns office. Scrapper wanted to know if Merritt could
get access to Ray Twohig's files at the Georgetown Legal
Intern office. Merritt stated that he knew where they were
but could not get access and Scrapper asked Merritt if he knew
how to use burglar's tools and said that Scrapper would provide the tools. Merritt stated that he remembered this
incident quite distinctly since it was the first direct, open
illegal instructions that Scrapper gave him. Scrapper stated
that he would get back to Merritt in a few days, which he

did, and told Merritt that it had been postponed temporarily.
Scrapper had stated that they wanted Twohig's files on Jack
Davis and Rennie Davis.

Merritt stated that in May he was contacted by phone
by Connie Fredericks who stated that "we would like to know"
who is in the Community Bookstore Building. Merritt stated
that his understanding of the request was that the MPD wanted
to know who was receiving mail there since a lot of mail
was going to people using aliases. Merritt's understanding
of the assignment was that he would get the mail from the off
and that it would be opened by the MPD to find out who the
mail belonged to. Merritt stated that later, the first week
in June, he was contacted by phone by Scrapper. Scrapper
asked Merritt to get into the Community Bookstore without
using burglar tools and Merritt stated that he could do this.
Scrapper stated that he wanted any anti-war petitions, any
mail and any anti-war leaflets that Merritt could get a hold
of. Scrapper also stated that if Merritt were caught by a
patrol car, he should use an alias and then call the MPD offi
number 626-2684 or 2685.

Institute for Policy Studies

Merritt stated that his first contact with the Instit
for Policy Studies was on July 15, 1971, when he obtained
a flyer on Studies of Marxism to be given at IPS. He gave
this flyer to Officer Robinson. Later, Robinson and Scrappe:
asked Merritt if he knew IPS and said that IPS would be his
next assignment that he was to take classes there and subsequently, Merritt did take classes there. On September 1,
1971, there was a job opening at IPS and Scrapper told Merri
to apply for the job. Merritt applied for the job but never
got it.

Also in September, Merritt found that he could not
get along with Scrapper and he was then assigned to Dixie
Gildon of the MPD.

Later in September, Special Agents of the FBI O'Conn
and Tucker came to Merritt's apartment with Officer Schoffle
At this time they were trying to locate the residence of
[FOIA(b)6] At this time Merritt mentioned his
financial problems and O'Connor suggested that he come to
work for the FBI. Shortly thereafter, Merritt was informed
by Dixie Gildon that he had been terminated due to lack of
funds and the next day he received a call from O'Connor

asking Merritt to work for the FBI. Merritt's assignment was to be the Institute for Policy Studies, and he was to continue his work there. Merritt attended meetings such as a Prison Reform meeting given by Philip Hirschkop and other meetings held at the Institute.

On November 23, 1971, Merritt was passing the IPS building at approximately 7:30 or 8:00 p.m. At this time the was a womens' meeting going on on the second floor and Merrit went into the lobby. Merritt saw a girl in the front office who then dropped a bag of mail which she had been filling with mail from the mail box of the IPS fellows. Merritt state that she was surprised and startled to see him and that Merritt then asked her if she had seen Art Waskow. The woman said that she had not seen him and that she was looking for the rest room and she was attending a meeting upstairs. Merritt later left the building and went down towards Dupont Circle. He looked back at the building and saw the girl come take the bag that she had filled with mail and throw it by the side of the door. After she did this, a car pulled up with two white males. The car stopped, one of the men got out, picked up the bag and put it in the car and then they lef

May 24, 1973 - Alleged Burglary

Merritt stated that while walking past the IPS office at 1:53 a.m. on May 24, 1973, he noticed a car parked near the IPS building. He noted that the car was a police cruiser since he saw the radio underneath the dashboard. Merritt also saw a window open near the fire escape and some lights on. Merritt then walked to the corner, stopped, and looked back. Merritt took down the license plate number of the car (774-443). Merritt then went across the Dupont Circle park and made a telephone call to Mrs. Raskin and told her that he believed there were people inside IPS. He then returned to the corner near the IPS building and saw two people come out and get into the car. Both were males, one came out of the Dupont Plaza Hotel and one came out of the alley-way between the Dupont Plaza Hotel and the IPS office. The two people in the car drove directly towards him at the corner of New Hampshire Avenue and Dupont Circle, apparently looked directly at him, and then accelerated and then went down 19th Street. Merritt then went home and called Mrs. Raskin and gave her the license plate number of the automobile. Merritt stated that in late June 1973, he met with Officer Schoffler who made reference to the "letter of May 25," referring to Mitchell Rogovin's letter concerning the alleged burglary. Also, in

July 1973, Dixie Gildon mentioned to him that she had learned
in late June of the letter of May 25, 1973.

November 1, 1973 Interview:

August 2, 1973 - Alleged Burglary

At approximately 3:15 a.m. on August 2, 1973,
Merritt was walking down New Hampshire Avenue towards Dupont
Circle. Merritt noticed a police cruiser in the alley-way
between Church Street and Q Street and as Merritt approached,
the cruiser turned on its siren, came out of the alley, turned
up 18th Street, and then took a right on Q Street. Merritt
stated that he thought that this was some sort of a warning
to the people who he thinks were burglarizing IPS. Merritt
proceeded down New Hampshire Avenue and saw a man come out of
the Dupont Plaza Hotel. The man was wearing a suit, tie,
and had a moustache, and white hair. Merritt then proceeded
to the corner of New Hampshire and Dupont Circle where he saw a
white unmarked car with a policeman in uniform sitting in the
car. When the officer saw Merritt he started the motor, pulled
out and turned north on 19th Street. Merritt then proceeded to
cross Dupont Circle where he called the Raskin's home to inform
them of what he believed to be a burglary. The Raskins were not
home and Merritt spoke to a house sitter who gave him the Raskin
address in Sweden and the name of the Raskins' secretary.
Merritt stated that he was unable to get the secretary's telephone number since she was not listed in the telephone book.
Merritt then tried to call Arnold and Porter and got no answer
and also he could not reach Mitchell Rogovin. Merritt then
went to the gas station at 22nd and P Streets, N.W., and called
the Washington Star where he told the person on the phone that
"something was going on in the Institute." Merritt stated
that he was later informed by personnel at the Star that a
woman had called the police and said she was a caretaker from
IPS and that there was a burglary going on. After calling the
Star, Merritt went back to Dupont Circle and saw a police cruise
with a dog arrive at the location of IPS and that the policeman
got out, looked around, and called for more cruisers. Several
cruisers and unmarked cars arrived and Merritt assumed the
unmarked cars belonged either to the Star reporters or possibly
the FBI. This was around 4:00 or 5:00 a.m. At 6:45 a.m.,
Merritt again passed by IPS and one of the unmarked cars was
still there.

Surveillance of IPS

Merritt stated the following concerning surveillance of IPS. Merritt stated that he believes that there was surveillance going on from the Dupont Plaza Hotel because the police always went into the hotel before going to IPS. Also, Merritt had been told in conversation with Schoffler and Seals (shortly before May Day) that the 4th floor front corner room of the Dupont Plaza Hotel was used for surveillance of IPS. Merritt stated that Tucker had told him that a boom and/or sourcer-type microphone was used for surveillance of IPS. Tucker told Merritt this in November 1971 right after the meeting at IPS at which Robert Wall spoke. Tucker wanted to know from Merritt whether Wall told the people at IPS that such devices were being used against them. Merritt stated that around the time of May Day he was told that the Solgrave Club was used by the FBI for surveillance of IPS. Merritt stated that he could not recall who told him this, but did remember someone pointing to a window in the Solgrave Club as the room that was being used for surveillance. Merritt stated that Seals, of AFT, told him on November 18, 1971, that the MPD, the FBI, and ATF all had IPS under surveillance and that, in addition, their tax records were regularly checked. In July or August 1971, Schoffler told Merritt that This occured in December 1971 shortly after Wall spoke at IPS.

Merritt stated that on August 14, 1973, he was passing IPS and saw a painter working in the building at approximately 3:00 a.m. Mr. Isbell stated that this was checked out with the people at IPS who said that there was some painting going on but that no one should have been there at 3:00 a.m.

Schoffler [ ] Incident

Merritt provided the following information concerning the Schoffler [ ] incident. Merritt stated that a few days after June 17, 1972, the date of the Watergate arrests, he was contacted by Schoffler and Leper who came to Merritt's home. Schoffler and Leper asked Merritt if he knew and

FOIA(b)6
FOIA(b)7 - (C)

9

Merritt stated that he did not know him. They then stated that [ ] was a homosexual with pro-Cuban contacts and was involved with the Young Americans for Freedom. They then asked Merritt to take the assignment of getting close to [ ], know him intimately, socially, and to get any names, addresses, and phone numbers of people [ ] was in contact with. Merritt asked why they wanted him to do this and all they stated was that this was the most important assignment that they had ever given to him and that it came from a high source, and that he would be paid well. They stated that the assignment was not for the MPD, CIA, FBI, or ATF. Merritt stated that he would think about it and let them know. A few days later, Merritt called and told Schoffler that he would not do it. Schoffler was annoyed. Schoffler also denied that the assignment had anything to do with Watergate. Several months later, in the fall of 1972, Merritt was talking with Schoffler and arguing about various things concerning the police and Schoffler told him that the assignment to get close to [ ] was involved with Watergate.

In June 1973, after the testimony of Schoffler and Leper before the Senate Select Committee, Merritt made an anonymous call to Jim Flug, of Senator Kennedy's Subcommittee on Administrative Practices and Procedures, and told him that he thought Schoffler and Leper had been lying to the Select Committ Flug suggested to Merritt that he call the Senate Select Committee, which Merritt did. Merritt spoke to Wayne Bishop of the Senate Select Committee and began to tell him his story concerning Schoffler. At first, Merritt would not identify himself and then later he called Bishop back and identified himself and began to tell his story. As he proceeded, he decide it would be better if he had Bishop contact his lawyer, Mr. Isbell. Shortly after this, Schoffler came to see Merritt. Merritt stated that Schoffler appeared to come on a friendly pretense, but then stated that he understood that Merritt was trying to get involved in Watergate and that if Merritt kne what was good for him, he would stay out of it. Schoffler then reminded Merritt of certain things that had been said to him by Tucker of the FBI at the time Merritt stopped working for the FBI. The conversation with Tucker had taken place in May of 1972, at which time Tucker told Merritt to remember the bad checks he had passed in West Virginia and not to participate in any further demonstrations because "we'd hate to see you get shot accidentally." Tucker had gone on to tell Merritt that he should remember what happened to someone else who he knew and stated "we'd hate to find you in the Potomac with cement over-shoes."

FOIA(b)6
FOIA(b)7 - (C)

97

Merritt stated that there were several attempts to plant narcotics on him and in his apartment. Merritt stated that at various times he destroyed the narcotics, put them in a police car, and on one occasion, he gave some heroin and a syringe that had been planted on him to Dixie Gildon. These incidents occured in the fall of 1972. Merritt stated that there were also attempts to plant informers close to him and that one informer actually moved in with Merritt.

Merritt stated that there were two burglaries of his residence at 1703 R Street, N.W. On July 11, 1973, his apartment was ransacked. That night he received a call from [redacted] who stated that [redacted] would meet him the next day at his doctor's office. Merritt stated that there was an appointment slip in his home at the time it was ransacked and this would be the only way that [redacted] would know he had an appointment. Merritt did not go to the doctor's appointment, and instead, Mr. Isbell went and confronted [redacted] Merritt stated that there was another burglary of this house on August 6, 1973.

Merritt stated that he was followed on several occasions and on June 15, 1973, noted that he was being followed by a car bearing D.C. tag 781-456. Merritt confirmed through Dixie Gildon that this was an FBI car. Merritt stated that on Sunday, October 28, 1973, there was an entry into his house through the back door. On October 31, 1973, Merritt was told by a repairman that the flu to his hot water heater had some how been stopped up and that poisonous carbon monoxide was accumulating within the house.

Merritt and his attorney, Mr. Isbell, stated that they would provide further documentation on Merritt's allegations.

WATERGATE SPECIAL PROSECUTION FORCE   DEPARTMENT OF JU

Memorandum

TO   :   Files   DATE: November 27

FROM :   Frank Martin

SUBJECT: Earl Robert Merritt

On the several occasions when Mr. Merritt was interviewed (October 18, 19, and November 1, 1973) and in subsequent telephone conversations, David Isbell, Merritt's attorn
has provided certain additional information concerning
Merritt's activities. It was agreed with Mr. Isbell that
providing this information would not constitute a waiver by
his client of any attorney-client or Fifth Amendment privilege

May Day

Merritt did, in fact, cut wires leading to speakers
and pulled tubes to disrupt one of the demonstration meetings,
which occurred two or three days before the major May Day
demonstration. This meeting took place at the May Day site
at Potomac Park.

Community Book Store

On one occasion Merritt entered the Community Book Stor
and took mail and delivered it to the MPD. On a second
occasion, he taped the door lock to the office and later
entered and took petitions and mail and delivered it to the
MPD, and that this material was not returned through him
to that office. Merritt was told that, "We are going to open
files on individuals," which he assumed meant the individuals
whose mail had been taken and whose names were on the petitions.

Merritt was later contacted by Connie Fredericks who

stated that one of the pieces of information he had supplied
was very interesting. She then read to him a letter from a
physician at St. Elizabeth's Hospital (a mental institution).
The letter was to a [FOIA(b)6] concerning the fact that h
had run away from the hospital and was later discharged.
Merritt stated that Connie Fredericks wanted him to get more
information about the individual who was discharged from St.
Elizabeth's. Merritt stated that in October 1971, when he
related this incident to the FBI, he was told that the MPD
had no right to give him such instructions. On the occasion
of the second break-in to the Community Book Store, two large
boxes weighing 40-50 pounds were taken.

Novem   ## November 23, 1971 - IPS Burglary

        After startling the girl at IPS, Merritt picked up
one of the bags of mail and left with it. He left the buildin
and went down towards Dupont Corcle and looked back at the
building and saw the girl come out and throw a bag that she
had filled with mail by the side of the door. After she did
this, a car pulled up with two white males. The car stopped,
one of the men got out, picked up the bag and put it in the
car and then they left. Merritt then called the Washington
Field Office of the FBI to attempt to contact Tucker to see
what he wanted him to do with the mail. Tucker was not there
and finally called Merritt back and asked Merritt to describe
the mail and to open an envelope with a plane ticket in it.
Merritt did this and xeroxed the ticket and envelope. Later
Tucker picked up the mail and returned it to Merritt approxi-
mately two days later, telling him to return it to IPS.
While speaking to Dixie Gildon, Merritt told her that he had
the mail and that he had to get it back. Gildon told him that
Officers Bittenbender and Oglmyer would like to see the mail.
Merritt then delivered the mail to the 5th floor of the MPD
headquarters where he called Oglmyer and was told by Dixie
Gildon to leave the mail beside the phone booth on that floor.
Merritt did this and then left the floor. Merritt later asked
Dixie Gildon if the mail had been returned and she told him
that it had not been returned that it had been put through the
shredder.

        Merritt described the girl he saw at the IPS office
who was taking the mail as a white female in her early twneties,

wearing glasses, long, light brown hair, approximately 5'7"
and 120 pounds. Merritt recently (late October 1973) saw a
girl he can now identify as the girl who took the mail from
IPS. Merritt saw her at a demonstration at the White House
where she was talking to Officer Bittenbender. Merritt
believes she may be Ann Kolego. Merritt was later told by
O'Connor that Merritt should have known better than to take
the mail and that Merritt should forget the incident and never
do it again. Merritt stated that from his examination of
the material when it was returned to him by Tucker, he knew
that at least the following material had been opened: the
airline ticket of Arthur Waskow, the manuscript that had been
delivered to Waskow had been unstapled and apparently xeroxed
and restapled, there was a personal letter from Mexico to
Waskow which had been opened and Merritt later learned from
Tucker the contents of the letter since Waskow was referred
to as "comrad" in the letter. There was also a letter to
Waskow concerning the salary increase. Mr. Isbell stated
that Merritt would provide notes of addressee and senders
on various of the letters.

TE 11/28/08

4

WATERGATÉ SPECIAL PROSECUTION FORCE

DEPARTMENT OF JUSTICE

Memorandum

TO : Files

DATE: December 20, 1973

FROM : Frank Martin

SUBJECT: Interview of Carl Schoffler

FOIA(b)6
FOIA(b)7 -
(C)

    Sgt. Carl Schoffler of the Metropolitan Police Department was interviewed on December 3, 1973, by Horowitz, Akerman and Martin. Horowitz advised Schoffler of his right to counsel and his right to remain silent and Schoffler voluntarily provided the following information.

    From 1970 until April 1973, Schoffler worked in the Second District as a TAC officer doing semi-undercover work on street crime. Schoffler stated that he did not normally report on intelligence information but would occasionally do so if while he was working on street crime he came across any information of interest to Intelligence. Schoffler stated that he met Robert Merritt, whom he knew as Robert Chandler, in 1970 and that Merritt did some informant work on street crime for him. Schoffler stated that Merritt was giving him information almost every day and did provide some good criminal investigation work. Schoffler noted that he once provided a notebook [____] and was accused of various rapes and that the notebook showed the addresses of various places where this individual had been accused of committing rapes. Schoffler stated that he saw Merritt every three or four days for almost two years.

    Concerning May Day, Schoffler stated that he occasionally supplied information on May Day and would phone the Intelligence office and give the information to whomever answered the phone. Schoffler stated that he had some contracts with ATF and with the FBI but none with regard to May Day. Schoffler also worked some on crowd control during May Day. Schoffler introduced Merritt to Scrapper, and Merritt worked with Scrapper and with Dixie Gildon. Schoffler noted that Acree, who headed much of the intelligence work, did not like Schoffler.

Screened

By: Heather Macrae   Date:
11-24-2008

102

2

Schoffler was questioned concerning the incident
involving [   ] Schoffler stated that at some
time after the Watergate arrests, Schoffler and Leper were
in their car and met Merritt near his residence at 2121 P
Street. Schoffler stated that he had first seen [   ] the
day after the Watergate arrests when [   ] came to represent
the Cubans. When Schoffler and Leper met Merritt, Merritt
stated that he might know [   ] and Merritt had an article
from the newspaper with a picture of [   ] in it. Schoffler
told Merritt to let him know if Merritt found out who [   ]
was and if he was "funny", i.e., homosexual. Schoffler
stated that this was an off-hand comment and he never expected Merritt to do anything, and Merritt never told Schoffler
anything about Caddy.

Schoffler stated that in the summer of 1973, after he
had testified in the Watergate hearings, Schoffler met
Merritt. Merritt stated that he had made all sorts of calls
to Senators concerning Watergate and the Caddy incident with
Schoffler. Schoffler stated that he told Merritt that if he,
Merritt, reported a crime then that was one thing, but that
if he reported something that was only in his head it was
going to come back on him. Schoffler said that he did not
in any way threaten Merritt.

Schoffler stated that he introduced Merritt to FBI Agents
O'Connor and Tucker and that it took about a week for them to
find out that he was a liar. Schoffer stated that of the leads
that Merritt gave, only perhaps one in ten or twenty would
turn out to be of any value but that Schoffler always followed
the leads because of that one in twenty chance. Schoffler
stated that he had never worked with Ann Kolego.

cc:
    Chron
    File
    Akerman
    Horowitz
    Martin

2010 view of Merritt's apartment at 2035 P St. NW used to surveil Dupont Circle.
Photo: Author's Archives

CHAPTER EIGHT

HIGHLIGHTS OF THE POST WATERGATE BREAK-IN ERA 1972-1985

July 1 – July 31, 1972

Two weeks after the Watergate arrests, Carl Shoffler instructed me to move to a nearby location where I would have a commanding view of the overall Dupont Circle area. The address was 2035 P St., N.W., where I was on the third floor over a dry cleaning establishment. The apartment had windows facing in all directions but was inconspicuous for police activity. Carl wanted to use the location for visual and camera surveillance.

Actually, the Georgetown House apartment building, at 2121 P St., N.W., was a taller building. This was where Douglas Caddy lived, and I later found out was also the residence of an Assistant U.S. Attorney and Watergate Special Prosecutor Archibald Cox.

But my new apartment overlooked most of the area of radical activity, including the Community Bookstore. This observation post lasted for only one month. During that period I continued to work closely with Carl but was increasingly upset with some of the distasteful assignments that he was giving me. So while I assisted Carl and the intelligence agencies with which he was working, I began to lay the groundwork for exposing the illegal activities of the government in its monitoring of the Institute for Policy Studies. I met secretly with attorney Mitchell Rogovin at Arnold & Porter and also with David Isbell at Covington & Burling, and told both attorneys what I knew about the matter. David Isbell agreed to represent me pro bono, which pleased me greatly as he was a key figure in the American Civil Liberties Union (ACLU).

August 1, 1972

I moved to the 1700 block of R St., N.W. into a three story house. I had the second floor all to myself and even had a working fireplace in the center of the house. The *real* Robert Chandler reappeared and I let him live on the third floor. His drug activity became so bad that I had to throw him out. I heard later than he had become a minister in the House of Prayer and had sexually assaulted a boy whose grandmother was in the choir.

I found this somewhat ironic because Carl Shoffler had selected the House of Prayer as one of his targets. He had been focused on the activities of Daddy Grace McCullough, who had started his House of Prayer churches a few years earlier in New York City. Daddy Grace was a pimp and drug dealer. He wore a diamond on every finger, a red cape and a feather plumed hat. Daddy Grace used to pass buckets in his churches and would tell the congregation to put only paper money in the buckets because he didn't like to hear anything that jingled.

I sometimes thought I led parallel lives: Being a CI for government agencies that ordered me to do some illegal and wild things and at the same time having a private life that acted as a magnet in attracting undesirables and unpopular causes.

August 15, 1972

MDP Sergeant Dixie Gildon showed up at my door at 1705 R St., N.W. She entered the house acting strangely and immediately walked over and turned off the TV set. She was in uniform, which was unusual because as an undercover officer she normally wore civilian clothing. I concluded that she had to be wearing a wire to record our conversation.

Dixie told me that the police knew that I was revealing my role as a CI to some press people and certain organizations through attorneys Rogovin and Isbell. She said that if I were to reveal everything that I knew and had done, it would be devastating to the national security. She wanted to know what it would take to keep me quiet – my very first offer of hush money.

She said that if I accepted her offer to keep quiet I could get a large sum of money. The exact amount was never disclosed because I immediately declined. Once I had made this quite clear to her, she asked that I escort her to her car, which was parked a block away even though there were ample parking spaces nearby. While walking to her car I noticed two police agents taking our pictures together. The walk was merely a pretext for the taking of photos of me as I realized that the police had never taken any pictures of me in the past. Had I accepted Dixie's offer I undoubtedly would have been arrested on the spot and charged with extortion or some other trumped up charge.

August 22, 1972

Dixie telephoned and asked to me to meet her on K St., N.W., apparently in a renewed effort to offer me money. I immediately called David Isbell and he decided to attend the meeting with me. Sure enough Dixie showed up at our agreed upon location, which was my doctor's office. Isbell wasted no time in approaching her and demanding that she cease contact with me forthwith. I loved the priceless look on her face when he told her.

October 16, 1972

I began to get sick, really sick. A friend, Leroy, came by to visit me and noticed a faint odor in the house. When we investigated we found a yellow flame burning at the bottom of the hot water tank. I telephoned the gas company and an inspector soon arrived. He found rags and pieces of brick stuffed inside the flue of the hot water tank. The inspector told me that it was rather ingenious because whoever had done it knew that it would cause carbon monoxide to flood the chimney of my fireplace and into my bedroom. He said that in another day or two I would have been dead.

* * *

A few weeks earlier two men almost at point blank had fired pistol shots over my head while I was walking on Connecticut Avenue, near Dupont Circle. I took this as a warning from federal agents whose agencies were upset with my exposing my role in government illegal activities.

November 1972

One day when I had the fireplace going in the center of the house and it was snowing outside, I happened to look out the window. I saw a young man walking down the street in the snow with no shoes or socks on. Of course, I rushed outside and offered him assistance. This turned out to be a whole new episode in my life. His name was Andre Duvall.

Andre told me that he lived up the street from me at 17th and U Sts., N.W. in a house full of male prostitutes and drag queens. He said that someone earlier that day had entered the house and stabbed six roommates, all drag queens, to death. He had managed to escape by climbing through a window, leaving everything behind, including his socks and shoes.

Andre was scared, frightened and hungry. From that day on he became my new roommate. In a sense Andre was replacing Rita Reed in my life, filling an emptiness that started when Rita disappeared. There was nothing sexual between Andre and me; we merely became close friends. Andre was in his early twenties and was an extremely handsome mixed Black guy. He told me that he had served in the military in Vietnam as a gunner on a plane. He said that one day the plane was flying over Vietnam when a rocket came through the floor and decapitated one of his sergeants. The plane then crashed in the jungle. He managed to survive and lifted up and began carrying a wounded sergeant. They had not traveled far when suddenly they came upon an unarmed Vietnamese boy of about 10 years of age who was attempting to operate a radio, apparently with the intent of disclosing their location to the enemy. The sergeant ordered Andre to shoot the boy in the head. Andre began crying and so did the boy who sensed what was happening. The boy appeared to be begging that his life be spared. The sergeant was adamant, ordering Andre to shoot to kill the boy or face court martial. Andre said that he shut his eyes and with tears flowing fired his weapon, killing the boy instantly.

Not long after Andre told me this story I caught him in our house with a syringe in his jugular vein and a belt tying off his neck so that he could get a hit of heroin. I demanded to know why. Andre remained speechless. So I jerked up his shirt sleeve and saw needle track marks. Andre confessed that he had more track marks in his feet, legs, penis, under his tongue and even in his eye lids. He said that after killing the boy in Vietnam he had turned to drugs, which in turn had led to the military granting him a medical discharge.

Gradually I revealed my identity as a CI to Andre, who really did not seem to care about my CI identity. If anything, it made him feel more secure about his situation in the aftermath of the murders of his six roommates.

It is hard to believe but about three weeks later when I was again looking out my front window I spotted a young girl walking down the same street as had Andre in freezing rain. Her face was bleeding. Well, like a well-meaning idiot, I rushed out to rescue her. It turned out her name was Angela Pennycook and that she was running from her pimp. Angela turned out to be a bat out of hell. Soon I was to wish I had left her alone on the street. At that time, she was a whore, lesbian, junkie, thief, back stabber and pathological liar. And these were her good qualities.

Angela was a Black girl of about 15 years who had gold capping on two of her front teeth. She was somewhat plain looking and chubby but boasted of two huge breasts. She had tried every drug imaginable and was such a pig that when she turned tricks while on her period she would stuff a sponge in her vagina to stop the bleeding. Her mother, Mae, lived in Rockville, Maryland but years before had ceased having contact with Angela after the latter at age 12 years had dropped off her baby for her mother to raise. Angela's dealings with everyone that she came into contact with were devastating and in the end that was exactly how her life ended.

I rented the first floor of the house to two friends, Kevin and his boyfriend, Rick. Kevin was always enterprising in his business pursuits while Rick was a young Black hippie. Rick was extremely talented at playing rock music on his guitar. His idol was Jimmy Hendrix. A few months later, I discovered Rick's body lying at my front door. He had been murdered. The case was never solved. I have often wondered if his death was meant as a warning to me to keep my mouth shut about certain activities I had undertaken for the government and for Carl Shoffler.

This was because my role as an informant for the police and various agencies was quickly coming to an end. Mainly I was still working for Carl and freelancing on the side for some agencies. It was strange but these agencies would seek out my services for intelligence gathering even though they knew I was becoming increasing hostile towards them. Apparently they found my work to be invaluable.

January 1973

I moved to 1700 block of 17th Street, N.W. because I was in fear of my life at R Street, N.W. My new landlord allowed me to stay there rent free because he was sympathetic with my situation. My new place was actually a three story mansion that was empty and in need of repairs. I lived in the carriage house directly behind the mansion with my only entrance being through the mansion itself. I had to enter the mansion, walk to rear of the second floor where there was a bridged hallway that went to the carriage house. It was almost like a maze or secret entrance.

I lived there with Andre and my cat, Puss, for a short time when one night all hell broke loose. Someone rang my door bell that was located on the front door of the mansion. When I inquired on the intercom as to who it was, the party refused to answer. Suddenly the intercom went dead. Then I spotted several men climbing up a ladder to my window in the carriage house. I naively opened up the window to ask them what they wanted. They identified themselves as police detectives and said they wanted to talk to Andre, who was not home, about the murders of the six drag queens. The detectives then climbed through the window and began threatening and cursing me. I managed to get to a telephone and called David Isbell and placed the phone in the hands of the lead detective. When he found out from Isbell that I was his client they left. The following day Isbell telephoned the chief of police and threatened a lawsuit and demanded an apology. No lawsuit was ever filed but the police did repair my intercom and doorbell and did apologize to me. The chief of police also reprimanded the detectives by forcing them to attend a courtesy school for six days.

Andre, to his credit, on his own initiative decided to submit himself voluntarily to police questioning about the six murders. His attorney accompanied him. He answered all the questions and was cleared by the police because he told the truth and had nothing to do with the incident.

After the police raid I never again felt comfortable living in the carriage house. I knew it was time to move. I telephoned Carl Shoffler about my decision and he told me to check the classified advertisement section of the *Washington Post* for apartments and by doing so I would learn about my next CI assignment, which would include a guarantee of free rent.

Carl and I also talked about a *Washington Star* reporter named Jared Stout. Stout had interviewed me several times about my illegal activities in behalf of government agencies. Carl informed me that Stout was connected to the Houston Plan that had been hatched in the Nixon White House and that he had a military intelligence background. Shortly after interviewing me Stout resigned from the *Washington Star* and became chief of police for Rockville, Maryland. I thought it strange that he could go from being a newspaper reporter to chief of police of a sizeable municipality. He worked in that post for awhile and then completely vanished, though I did find traces of him later in Texas and Utah.

February 1973 to September 10, 1977

Carl Shoffler was right once again. There was an ad in the *Washington Post* that read: "Free apt. 18 St./Col. Rd. NW. Top of book store in exchange for repairs. Call Buster 265-1975." I never found out how Carl knew about Buster's decision to place the ad in the newspaper, but guessed that it was through Carl's use of wire-tapping.

The address in the ad was the book store on Columbia Road NW. It was located four doors from a McDonald's and right beside a Christian Science Reading Room. This was an adult book store in a three-story townhouse. Buster and I hit it off right away and he told me to take the second floor apartment. On the first floor and street level was a store that was approximately fifty feet by one hundred

2010 view of Buster Riggin's bookstore on Columbia Road NW
Photo: Bob Dodds

feet. In the rear of the store was a movie arcade room that was about fifty by fifty feet.

Buster gave the apartment on the third floor to a man named Kevin and his wife. Kevin was a macho homophobe. Obviously I did not get along with Kevin due to his warped personality and his resentment that Buster had given me the choice apartment and later the job of managing the book store.

Buster's real name was Walter Francis Riggin. He had a son about 18 years old named Ricky. Ricky was a midget type of guy who had a disability. He was married to a girl named Suzie, who was the same size as Ricky. Both were hard-core drug addicts and were stealing from Buster to support their addictive habits.

Buster was of Italian descent. He was a short man, about five feet two inches in height and about 155 pounds. He was in his mid-fifties and was bald, a feature he tried to cover up by wearing a woman's black wig that was cut short to his shoulders. He was a fast talker and thought he could outwit anyone. He was also very energetic and always enterprising.

His principal enterprises were prostitution, pimping, counterfeiting of plancheons (counterfeit quarters), drugs, gambling, racketeering, fencing stolen merchandise, and pornography. He specialized in child pornography, bestiality and snuff films, where the victim was murdered. He had other vices but these were his principal ones. His close associate in these vices was a man by the name of Joe Nesline, a small time Mafia don from New York City who lived in the Adams-Morgan area of Washington, D.C., where the book store was located.

I don't think I have to explain explicitly what my CI assignment was for Carl and for the U.S. Attorney for the District of Columbia.

Employing my usual candor I early on told Buster that I was a former informer for the government and had worked for Carl. I also told Buster that I hated the cops, FBI and Carl. Buster was stupid enough to believe me. Actually I had no choice but to be candid with Buster because my name was soon all over the local newspapers and radio and TV media. The news about my exposing government illegal activities was virtually non-stop. One day Buster and I were right outside the book store on the street when a black limousine pulled up and three men in black suits got out and handed me a subpoena to testify before the Senate Watergate Committee headed by Senator Sam Ervin, Jr.

Once Buster named me the manager and only employee of the book store he embarked on a campaign of non-stop talking, just like John Gotti did years later in New York City. In no time at all I learned almost everything there was to know about him and his business enterprises. I quickly concluded that Buster and his buddy, Joe Nesline, were nothing but small time crooks.

I didn't like my job running the book store. I quickly became tired of selling Rush and Locker Room to perverts who inhaled these to heighten their orgasm. I was also sick of the pedophiles that came into the store to purchase Lolli-Tots. I came to despise the freaks that purchased bestiality books and films about S&M and golden showers and fist to the elbow up someone's anus. I was also disgusted with having to clean up the film room at the rear of the store where the floor became cluttered with used condoms, tissues, urine, shit and cum. For all of this I was receiving free rent and $100 a week from Buster plus another lousy $100 a week from Carl and intelligence agencies, with small expenses being picked up also.

It always amazed me how gullible and stupid the customers of the book store were. My name and picture appeared frequently in the local media but no one ever connected me as manager of the book store with the CI who was exposing illegal government activities.

This characterization even applied to the book store's most famous regular customer, who walked in the front door only a few days after I became manager. When he entered Buster wasted no time in introducing me to Carl Bernstein, ace reporter for the *Washington Post*. Buster even told Bernstein that I had worked for Carl Shoffler of Watergate fame, the police and the FBI. This information did not seem to register with Bernstein. He was too preoccupied with perusing and buying S&M, bestiality and golden shower films. One of his favorites was Big Black Studs Love White Chicks. Years later, after I had left employment at the book store, I telephoned Bernstein at the *Post* and asked him to reveal the truth about my true role in the Watergate arrests and being an informant for the government. Bernstein had the balls to claim that he had never met me and as far as he was concerned he and Bob Woodward had left no stone unturned in pursuing the Watergate scandal. I talked to Woodward and got the same attitude and feed-back. Woodward even refused to believe anything I told him about Bernstein and Buster. He called me a liar. After he said this to me I told him that he and Bernstein could both kiss me where the sun doesn't shine. The truth was that Bernstein besides purchasing porn films also bought Rush and items such as paddles, whips and handcuffs. He even bought a female blow-up doll. He was a porn addict and would come into the store at least two to three times a week. He would always get a $10 roll of quarters to watch porn films in the movie room at the rear of the store, invariably returning $9 in quarters to me before he left to store. It always took him four minutes or less to watch four 25-cent movies. He was a quick shooter, reaching an orgasm in no time and having the bad habit of squirting his cum all over the sides of the movie machine and the floor. I got sick and tired of having to clean up his mess. I told Carl Shoffler about Bernstein and he said that intelligence agencies had known for years about his freaky sexual appetites and thought him to be a first-class weirdo.

May 15, 16 and 17, 1973

With David Isbell at my side I testified in executive sessions on Capitol Hill before members of the Watergate Senate Select Committee in total secrecy. This was just before the May 18th, opening day of the committee's public hearings.

I recall Senator Ervin telling me that 'Mr. Merritt, your testimony is incredible. But I don't think the American public is ready for the malicious acts that you have committed at the requests of the police and FBI. I am appalled at the fact that they asked you to commit these criminal acts against the American people and for the sake of national interest and security reasons.'

I never told the whole truth to anyone at the height of the Watergate scandal about my learning of the planned break-in two weeks ahead of the arrests. At the time I was fearful for my life. I was still working with Carl Shoffler and protecting what he had done after I gave him the information about the break-in. Rita Reed had disappeared off the face of the earth. I thought the same thing could happen to me. I knew too much.

June 25, 1973

The Senate Watergate hearings were a hit on national TV. John Dean was testifying. Carl and I were watching the drama together. I remember Carl commenting, "Dean is full of shit."

September 1, 1973

I was still living on Columbia Road, N.W. and working for Buster Riggin. Buster decided to open a new store next door to his book store. He asked me to run it for him. It was a variety store selling candy, sodas, chips, and drug paraphernalia and had a game room for teens. I gave the store its name: The Dragon's Nest. I got the idea to do so from the code name of my CI assignment to monitor Buster's activities. Carl Shoffler became somewhat angry that I dared to name the store after a secret police code.

October 1973

Newspapers in Washington, D.C. begin to publish stories about my role as a CI for the Washington, D.C. Metropolitan Police Department and the FBI. Among these are "Informants For Police Exposed," *Washington Post*, October 7, 1973; "Informers Spied on D.C. Activists," Washington, D.C. *Star-News*, October 7, 1973; "Informant Tried To Spy on Kennedy," by Jack Anderson, *Washington Post*, October 23, 1973; "FBI Informer Confesses," *The Daily Rag*, October 5-12, 1973; and "Two Lift Curtain on Undercover Work," *Washington Post*, November 26, 1973.

October 3, 1973

The Institute for Policy Studies filed a lawsuit against named Nixon Administration officials alleging its offices and officers had been illegally wiretapped. Attorney Mitchell Rogovin signed an affidavit that was based on the inside information I had supplied him, although my name did not appear in the document or the lawsuit papers.

October 18 and 19, 1973

With David Isbell at my side I gave testimony to Watergate Special Prosecutor Archibald Cox regarding my CI role.

October 20, 1973

President Nixon fired Special Prosecutor Archibald Cox and attempted to abolish the office of the Watergate Special Prosecutor.

September, 10, 1977

Carl Shoffler ordered me to pull out immediately from working for Buster Riggin. The assignment was over. Weeks later government agents raided Buster. It was a devastating blow to Buster as he and his associates lost all of their business enterprises.

November, 1977

I moved to 1630 Kalorama Road, N.W., near the Meridian Hill Park. I lived there for about three months and had to move again when Buster managed to serve a subpoena on me. He was attempting to sue the police and FBI based on my CI activities. For some reason he had it in his head that I would be his star witness and support his legal action. He even offered me a nice chunk of money if I would do so. So Carl Shoffler and the U.S. Attorney for the District of Columbia decided that I should allow Buster to think I would be his flunky star witness. When the trial took place my testimony had the effect of destroying Buster's lawsuit. So again I had to move for personal security reasons.

June, 1980

Carl Shoffler had some family emergency and left me without any money. As usual I was living daily mouth to mouth. As if this was not bad enough I kept getting new threats from Buster who wanted revenge against me for sabotaging his lawsuit. When someone tried to set fire to the front porch of the house where I was living, I decided evasive action was necessary. By a stroke of luck I ran into an old acquaintance whom I could trust and who owned several houses in the nation's capital. I told him of my situation and he gave me the keys to an empty house at 1824 Swann Street, N.W. and told me I could stay there as long as I wanted. The major drawback to this offer was that there was no gas, no electricity and no furniture. With my cat, Puss,

I managed to live there for a month but both Puss and I nearly starved.

Carl finally returned and apologized profusely because someone else was supposed to have dropped off the money owed me but didn't. It was an honest mix-up, but one I barely survived.

August 1 to March 31, 1983

I moved back to a former residence at 1818 Riggs Place, N.W,. I decide to take a reprieve from working for Carl and the government agencies. I got a job for a short time at the Georgetown University Hospital as an operating anesthesiologist for the famed Dr. George Hufnagel. The renowned doctor had served as Nixon's private physician. Dr. Hufnagel was more effeminate that any female in the hospital – and he didn't care who knew it.

Andre moved back to live with me. I discovered that not only had his drug habit not gone away but it was worse than ever. So I got him an apartment next door and paid for his first month's rent. I also got him a job as a clerk in the admitting office at Capitol Hill Hospital where I was then employed.

My job at the hospital was working as the emergency room supervisor. Capitol Hill Hospital had a unique triage system that was based on racial and financial profiling, not on the condition of the patient. Triage one meant that the patient was VIP white and/ or money; triage two meant that the patient was Black and triage three meant that the patient was poor and had no insurance. The medical personnel in the emergency room were usually interns with no licensed physician being present. One day a lady came to the hospital with a chicken bone caught in her throat. The interns pushed the bone down into her lungs, which caused her lungs to collapse. She was put on an artificial respirator and soon died. This tragedy did not go unnoticed as she was the mother of a member of the hospital's board of directors.

Other unusual events occurred in the emergency room. One day two men were admitted who were stuck together anally. A female patient came in with a small glass coca-cola bottle in her pussy. A young man arrived covered with crabs so thick that the interns had to scrape them off with a putty knife. One Black patient came in with serious chest pains. Since he did not have insurance he was denied

119

treatment and ordered to leave the hospital. A policeman escorted him to his home and while he was getting out of the vehicle, with one foot inside the car and the other on the ground, he fell dead of a heart attack.

It was this latter incident that got me fired from the hospital. I was so angry at what I had seen that I went to the media and revealed the whole story, an action that subsequently cost the hospital millions of dollars in out-of-court settlements. So ended my employment at the Capitol Hill Hospital.

A few weeks later a doctor at George Washington University Hospital telephoned to inform me that Andre had died of an unknown disease. Andre's was the first known death from AIDS in the nation's capital.

When Andre died I was still mourning the death of my mother ten years earlier. Since then I had never stepped a foot inside a church as I had not forgiven God for taking my mother. Then, almost 10 years to the day on which she died, I was walking by St. Matthews and went inside and took a seat. I closed my eyes. I was not really praying. I began to wonder why I had entered the church. When I opened my eyes I saw a large statue with several angels and a woman kneeling before Jesus. The woman was my mother and I heard her say distinctly, "Butch, I love you and I am happy." I never knew if this was my imagination or a miracle from On High. But my mourning ended then and I no longer dressed in black. For the first time in ten years I felt contented and had peace.

A couple of days later I went to see a movie at the Town theatre just three blocks from the White House. Unbeknownst to me a regrettable episode was about to begin in my life. The movie I saw was *The Black Mamba*. Its name was ironically most appropriate for what was about to happen to me. I left the theatre, which was on 13th Street at New York Avenue, N.W. As it turned out the number 13 was going to be a sign of bad luck for me and New York Avenue was going to lead me to New York City. Actually, New York Avenue in Washington, D.C. does lead all the way to New York City.

After I left the theatre, I walked across the street to the Trailways bus terminal to get out of the rain, grab a bite to eat, use the bathroom and then head home. Everything was going fine until I headed for the bathroom. That's when I came face to face with a real black mamba, whose named was Norman Edriss Pannell, Jr. He was a young handsome black man with a lot of charm even though he dressed shabbily. He panhandled me for food and it was obvious that he was both hungry and poor. I committed one of the biggest mistakes of my life by making friends with him that night. It was a friendship that turned into a nightmare. Edriss, who was named after an Arab prince, was not worthy of anything connected to royalty. He was, as I later came to realize, more likely the son of Satan. His own mother, Valerie, who was a heroin addict, warned me to stay away from him. I chose to ignore her wise advice. She told me that she had a dream that he was nothing but pure evil. She confessed that she had tried to abort him with a coat hanger and had even poured chemicals into her vagina to get rid of him, having the premonition that she was about to give birth to a being who would be dedicated to wreaking havoc and hell on his fellow man.

Edriss was in his early twenties. His skin was lightly black, his hair brown and curly and his eyes green. Most people upon entering his presence became afraid of him. He had an instinctive way of instilling fear in people. He used to beat his own mother and his younger brother, Jamal. One time he threw a spear at Jamal that entered his right cheek and exited his left check. He beat and tried to rape his younger sister, Natosha, sometimes called Tick. He even screwed his own daughter at age 11, boasting that he wanted to be her first.

Edriss used various types of drugs, but these were not the cause or excuse for his conduct. Edriss started off with pot, went on to PCP, called whacky weed, and then became a crack head. After a judge committed him for psychiatric examination at age 16, Edriss pushed another male patient down a staircase, killing him. Edriss claimed the patient was trying to sexually molest him. He later told me that the only reason he killed the man was because the he was white.

One night Edriss broke into the Gonzaga St. Aloysius Catholic High School just two blocks from the Capitol building and stole typewriters and other equipment valued at thousands of dollars. I decided to turn him in to the police but before doing so I telephoned the St. Aloysius rectory and spoke to a person who answered the phone by the name of Father Horace B. McKenna. Father McKenna ended up going to court when Edriss was arraigned to ask for third party custody of Edriss, which the judge granted.

Father McKenna was a true saint and he and I became best of friends. Under his influence I decided to renew being a Catholic. Because I was had never been confirmed in the faith, I telephoned the bishop and asked him if Father McKenna could administer the confirmation to me at an upcoming Easter service. I knew that this was against tradition, which mandated that the sacrament could only be done by the bishop. I pleaded for an exception, citing that Father McKenna was in his eighties, but the bishop was adamant that only he and not a priest could perform confirmation. Later I attended the Easter Sunday service at a small Catholic church in northeast Washington, D.C. The bishop called my name to be confirmed and then handed the holy oils to Father McKenna to perform the confirmation. Thereafter I took on Father McKenna's middle name as my saint name, which was Bernard.

As a result of Edriss' arrest and with the help of Father McKenna, Edriss turned a corner in his life and stopped getting into trouble with the law. He even worked with Father McKenna in the church and with the poor and homeless.

The last time I ever heard from Father McKenna was at 6:30 A.M. on May 11, 1982. He telephoned me from the Georgetown University Hospital to ask how I was doing and if life was treating me well. He said that I was in his thoughts and then he wished me love in the name of God. He died at 6:33 A.M. Over 2500 persons attended his funeral mass. Edriss and another friend by the name of Philip Veney were two of the pall bearers when Father McKenna was buried on the grounds of Georgetown University.

Prior to his death Father McKenna and I had helped found an organization called the Young Dillingers, which eventually had a at one time a membership of over 2500 Black men and women, all of whom were ex-offenders. The purpose of the group was to combat crime, help the homeless and beautify the city of Washington, D.C. The Young Dillingers became a role model for the youth in the nation's capital and surrounding areas.

April 1, 1983 to early 1984

I moved to 1212 Massachusetts Avenue, N.W. This address became the central headquarters for the Young Dillingers. The organization had acquired 36 houses at a cost of one dollar each from a public spirited citizen named John Garrison. Under an agreement with Garrison the group would renovate and use the rental properties to fund the organization, with Garrison receiving only 25 percent of the rentals and after three years the properties would be deeded jointly to the Young Dillingers and to me.

The group also received a contribution of $10,000 from Boeing Airlines and $20,000 from Mayor Marion Barry in behalf of the District of Columbia. A major breakthrough in fund raising occurred when a lady named Sonja Larson became a prime fundraiser for the organization. She expressed an interest in helping the black youths in the nation's capital. Sonja introduced me to a lady named Madeline Furth, who over a year later became my godmother. Ms. Furth, who like Sonja was enamored of the idea of helping disadvantaged black youth, told me she wanted to contribute $250,000 to the Young Dillingers. She said there was a catch: I was to state that it was needed by me to pay legal expenses to defend a family inheritance as opposed to her publicly acknowledging that the money was going to help black kids. Madeline was eccentric and her method of making the contribution was convoluted to say the least. But I acceded to her request.

Several months later Madeline was called for grand jury duty and being bored at the proceeding decided to liven things up by presenting me for indictment. Madeline apparently had a back-up scheme that if the Young Dillingers did not meet all of its financial goals she would have me arrested; then attempt to collect the money from the victims' fund. So without any warning I was indicted. Madeline promptly called me and excitedly told me the news. As I mentioned before, Madeline was somewhat eccentric.

The Young Dillingers were becoming so popular and powerful in Washington, D.C. that Curtis Sliwa of the Guardian Angels traveled from New York City to set up a recruiting booth in front of the Capitol building. This effort was short-lived. Edriss and other Young Dillingers met Sliwa and his group and in so many words told them to get the hell out of Dodge. They resisted. The local media the next day reported that Sliwa and two of his Guardian Angels had been rescued after being thrown into the Potomac River. This ended any effort on their part to encroach on the turf of the Young Dillingers.

The success of the Young Dillingers brought national publicity to the organization. This made Edriss a celebrity overnight as he was president and the leader of the group. Each member took on the name of famous mafia figures and gangsters. The idea was not to portray themselves as imitators of famed hoodlums but to say that even ex-offenders could be rehabilitated and become good citizens.

The Young Dillingers received recognition from the police department, churches, Mayor Barry, and even from First Lady Nancy Reagan. When Pope John Paul II came to visit Washington, D.C., Mayor Barry arranged for Edriss and me to be on the front line of the greeting committee that met the Pope. The Pope landed on the Capitol Mall in a maze of six helicopters. Mayor Barry and his wife, Effie, kissed the Pope's ring but I chose simply to gently shake his hand. Even though I had become a converted Catholic there was still enough Presbyterian blood in me to prevent me from bowing to any man. The greeting throng was chanting that it loved the Pope and the Pope was responding that he loved them, too. When the Pope reached me he was repeating the same line and looked somewhat surprised when I responded, "I love you, too, Papa."

The Young Dillingers stroke of good luck began to turn sour. It started with dogs of all things. Edriss and his family lived in a small house next door to the organization's headquarters mansion at 1212 Massachusetts Avenue, N.W. where I resided.

Unbeknownst to me, he kept his two Doberman pinchers in the basement of the mansion. One day two police officers showed up at my door, accompanied by a representative of the SPCA, and arrested me for animal cruelty because the dogs were emaciated. I had no idea. I love animals and would never have allowed this to happen. Fortunately, the charge against me was later dismissed.

However, this incident seemed to set off a series of other events that ultimately led to the end of the Young Dillingers. The next crisis that occurred was the murder of a Young Dillinger named Johnny K. His real name was Johnny Washington and the K stood for knock-out because he was training to be a professional boxer. He was patrolling the neighborhood where he lived when he was stabbed to death. The killer was arrested a few days later after Young Dillingers identified him to the police.

Not long after that another Young Dillinger named Walter "Baby Face" Turner was shot to death. His killer was arrested soon thereafter, again with Young Dillingers identifying him to the police.

Then Carl Shoffler, the police and the FBI began to harass the Young Dillingers to extract any information its members might have on Mayor Barry and to get their cooperation in setting up and entrapping him on a crack cocaine charge. When I learned of this effort I refused to cooperate as did members of the Young Dillingers. This resulted in the police and FBI putting intense pressure on the organization to force it to cooperate. Again we refused. The next thing I knew I was hit with an unsealed 13-count indictment regarding the money that Madeline Furth had contributed to the Young Dillingers.

Shortly thereafter Mary Treadwell, an ex-wife of Mayor Barry, visited me to discuss the police and FBI campaign to frame her former husband.

One of my next visitors was Yvette Terry, a lesbian who was a Young Dillinger. She confided in me that she had engaged in a sexual three-some with the singer Chaka Khan, also known as Yvette Stevens, and the District of Columbia's delegate to Congress. This allegedly took place at the Howard Inn Motel on Georgia Avenue, N.W. Yvette Terry also told me that she was receiving blackmail from the delgate to keep her mouth shut.

One day I was in the District of Columbia courthouse with Yvette Terry in an attempt to get Angela Pennycook out of jail on a prostitution charge. Yvette was also having a lesbian affair with Angela. While we were at the courthouse waiting for Angela's case to be called when this delgate suddenly appeared. Yvette Terry walked up to him and introduced me by saying, "Butch, this is the Congressman _____, me and Chaka Khan had the orgy with." The delegate was so embarrassed that he turned and ran out of the courthouse.

About three weeks later Yvette Terry told me she was going to pick up more blackmail money. Not too long thereafter I got a phone call from police detective Joe Schwartz of the homicide division informing me that Yvette Terry was murdered just three blocks away. She was stabbed in the heart. I told the detective about the blackmail scheme. He in turn stated that he believed Angela

Pennycook and her gay "boyfriend," Dominique, were in on the blackmail and might have had something to do with the murder.

I contacted Angela Pennycook about the murder and demanded that she go to the police and tell them what she knew. Instead she went to the police and told them I was threatening her. I was arrested the next day and charged with obstruction of justice and spent 60 days in jail for bullshit, when all I was trying to do was get Angela to tell the truth.

All these incidents took a toll on the Young Dillingers and the organization began to fall apart.

While I was in jail for the 60 days, Edriss and a handful of his cronies started stealing from the Young Dillingers. They stole the rent money that the tenants in some of the 36 houses had paid. This led to these tenants being unjustly evicted. Edriss also failed to pay the utility bills, which caused electricity and gas to be cut off to many tenants. He ransacked my office and stole all my equipment.

After I got out of jail I found all my clothes in my residence were missing. I had no street clothes to wear. I managed to scrape up about $1000 by selling my car and a few other items. Sonja and Madeline bought me clothes and gave me some money. I was then only a few weeks away from being sentenced by Superior Court Judge Reggie Walton on a forced plea-deal of three counts of false pretense charges stemming from the 13-count indictment. I'd had enough, not only of jail, but of everything.

CHAPTER NINE

FIRST ESCAPE TO NEW YORK CITY (1985)

T he year 1984 witnessed the fall of the Young Dillingers. Lead members were being murdered, maimed and assaulted. It was a year that people were at each other's throats. Washington, D.C. had a stench in the air that had remained over the city since Watergate.

Carl Shoffler was becoming a pain in the ass with his out-sized egotistical attitude. Both he and the FBI had been demanding that I use the Young Dillingers to spy on D.C. Mayor Marion Barry regarding his alleged crack habit. I refused. Even the U.S. Attorney attempted to make a deal with me to dismiss the criminal charges of false pretenses if I cooperated with the campaign to destroy Mayor Barry.

It was getting closer to my sentencing date in May 1984. When Carl saw that I was not going to be cooperative regarding Mayor Barry, he suggested that I might be more valuable to the government if I took a new twist and became a federal fugitive. Carl wanted me to skip out of my sentencing and leave immediately for New York City. He had lined up a CI assignment for me that involved international interests. Carl told me he could easily rectify my federal fugitive status at a later date through his law enforcement connections.

So I began to secretly get ready to go on the lam. But first I had to take care of some pending matters. I had houses with tenants and they depended on me, especially since Edriss and some of the Young Dillingers had robbed the properties blind while I was in D.C. jail a few months before. Carl said he was going to give me money to live on when I arrived in New York City, but it wasn't enough. I had to make an arrangement for someone to collect the rents on the houses, pay the bills and get some of the money to me. The person designated was Sonja Larson, who was one of the complainants against me in the false pretenses case. Things were definetly getting strange.

Before I could manage to get my affairs in order, Edriss was in a neighborhood heavily infested with drug activity, someone recognized him and shot him several times at point blank range. Somehow, he survived snd made it to the nearby Howard University Hospital.

Although Edriss was the titular leader, in reality I was the hidden head of the Young Dillingers. My position made it impossible for me to just abandon the members and leave their organization leaderless. To the kids it did not matter that I was facing a pending criminal case because the neighborhood didn't believe the criminal charges had any merit. I was the only white man who was sticking his neck out for them. I shall never forget one white Assistant U.S. Attorney who stopped me in court one day and asked why a white man from the Deep South was "helping these fucking niggers." I replied that West Virginia was not part of the Deep South and in any event it was about time that someone tried to give these black kids a chance at getting a better life.

Since the criminal case against me had been widely publicized, I felt that I was trapped in the law enforcement capital of the world. Sonja Larson suggested that I begin wearing a disguise. She bought me a wig, mustache and a different style of clothing and moved me from hotel to hotel each day. Even though I was accused of stealing over $250,000, I had no money. Every penny of the $250,000 had been funneled into the running of the Young Dillingers. The only reason I was indicted in the first place was because Madeline Furth was sitting on the local grand jury at the time. She had told me that the other cases heard by the grand jury were boring and mine would bring excitement and be fun. She also said that she needed a cover to serve as an explanation as to why she had taken money from her family accounts and donated it to the Young Dillingers, an organization that had consisted of over two thousand Black youths, all of whom were ex-offenders. After she got me indicted, Madeline started to give me money to survive on. All of this was done as an elaborate scheme by her, she told me, to get reimbursed by the government's Victims of Crime Fund.

Carl was becoming increasingly upset that I had not yet fled D.C. for New York City. He knew my whereabouts at all times but would not do me any harm or jeopardize my freedom. Finally, after hiding out in the nation's capital for about six weeks and after the fugitive warrant had been issued, I decided to leave the city.

So with some cash on hand, and many disguises, I first went to Baltimore, Maryland and rented a room under the name of Tony E'Damiano in a middle-class but clean hotel. I bought a small TV and a pair of parakeets to keep me company in my room. After a few weeks I moved into an attic apartment over a book store that had a defunct restaurant in the rear. A nice lady, Anne, owned it and offered me a job to manage the bookstore and reopen the restaurant, which I did. After a while I found it boring to be selling books while making salads and cooking spaghetti and steaks. So I placed an ad in the *Baltimore Sun* newspaper that indicated I was looking for a free lease while I fixed up and renovated a house. A man by the name of James responded to the ad and gave me a free lease for three years on several houses that he owned. As it turned out the repairs on the houses were minor. I chose to live on West Baltimore Street in an apartment in one of the houses.

I found Baltimore to be tiresome. This was before the city reinvented itself and made its wharf area a major tourist attraction. My boredom caused me to make a major gaffé one night. I decided to use a pay telephone to call Carl Shoffler at his work but the phone was answered by a co-worker who knew me but didn't know about the secret arrangement that Carl had with me. The co-worker kept me on the line long enough to run a trace on it. When I heard the tell-tale click, I knew I had only minutes to get away. There were some construction workers in the area and immediately after I hung up one of these workers picked up the pay phone to make a call. I went inside a pizza shop nearby and sat down. Within a matter of a few minutes the police swarmed the pay phone with guns pointed at the head of the construction worker, who appeared to piss in his pants. Of course, I immediately left the area and knowing that my picture would appear on the 11 PM local news I decided to leave Baltimore immediately. I did not stop to retrieve my personal belongings but instead began to head for the bus station. On the way there a cop stopped his car in the middle of the street and got out and peered closely at me. I reached down and picked up a cigarette butt in front of him and made an effort to light and smoke it. The cop quickly got disgusted with me, concluding that I was a street bum, and drove off. I began walking and soon approached a police station. I got really bold and went in and asked for directions to a hospital emergency room. This occurred during a change in shifts and I casually walked out after hearing what I thought was my name being bantered about by those on duty.

About four blocks away I came upon a truck stop. I asked one of the drivers as he came out of the coffee shop if I could hitch a ride with him, if he was heading for New York City. He wasn't but did give me a ride to Wilmington, Delaware, where I managed to get another ride from two guys who had stopped to change a flat tire on their vehicle. They dropped me off at the Port Authority Bus Terminal near Times Square at 5 A.M. This was my official welcome to the Big Apple.

After staying in the Times Square Hotel for a couple of weeks, I decided to seek a more permanent residence. I checked the ads in the *Village Voice* and found a room on the Upper East Side on East 102nd Street, which, by coincidence, happened to be directly across from the police precinct and three blocks from the mayor's mansion. My new roommate was a 93-year old gay man by the name of William Gussie, who claimed to be a retired professional chef. His specialty was a vegetable soup, which he made with everything in it – including his dirty socks and underwear. He was Jewish and used to walk around the apartment wearing nothing but his yarmulke. While his personal habits were disgusting, he was a very nice man.

I stayed with William for about four months until I got a job at Temple Israel as a superintendent. The temple was located on the east side on East 75th street near Central Park. I had a new job, a new place of residence, and a new identity. Everything was going great until I made another major gaffé that rivaled the one I made in Baltimore. On the spur of the moment I contacted Edriss Pannell, who was still in Washington, D.C., and invited him to visit me in Manhattan. Within a day or so after he moved in with me, I fell into a trap that he had set up. He asked me to go to Times

Square to get crack for him. To this day I don't know why I made such a stupid move, because waiting for me in Times Square was Angela Pennycook, who supposedly by sheer coincidence just happened to run into me. She promised faithfully not to double-cross me if I let her stay with me. She had not changed since I first met her at age 13 when she was naked, homeless, dirty and hungry and refused assistance by her mother. After we returned to my apartment, which happened to be in the Temple, Angela and Edriss started smoking crack, which quickly led to sexual intercourse between them. Edriss, while high on crack, suddenly went into a rage and struck me twice with a crow bar, breaking my left arm in two places. I had no choice but to go immediately to the emergency room at the Lenox Hill Hospital around the corner at 100 East 77th Street to have a cast put on my arm. While I was there Angela and Edriss telephoned the police and FBI to get me arrested so that they could claim the $500 reward being offered for my head. Such was the action by two "loyal" friends for whom I had made countless sacrifices and ruined my life.

The officers of the New York Police Department Warrant Squad, who arrested me, introduced themselves as New York's Finest. When this occurred I was not afraid or intimidated because I secretly knew that I had the protection of Carl Shoffler and the government.

I soon came to realize that the few months that I had spent previously in D.C. jail on a phony charge of obstruction of justice was time well spent in preparation for what was about to come. It turned out that I was going to be a guest for a few months at the Metropolitan Correction Center in lower Manhattan beginning just a few days before Christmas in 1985. I was placed on the tenth floor with incarcerated Mafia dons. My arm was now in a cast, and my new Mafia cell mates wanted to know if the police were responsible. Of course, I said yes. I then told these Mafia guys about the night that I was walking near Spark's Steak House on East 48th Street and heard the shots ring out the night that John Gotti had Paul Castellano killed.

On January 28, 1986 at 11:39 AM, I was with these same cell mates watching TV when the space craft Challenger blew up, killing those on board. The Mafia dons broke into a cheer. A couple expressed the wish that U.S. Attorney Rudolph Giuilani had been on board at the time of the explosion.

Of course, Carl Shoffler knew exactly where I was spending my days and started to call me using the legal phone lines by claiming he was my lawyer. This was to prevent the jail guards from listening in on the conversations. Carl began to instruct me on the power of the Mafia in New York City and said he wanted me to get information from my new cell mates on John Gotti and others Mafia kingpins. Carl arranged for the FBI to debrief me by faking visits from my lawyers. The FBI would take me to Assistant U.S. Attorney Louis Grabois to be debriefed..

Carl Shoffler, true to his modus operandi, managed to exploit me as usual by keeping me in the MCC until the legal time was up to be extradited to Washington, D.C. During this period of time he and the FBI learned a lot of valuable information from me regarding Mafia activities that I had picked up from my cell mates. One thing that I had learned was that the incarcerated Mafia dons used some sort of Morse Code by flashing the dormitory lights on and off to their counterparts outside on the street on which MCC was located. This same method may still be in use today.

One day I was placed in a private car and taken to an undisclosed location, which was a holding center, and then given a McDonald's hamburger after riding 12 hours to get there. After that I was placed in another private car, accompanied by two U.S. Marshals, and driven to a private air strip. I found myself standing in an airfield wearing just a T-shirt in a March 1986 snow storm waiting for a military aircraft. From the undisclosed location in Pennsylvania I was taken to the Lewisburg Penitentiary. This prison was one of the oldest and worst in the nation. Once there, I was stripped and cavity-searched, given new clothes, fed an apple and assigned a 5 by 8 foot cell that I shared with another prisoner. In the cell was a bunk bed, a toilet and a tiny window that could be opened. But before I entered the cell I was informed that my lawyer, Carl Shoffler, wanted to speak to me on the phone. Carl informed me that I was being assigned to another cell, one that I would share with a prisoner who was a certified public accountant from the country of Colombia. This man had been arrested in New York City and caught with over $50 million in cash that was to be laundered. Carl instructed me that my job was to pick the brain of this prisoner, which I proceeded to do over the next week. On my last day at the penitentiary the Colombian thought he could get more than he bargained for. He made the mistake of pulling his penis out when I was trying to eat my food, so I stabbed him in the balls with a pencil. He had to get treatment, but I was not charged. Within hours I was placed on a bus with some other prisoners to go to the D.C. jail.

I remember getting to the D.C. jail and being processed there right before dinner. I was placed in a protective custody dormitory. The next day I was taken before District of Columbia Judge Reggie Walton to have the fugitive warrant quashed and a new sentencing date was set. Meanwhile the media was having a field day with me. There was turmoil in the Black community, especially among those relatives of the two thousand sons and daughters whom I had helped as members of the Young Dillingers. No one in a position of authority knew exactly what to do with me.

In January 1986, on the way back from the courthouse following a hearing on my case, another inmate on the bus identified me as being the head of the Young Dillingers and having celebrity status. That inmate was Tony, a former Young Dillinger who had gone bad. He and a gang of about 12 other inmates on the bus began assaulting me. There was nothing I could do to defend myself since I was chained at the feet, waist and handcuffs. The three guards on the bus had purposely turned their backs while the assault took place. When the bus finally arrived in the compound of the D.C. jail, I disembarked in a bloody pulp. I was taken to the D.C. General Hospital, which was next door to the jail, where I was kept in its infirmary for about six weeks until I recovered. During this time I was visited by my attorneys who had filed a multi-million dollar law suit against the District of Columbia and its Department of Corrections, which, of course, was publicized in the media. Due to the possibility that legal discovery arising from the lawsuit could prove embarrassing to the government, Carl Shoffler demanded that I back out of the litigation and not cooperate with my lawyers.

When I was finally discharged from the hospital, I was transferred to the Fairfax County Jail in Virginia, which had a white inmate population. Little did these fellow prisoners suspect that I wasn't all white. While incarcerated there I was almost released by mistake.

Someone in the jail's bureaucracy had made an error in my papers. When I was almost moments away from being released, there was a brazen escape, and the jail's authorities ordered a head count of all prisoners, during which my papers were rechecked and the error found and my release cancelled.

Right after this incident I was returned to the D.C. jail. The authorities at the Fairfax County Jail tried to cast blame on me for the error in the my papers that almost caused my release despite the obvious fact that I had no access to my files in their records room. Carl Shoffler found the whole thing amusing.

My transfer back to the D.C. jail was part of a strategic plan by Carl and others in law enforcement. This was because I was placed in a cell next to the infamous Israeli spy, Jonathan Pollard, who was in the protective custody wing. Naturally my assignment was to spy upon the spy and learn what I could from him. This included secretly taping our conversations. Carl had arranged for me to have a small pocket tape recorder to record the exchanges between Pollard and me. Pollard was in the end cell and I was in the cell next to him. Pollard and I were the only white prisoners in the entire wing which housed about 60 prisoners.

During the daytime all the prisoners in our wing were let out of our cells so that we could shower, use telephones, socialize or whatever. It was easy for Pollard and I to become friends because of my Jewish grandmother. Pollard told me that he was a civilian working in U.S. Naval Intelligence where he handled classified sensitive material on the U.S., Middle East and Israel. He said that he was appalled that the U.S. was deliberately suppressing and holding back valuable and vital information that affected the security and welfare of Israel. He maintained the reason was simple: oil and money.

Pollard was no James Bond. He simply used a dolly and wheeled boxes of confidential and top secret documents out the front door of Naval Intelligence, all the while in the presence of guards. He said that he had lived on 19th Street, just above Dupont Circle. He took the secret documents to his apartment and rented a copy machine and copied the materials. He did this on many occasions, returning the secret documents to their storage area at Naval Intelligence each day before his co-workers arrived. He told me that he did this until things started to get out of hand. He had become greedy and removed so much material from Naval Intelligence that he had to store boxes containing the secret documents in the hallway outside his apartment, even though the boxes were clearly marked Top Secret and Confidential.

Finally, one of his neighbors got curious and started asking him questions. He told the neighbor not to pay attention to the boxes because they were thrown-away containers from where he worked that he was using on a project conducted from his home.

Pollard told me that he had been in contact all the while he was copying the documents with two agents from Israel who gave him between $20,000 and $30,000 for his expenses in renting the copy machine and buying copy paper. He said that he was told to meet an Israeli Lt. X in New York City to deliver the documents that he had copied.

It was the nosy neighbor that alerted the federal authorities to his activity. When Pollard got home from New York City he noticed immediately that he was under surveillance. So he jumped in a taxi and fled to the Embassy of Israel, where he banged on the door. The person who opened the door refused to let him in. It was at this point that FBI agents arrested him. He was charged with espionage. The same day his wife, Esther, was also arrested.

Pollard said the only reason he made a deal to cooperate with the federal authorities was that his wife was extremely ill ,and as part of the deal his wife was released and charges dropped against her. He told me that the government had kept its word on the deal.

Pollard felt comfortable in my presence and told me many things. However, I'd been in jail and therefore, before meeting Pollard I knew nothing about him or his case until later when I was briefed by Carl. So if Pollard was a traitor, then so was I in a sense, when I betrayed his confidence,

My next assignment was to be in a cell next to a prisoner who personally knew Boston Celtics first-round draft pick basketball star Lenny Bias and D.C. Mayor Marion Barry. Again I was successful in extracting valuable information about Bias' death from a cocaine overdose and who had supplied him with the narcotics. Carl Shoffler immediately arranged for me to be served with a subpoena to testify before the grand jury investigating Bias' death and the possible involvement by Mayor Barry in supplying him the narcotics. I

135

was transferred from the D.C. jail to the Upper Marlboro Jail in Maryland so that I could testify before the grand jury. However, I made it quite clear to Carl Shoffler that I would refuse to testify about Mayor Barry, who was a target of law enforcement because he was, in Carl's words, "a cotton-pickin' nigger from Georgia." Although my transfer to the Upper Marlboro Jail was done in secrecy, another inmate somehow managed to get the word out that I was incarcerated there and the circumstances surrounding it. That same evening I received a visit from a TV reporter who put the story on the air about my proposed testimony on the Bias' case. This caused the Upper Marlboro District Attorney to vent his anger by having me transferred immediately back to the D.C. jail.

My refusal to testify prompted Carl Shoffler to arrange that I be placed in the same cell with James C. Howard, III. Howard had been convicted of a murder in a case based on information I had supplied. The jail authorities were shocked the next morning to find Howard and me laughing and talking. Howard was not upset at me for fingering him for the death. In fact, he was happy. He received only a six year sentence for his action and claimed that he had found Jesus and was glad that I had help him clear his conscience.

Over a period of time I figured out how to manipulate the staff of the D.C. jail. I even had a young Dillinger, Phillip Veney, as one of my guards. Phillip would bring me cigarettes, commissary items and money whenever I needed these. He also agreed to deliver a message from me to Karen Johnson, a close ally of Mayor Barry, who was being held in the penthouse suite on the top of the jail, where she enjoyed the comforts of nice furnishings and a TV and phone. Karen was incarcerated for grand jury contempt for refusing to testify against Mayor Barry regarding alleged drugs and other activities. Karen was even allowed to have overnight visitors and to spend nights outside the jail.

Carl Shoffler's assignment to me at the time was to investigate corruption by the guards regarding drugs and bribes. I was making great headway in compiling information about these when Carl made the mistake of using a legal phone line to contact me while the line was being monitored by a party in the Corrections Department involved in the corruption. Immediately I was transferred to the Lorton Maximum Prison Facility in Lorton, Virginia, where I was the only alleged white among 550 Black inmates, with the exception of one Hispanic from New York City.

Muslim inmates prepared and cooked the food for the prison population. Any type of food not considered adhering to the Muslim diet, such as pork, had extra ingredients added to it, such as body excrements. It was pretty obvious to me that the government had transferred me to Lorton to have me killed. My lawyers had requested that I be sent to a federal facility for my safety. As it turned out the joke was on the government because the Black and Muslim inmates loved me and were protective of me.

The Lorton Facility, which was dark and drab, was my home for the next 18 months. I saw inmates lose their minds and commit suicide. The guards were corrupt and routinely brought in drugs and booze. The guards had their own goon squad and if they did not like you they would electronically pop open your cell door at 3 A.M. for masked inmates to enter and do to you whatever they wished.

I never had any problems because the inmate population liked and protected me. At times I served as their jailhouse lawyer and even managed to get some severe and lengthy sentences reduced.

No rapes took place because each inmate had his own cell, and showers were taken alone. Each cell was 5 by 8 feet and enclosed with steel bars and had a toilet, bed, desk and stool with no windows. Communication between the inmates consisted of holding a small hand mirror and talking to each other by looking into the mirrors. Inmates made string by tearing strips off of bed sheets. The strings were called fishing lines. A line was used to send or transport items such as cigarettes, matches, paper, pens, food or whatever from cell to cell. Secret messages that could not be reduced to writing were sent by a coded system by making clanging noises on the bars. No matter how hard they tried, the guards could never break the code.

Almost every day for the next 18 months I would get visits from my lawyers (that is, from Carl Shoffler and the FBI). I refused to cooperate with any of them. I felt this whole matter had gone too far. I was not supposed to be prisoner! But here I was serving time for a sentence on charges that were false and fabricated by the complainants and the government.

I had no one to whom I could turn to explain my circumstances and my identity. I was in a dangerous situation and was trapped.

One day a Catholic Franciscan friar from a nearby monastery was visiting the prison. When I heard he was going to visit I immediately prepared a secret letter for Mayor Marion Barry. When the friar came to my cell to talk to me, I pleaded with him to hand deliver my letter to Mayor Barry. And so he did. I was shocked that I could trust the friar because I feared he would turn the letter over to the prison officials.

About 4 A.M. the next morning an excited guard awakened me to tell me that I had a visitor, a Reverend Ferrell. I asked the guard who exactly Reverend Ferrell was and he told me that he was Mayor Barry's right-hand man. I was escorted by the guard to meet the Reverend who immediately asked if I was the person who wrote the secret letter to the Mayor that had been delivered by the friar. I replied that I was. The Reverend then asked me if it was true as stated in my letter that the FBI had been coming to the prison to confer with me about the Mayor. I replied affirmatively, adding that the FBI wanted to know certain personal information regarding the Mayor and drug activities. Reverend Ferrell asked me if I had told the FBI anything about this matter and I replied that I had not and would not. At that point the Reverend departed, indicating that he would be back in contact with me soon.

The very next day I was informed that a parole board had arrived at the prison to interview me about a release. I had been sentenced to 4½ years and had not even served half the sentence. I was the only prisoner interviewed that day by the parole board. The following day at 5 A.M. a guard told me to gather my bag of small personal items as I was leaving the prison. I was told to walk across the prison yard, which prisoners were never allowed to do, and did so without handcuffs or restraints. When I got to the gate the guard in the tower opened it and I walked into the outside world. Just before doing so a guard told me that I was making early parole and was in the process of being released, but that I would have to spend some more time at another prison called Lorton Minimum.

Upon walking through the gate I came upon a black limousine. I feared that I was going to be killed at any minute. Instead the driver opened the door to the limousine, indicating that I could get inside, which I did. The vehicle immediately departed and 15 minutes later I arrived at Lorton Minimum Prison Facility. I walked inside without any handcuffs and was told by the Warden to go to my dormitory and make up my bed. Before I could do so there was a call to breakfast in another section of the facility. I walked across the grounds to the food pavilion and while so doing noticed that there was only a small six foot wire fence around the prison compound and no guards. Just as I got in line for my breakfast I heard a voice on the loud speaker call out my name with instruction that I should report to the warden's office immediately. Upon arriving there the warden told me to forget about breakfast and my small bag of personal belongings because there was a car waiting for me on the other side of his door and I was to depart immediately. I stepped outside, again fearing that a bullet would end my life at any moment.

However, again there was the same black limousine and driver waiting for me. I asked the chauffeur if he had been sent to kill me and he laughed and said that "Mr. Merritt, you are a very special character and you have people in high places looking out for you." He informed that he would drop me off at another holding facility called Good Hope Halfway House on Good Hope Road in southeast Washington, D.C.

I entered the halfway house and was greeted by a councilor who gave me a twenty dollar bill and told me the money was for food and bus fare. He said that my lawyer had called and wanted me to meet him as soon as possible at a McDonald's located at 14th and K Streets, N.W. When I got to the McDonald's, I wasn't sure who would be waiting for me but I knew it was not going to be my lawyer. Within a few minutes another black limousine pulled up, and its driver entered McDonald's and approached me. He asked me to get inside the limousine and upon so doing he gave me $2500 in cash. He told me that money was for being loyal. He said that someone would be in contact with me within a few weeks and until then I should keep my mouth shut.

I was so happy with this turn of events and with my new freedom that I walked for hours around the nation's capital and then caught a bus part of the way to the halfway house. Because of the route of the bus I had to exit the vehicle about seven blocks from the halfway house, still having some time to myself before checking in by the 8 P.M. curfew.

About three blocks from the halfway house, as I was walking though an isolated area, there suddenly appeared what seem to be the same black limousine that I had encountered at McDonald's. It stopped about 20 yards from me and a tainted window rolled down a couple of inches. I saw a pistol and then two gun shots were fired over my head. Of course, I was afraid and through the whole day had feared I would be killed. So I jumped over an adjacent embankment and began running through an open field full of weeds before finally coming to a stop and catching my breath.

I made it back to the halfway house and the first thing I did was to check the envelope that the limousine driver had given me earlier at McDonald's. I counted the cash and checked to make certain the bills were not counterfeit. For a couple of days I stayed inside the halfway house, just watching TV and making phone calls to friends and people with whom I had lost contact.

One of the councilors approached me with an offer to arrange for getting some cocaine. He said that he could even arrange for me to get a clean urine test if one were demanded by the authorities. I declined as I was not into drugs at that time.

When Thanksgiving was a few days away I was told to pack up and move to another halfway house on North Capitol Street that was three blocks from the bus station. The halfway house was formerly a women's jail. I was there for less than a week when a guard came to my room and said, "Mr. Merritt, it is Thanksgiving eve. It is also 2:35 in the afternoon and I am supposed to release you at 6 P.M. Why don't you go ahead and leave now and I will mark down that you left at 6 P.M. Be sure to have a happy Thanksgiving.

The date was November 25, 1987. The guard had me sign my release papers indicating that date and told me to write down 6 P.M. He then affixed his signature to the papers. While I don't remember his name, I shall never forget his face.

Before I left the halfway house, which was around 3 P.M., I got a phone call. A voice told me to meet my lawyer again in two days at McDonald's.

I had a secret location on Kalorama Road, N.W. that no one knew anything about, including the Young Dillingers. I stayed there and bought myself a Thanksgiving dinner over which I thanked God for giving me my freedom back and for putting behind me the whole dirty affair from Watergate to that present time. It was finally done and over with. Or so I thought.

Little did I know but that it would begin all over again and last for the next 22 years.

On Friday, November 27, 1987 – the day after Thanksgiving – I went to meet my so-called lawyer again at McDonald's. Of course, I never knew exactly who would show up.

This time is was the same limo and chauffeur who had given me the $2500. He denied it was he who had fired the two shots at me. He reached into his pocket and extracted an envelope that contained $7500 and a one-way airline ticket to New York City. The chauffeur told me not ask any questions and never to reveal what I knew about anyone or anything. He also warned me never to return to Washington, D.C. He then drove me in the limousine to the National Airport where I caught a plane to New York City. The date was November 27, 1987 and I have remained a resident of the City to this day.

The Kenmore Hotel.
Photo: Author's Archives

Chapter Ten

New York City 1987 To Present

I arrived at LaGuardia Airport in New York City in late November 1987.

Carl Shoffler had previously told me to take an ad out in the *New York Times* seeking a job as a building superintendent in the New York City area. I had received a promising response to the ad. So I took a cab from the airport and went straight to 17 South Park Avenue in Manhattan. There I met a John and a Bruce who were the owners of an investment corporation. They hired me on the spot as a property manager in charge of 36 buildings in Harlem. I was given a white van for my personal use. It didn't seem to matter that I did not have a New York State driver license or, for that matter, a license of any type. I had just gotten out of prison after serving 18 months, and my District of Columbia driver license was expired.

I was also paid $1000 a week off the books and had a free apartment in Harlem.

Bruce was a young brilliant white boy in his early twenties from Kentucky who was being hired and exploited by the Mafia. John was a middle-aged white man from Australia who was new to America and was also being exploited by the Mob. John was always secretive about everything. Bruce was the brains behind the operation and rarely left the office.

My job as property manager was to *pretend* to make repairs on the 36 buildings for violations of the housing code. However, my real job was to create more violations of very serious nature, such as opening up a gas line in order to cause a serious fire or make the building blow up. Bruce wanted all of his so-called tenants to vacate the building forthwith because they were squatters and it was nearly impossible to evict them, because they would bring up publicly the multiple violations of the buildings.

On one occasion I did open a main gas line that could have caused the death of many people, but I immediately telephoned the city's fire department to report gas odors. Firemen arrived within minutes and shut the gas off to the entire building, which was precisely what I wanted as this left the tenants with no heat or hot water right before Christmas. When they found they had no gas to cook with, many tenants chose to move out but many did not.

After Bruce and John began pressuring me to commit arson for them, I decided it was time to call in Carl Shoffler and his boys and let them take care of the situation behind the scenes as I was not going to commit mass murder.

Also, I secretly took on another building superintendent job in Brooklyn at a building on Sterling Avenue, which was three stories tall and had about 20 apartments. The job paid only $250 a week off-the-books and came with a nice apartment with all utilities paid. The neighborhood and the building's tenants were all Jamaican and I found myself subject to racism, even though I was half Black, I had a light way of showing it. One day I stumbled upon a large trunk in the basement. It was full of blank Social Security cards. So I called in Carl Shoffler, the FBI, the Secret Service and the Immigration and Naturalization Service, it seems these folks were involved in counterfeiting government documents such as Social Security cards, birth certificates, green cards, INS papers and U.S. passports.

With the money that Carl was sending me and the money I had saved up, I found that I had enough to move back into Manhattan and get a room just before the Feds via Carl raided the Sterling Avenue building. I moved into the Hotel Vigilant at 28th Street and 9th Avenue. It turned out to be a nightmare. The police called it the Hotel Vigilante. I paid $100 a week for a room that was 4 feet by 6 feet. The bed was nailed to the wall and there was exactly 12 square feet of walking space beside my bed and that was it. The room had chicken wire for its ceiling. I discovered that my room was really a cubicle on a floor that had 100 other cubicles, all with chicken wire over the top. Each cubicle was separated by walls that were one-half inch thick. The hotel has six floors, five of which had 100 cubicles, and a Chinese restaurant on the ground floor. Each of the five floors housing cubicles had one bathroom with the toilet and shower being co-ed.

The Hotel Vigilant was essentially nothing but a giant crack house that had non-stop sexual orgies. I could only take this environment for a short time, so I placed an ad in the *New York Times* indicating that I was looking for a job as a building superintendent. I got a response to the ad immediately and was hired to be the superintendent of a residential building in Manhattan at 77 South Park Avenue. My salary was $1000 a week. I was given a free two bedroom apartment that had a fireplace and its own laundry room. It was fully carpeted and beautifully furnished. I had to wear a suit and white gloves. The building had over 500 tenants. Its lobby glittered with marble walls and chandeliers and had antique furniture. For the first time in my life I had a job that had fringe benefits, such as health and life insurance.

Of course, I was still a fugitive from justice. My new name was Antoine Leguerrier. And amazingly, a neighbor directly above was David Rockefeller. He had a secret staircase that led from his apartment down to the street level, where it opened up through a false wall inside a doctor's office. Another neighbor was the brother of the famous Rabbi Kahane. Yet another tenant, whose name I have forgotten, was a gentleman who owned a Canadian railroad. He was always dirty and never took a bath. His full-time hobby was to collect bottles and cans and any other garbage that interested him, which he proceeded to stuff into his apartment. He would go to nearby Grand Central Station each day to eat handouts with the homeless. I was told his net worth was over half a billion dollars.

The building with the distinguished address had its share of vices, too. A beautiful Swedish model lived in one of the three penthouses and earned her living as a prostitute, charging $2500 per date. The most controversial tenant was Ted Meegaten, who also lived in one of the penthouses. Ted was a former actor, rodeo rider and porn star. He was also a miser who, like his fellow rich tenants, had an obsession for collecting garbage. Every room in his penthouse was filled from top to bottom and wall to wall with everything one could imagine. He barely had enough room to open his front door, on the other side of which was a chair that he sat and slept in. He had to leave the building to eat, take a bath or use the toilet. Ted had gotten his rent-controlled apartment before 1950 and paid only $67 a month for what was supposed to be a beautiful penthouse. Ted's view from his apartment of the city was breath-taking. He could almost reach out and touch Grand Central Station and the Empire State Building.

Ted's next door neighbor (whose name I have forgotten) lived most of the time in California where he owned a cable TV station. He only stayed in his penthouse once or twice a year. The man hated Ted and wanted him out of the building. On one occasion he telephoned me and offered an undisclosed amount of money if I were to push Ted off the roof. He even wired me $5000 to consider the offer, which I received and accepted. I still declined the offer but arranged for him to be set up with a hit man who would do the job on Ted. Need I say more? Of course, Carl Shoffler got the hit man for him. I don't know what happened after that because soon thereafter I was working in my office when the owner of the building entered the lobby from the street. I knew my time was limited at the building and that I had to depart because of the *hit man situation.* So I decided to leave in style. I placed an ad in the *New York Times* to sublease my free apartment at 77 South Park Avenue. I managed to rent out my apartment for $3000 per month plus a $3000 security deposit, for a total of $6000. I rented out my apartment to 10 different people, and pocketed $60,000, leaving the owner to straighten out the inevitable chaos. I did hear after I left that Ted Meegarten died of natural causes. I also heard from an employee of the building I later bumped into on the street that on the day after I moved out six large moving vans showed up, each of which had instructions to move their truck's belongings into my former apartment.

Now I had a small war chest on which to survive as a fugitive from justice.

I placed another ad in the *New York Times* and soon had a job as superintendent at a building in Greenwich Village. I stayed there for three or four months. When I found that I was having problems from a couple of troublesome tenants, whom I felt were deliberately picking on me, I moved out without notice, leaving the building without a superintendent.

I had plenty of money to stay at various hotels in Times Square.

And then again, I placed another ad in the *New York Times*, landing a superintendent's job with a free apartment at a small building at 208th Street and Dickman Avenue in Washington Heights. All the tenants seemed to be drug addicts, gangsters and welfare cheats. I did not like the area, the building and especially the tenants. I had already decided to rent my apartment out *as usual* but decided to take my time and collect my thoughts. This was because Carl Shoffler had me working on what became a dangerous assignment. He had ordered me to infiltrate Muslims from countries like Algeria and Pakistan, and these Muslims knew exactly where I lived. Carl was having me work the telephones in Times Square. This meant making illegal phone calls for Muslims using telephone credit cards and third-party billings. However, the credit cards and third-party billings were in reality not illegal because they were furnished by Carl. The telephone calls were for Muslims to call their homes and friends overseas. Some of the Muslims had been identified as spies, so all their calls were being traced and monitored because of the "illegal" cards they used.

I lived for awhile near the foothills of Inwood Park and loved walking through the woods enjoying the wildlife, flowers, trees herbs and old Indian caves. I spent most of the summer there quietly enjoying myself. One day I found a small, beautiful fighting cock. I took it home and made a pet of it. But then I let some crazy homeless woman stay at my apartment one day to get her out of the rain and went out for a walk. When I came back I found her eating my pet chicken. I threw her ass out.

One day several undercover cops arrested me for making calls for the Muslims using "illegal" phone cards. Even though Carl secretly got the charge against me dismissed, I thought this was enough already. I made the decision that it was time for me to move on and rent out my free super's apartment. I did this using my tried and true formula but only made about $18,000.

Again I stayed in Times Square hotels until my money was totally depleted. Then I moved to subway track number one of the Pennsylvania Railroad Station under Madison Square Garden for about three months. I became so depressed that one day I decided to jump in front a subway train. As the train came in I was getting my nerve up to jump when a professional-looking man with a briefcase who had the appearance of a Wall Street broker, standing only three feet from me, suddenly jumped in front of the train. His body was ripped to shreds and decapitated. I was so shaken by what I had witnessed that I went upstairs and sat down in the lobby of Penn Station. While I was sitting there in a daze a man and a woman approached me. The woman said her name was Charlotte and the man said his name was Jim Cassidy. They told me they were social workers from the outreach office in Penn Station. They asked me to fill out an application for Section 8 housing. I found that I qualified.

I soon got my Section 8 certificate, which was for an apartment at 168th Street and Boston Road in the South Bronx, also known as Fort Apache. I lived only a few blocks from the old Fort Apache Police Precinct that had been taken over years earlier by hoodlum gangs. The situation became so nationally infamous that a movie was later made about it, *Fort Apache.*

On April 10, 1991 I had to go to Madison Square Garden to meet with Charlotte and Jim to pick up the lease for my new Section 8 apartment. I was walking by St. John's Catholic Church, which is right beside Madison Square Garden, when I spotted a beautiful white dove fluttering against the church windows like it was trying to get inside. I walked over and picked up the dove and took it back to my apartment in Fort Apache. I placed a bowl of water and food on a window sill. The dove would sit on the window sill all day and not fly away.

Just before midnight, under a full moon, on Friday, April 12, 1991, I decided to walk from my apartment to a nearby store to get a pack of cigarettes. I remember that the night was eerily quiet. About one block away I was directly in front of the Bronx-Lebanon Hospital's emergency room door when I felt a strong thud to my left jaw and a sharp pain to the back of my neck. Suddenly I was surrounded by a crowd of Hispanic teenagers. One of them pulled out a 12 inch butcher knife, just like what you would see in a Freddie Kruger movie. He plunged the knife into my right side going through my upper torso between the ribs, penetrating my right lung, cutting through a mammary artery and severing the bottom part of my heart by slicing it wide open.

At this point I recall a guard from the emergency room appeared swinging a 2x4 board at the crowd, causing it to disperse. The guard grabbed me and pushed me into the emergency room. I remember going into the waiting area and finding there was no registration clerk. So I sat down. The guard soon re-entered the hospital and saw me sitting there. He realized I was in a state of shock and didn't know what I was doing. He took me directly to the emergency treatment area and told the medical staff that I had been assaulted and stabbed right in front of the hospital.

I was taken immediately into treatment room number one and placed on a table. I recall about six doctors and three or four nurses around me and I was holding my chest with my hand. They were cutting my clothes off. They started asking me questions at the same time as did an Irish cop who was present. I remember the cop asking me my name and saying that he had found two sets of ID's in my pants and he wanted to know which name was really mine since they both had the same ID photo but different names. I managed to deliberately mumble something to him that was obviously inaudible. By a stroke of luck, the cop wrote down the wrong name. The doctors intensified their questioning of me. I suddenly realized that I could not talk because I was beginning to lose air and could not breathe. I remember one doctor who quickly stitched up the stab wound that was about two to three inches on the back of my neck. Then another doctor cut my stomach area open with a scalpel, making an incision about three inches long below my navel. He wanted to see if I had internal bleeding. I was losing my breath fast now and it was totally impossible for me to talk. So I grabbed a pen from the pocket of a doctor's white jacket with my left hand and wrote on the bed sheet *no air.*

At this point the doctors switched their attention to my face and upper body. I don't why but before they seemed to be concentrating on my lower body. A doctor pulled my right hand from my chest and suddenly blood shot through the stab wound and splattered on the ceiling. I found that I could breathe a little bit.

I remember being transferred from the observation table onto a stretcher and the doctors remarking among themselves that I was dying. They said I had to go to the operating room. I remember being rushed through the hallway on the stretcher and observing how fast I was being moved by the lights flashing over my head. The doctor placed me in an elevator that would take me to the operating room, but the elevator would not move. The doctors panicked and then rushed me through the hallways into the main lobby of the hospital and onto the hospital's guest elevator.

Upon arriving at the operating room a doctor asked me the name and number of a relative. I gave them my Aunt Peggy's number in West Virginia, who was my mother's sister-in-law. I don't know what would have happened if Peggy had not answered the phone at that time of night or if she had said no to the strange alias that I was using.

After that I remember a doctor who was Asian cutting me wide open, and the next thing I knew I was waking up several hours later because the hands on the clock had moved since the operation began. But there was a problem. I was at the top of the operating room with my back against the ceiling and I was looking down at my own body and the doctors hovering around it. I had a most pleasant and happy feeling. I felt calm and peaceful. I remember hearing the anesthesiologist telling the doctors that I had no pulse and no heart beat. Then I remember hearing the same voice suddenly exclaim that he was now getting a faint heart beat. At that point I remember falling back into my body on the operating table. I felt that I just wanted to be left alone because it was so peaceful where I was. I fell asleep again and this time when I woke up I looked down and saw my heart in a doctor's hands being sewed up. I could actually see my heart pulsating in the doctor's hands. I fell asleep again.

The next time when I started to wake up again I heard a nurse tell someone that my breath stunk from all the blood and she was not going to irrigate or cleanse it out with water. I threw a bed pan at her.

After three days I was out of my crisis. It was a miracle that I survived this and all the doctors concurred. After all I was on the operating table for 36 hours straight. Then I was in the ICU for three days before waking up. I had IV needles everywhere, along with wires, tubes in my mouth and nose, a catheter in my penis and a huge tube like a hose in my right lung.

After a few days I was transferred from the old Bronx Lebanon Hospital to the new Bronx Lebanon Hospital a few blocks away. This was done to repair my left jaw, which was totally destroyed. Eventually all the tubes and wires and huge hose disappeared from my body. I stayed in the new hospital for about two weeks before being discharged.

I left the hospital and caught a cab and went back to my apartment at 168th St and Boston Road. I was reluctant about entering my building but suppressed my fears and went into my apartment. I was in excruciating pain. Previously I had befriended some of the neighborhood guys who were crack heads. It was funny that I had turned down pain pills from the hospital because they were narcotics and I feared I would become addicted. But I succumbed to the urging of the local guys who persuaded me that using crack would take away all the pain and help me forget what had happened.

Taking crack for the first time was the biggest mistake of my life. It was the beginning of a whole new world that I knew nothing about. After taking just one hit on the crack pipe I stepped all the way into the twilight zone and it would be years before I found my way back out.

Smoking crack for the first time – and only the first time – was the best experience I ever had. Yes, all the pain was gone and I felt totally euphoric. It caused strong sexual desires. But it actually only lasted for one to three minutes and the after-effects were devastating. The worst possible thing was the fact that I was hooked from just one hit. It can take only one to turn someone into an addict.

Now I was a federal fugitive from justice, an assault and stabbing victim, and a new crack head. I decided I couldn't take anymore stress. Smoking crack causes extreme paranoia of your most subconscious fears. Since I was a fugitive from justice my fears centered on the police. I knew in my bones that I had to get away from my apartment and its environment. So I gave the keys to my apartment to my young crack-dealing friends and left with just a small bag of personal belongings and clothes.

I never returned to the apartment near Fort Apache.

I became homeless. I stayed temporarily with some friends who lived on Adams Street near the Bronx Zoo. These were two Puerto Ricans, Gwen and Danny, with whom I had become acquainted in the crack world. I soon found that I had jumped from the frying pan into the fire by moving in with these two. They had a little boy about nine years old who tried to stab people when ordered by his mother. They also had a three-year-old little girl. Gwen was almost nine months pregnant. She and Danny received welfare and sold their food stamps for crack. The children were hungry most of the time. The whole environment caused me to increase my crack smoking. The last straw came when Gwen gave birth to a baby girl whom she soon attempted to sell for crack.

A neighbor of Gwen and Danny invited me to move in with him and another crack friend by the name of Cecilia, who was from Panama. She had a Puerto Rican boy friend named Eddie. She had a 13-year-old son named Louie. Cecilia, who was also known as Cessie, received welfare and also worked as a cashier for the Webster Liquor Store in the Bronx. Cessie was making over $1000 a week as a cashier by stealing from the store, and made no secret about it. Eddie was a gypsy cab driver and a sewer rat. He and his brother were both sewer rats and were arrested after being caught in the city's sewer lines looking for valuables that were lost down drains. They boasted that they found a $10,000 diamond ring that some lady had dropped down her kitchen sink.

One day Eddie came home while Cessie was at work at the liquor store and raped her 13 year old son, Louis. I gave Louis some money to run away and stay with his grandmother in Brooklyn because Cessie initially filed a complaint with the police against Eddie but then within an hour withdrew the charge.

I left the Bronx and went to Manhattan, to be officially homeless on the streets of New York City for the next year-and-a-half.

I lived inside the Port Authority Bus Terminal near Times Square and in the doorways at night of stores in the gold and diamond district, not far from Rockefeller Center. I learned how to go to the soup kitchens and use a street sheet that was a directory and guide for homeless people. I also learned it was not safe to go to the shelters, especially the Bellevue men's shelters. When it was raining I would go to Penn Station at Madison Square Garden and sit in the lobby of the Amtrak station. I also learned how to hang out at public museums and the public spaces of many buildings.

Being homeless was a different world of none – in other words, there was literally no place like it. It was difficult to try to blend in with ordinary domiciled people, something most people take for granted. Until you have been homeless, you have no idea of what a different life it is. When it is too hot you don't have a home to go to in order to cool off. The same is true when it is cold, windy and rainy.

When you wake up you either have the bright sun beaming into your eyes or a cop's nightstick beating against your bench. When you need to go to the bathroom you must find the nearest convenient place and sometimes this is very public. You can carry with you only what you need to survive and sometimes that becomes too heavy.

When homeless even washing up or taking a shower can become a burden. Some homeless persons give up after a while and don't care whether they are clean or not. As a matter of fact some of the homeless prefer to keep dirty and carry a body odor to keep strangers away from them.

There were times when I would sit on a bench and watch people getting off work at 5 P.M. to head home – but I had no home to go to. Not only did I have to tolerate the elements, I had to sleep with one eye open for people who wanted to cause me harm or better yet the rats who were sniffing around looking for food and smelling crumbs on my clothing or in my pockets.

It is no fun to wash your socks and underwear in a public water fountain in the parks with people giving you dirty looks. I was not the type to beg for money. If I did not get any money from welfare I had to eat from the garbage cans at the rear of grocery stores. In other words, I was taking food away from the rats: the rats resented this and sometimes would try to take the food back. When it was pouring down rain and I couldn't make it to a public bathroom, I would just piss in my pants while walking down the street with throngs of pedestrians around me. Nobody noticed or even cared.

I remember one time it rained hard and I had just found a huge bag of sandwiches. I also found two large umbrellas and a blanket. So I went to a plaza beside Madison Square Garden and opened up my umbrellas and climbed inside a trash bag with my sandwiches. I slept there for two days while it rained, and no one bothered me. I thought it funny because if it were not raining, there would be tens of thousands of people walking through the plaza and they would be walking right over me. But I lay there on the sidewalk in the middle of the plaza with the rain pouring all around me, bone dry and cozy and amused at the few soaked persons running around me who were braving the rain.

New Years Day, Easter, Fourth of July, Thanksgiving and Christmas came and went and I was still homeless. It hurt. When the snow got so bad I would sleep on the A subway train that would travel back and forth from Washington Heights at 208 Street to Far Rockaway on Long Island, or if the hoodlums and gangs were patrolling the train and the subway platforms, I would go to the Twin Towers and sleep on the lower level. The Twin Towers before 9/11 were required by law, since they had subway exits, to provide public restrooms and public spaces for people. So the Twin Towers roped off a large section of the floor outside the public restrooms for homeless people to use for sleeping when it was freezing outside. There were even guards that stood by during the entire night. They did not do so to be nice but to protect the general public from the homeless.

Another place that was safe to sleep when cold weather hit was tracks nos. 1, 3 and 17 in Pennsylvania Station, just below Madison Square Garden. However, that practice soon came to a halt because track no. 17 was a storage train that carried valuables. The homeless were accused of breaking into a storage train and stealing millions of dollars of furs, when in fact the theft was carried out by crooked cops who put the blame on the homeless.

One of my favorite spots was Central Park. It was always beautiful and no one ever bothered me. It was peaceful and quiet. People were nice and gave me food. There were restrooms that I could use without being harassed, and there was always a lot of activity. I remember attending a Mafia wedding as an uninvited guest where I was butt naked and having fellatio performed on me while I smoked crack. Of course, the wedding was being held at the pavilion by the pond with paddle boats and I was in the adjacent black lagoon, where I was not visible to the public. The black lagoon was a peninsula that stuck out in the pond. There was only one way in and out and it was difficult to transverse because of the rocks and brush. It was a place known to gays who liked to have public sex and be nude in the woods 24/7.

As time went on I came to the conclusion that multi-millions of dollars were being made off homeless people, and their needs and causes exploited. I don't know about other cities but New York City has hundreds if not thousands of empty and abandoned buildings that could be used to house every homeless person in the city.

Poor people do not seem to realize that when they turn their neighborhoods into ghettos by drugs, prostitution, crime and graffiti that it is the rich developers who start coming in and quietly surveying the area and begin pushing the poor people out, making thousands of persons homeless.

Again, I don't know about other cities but New York City has enough food left over each day from grocery stores and restaurants that could feed almost every person in the city – homeless or not.

One thing that everyone needs to know is that lose your job, lose your health and you become one step away from being homeless. That was never more true than today.

I had been on the streets for some time and was beginning to discover a brand new world – a city underneath the City of New York. Another person who had befriended me took me to Grand Central Station where we went through the main lobby and down a small staircase that appeared obsolete. We descended down as far as we could go, perhaps four to six stories underground. At the end of the staircase we came out to a train platform that was no longer in use. We walked a couple of steps and then went onto an old unused railroad track where we walked about 20 feet and came to a small sliding metal door that was under the platform. The door was approximately three by four feet. When we opened it to my surprise there were two guards on the other side who, after we entered, searched us for weapons, drugs and alcohol. They were polite but cautious. I found myself in a vast open area. There were hundreds of people living in spaces or cubicles. The area was lighted by electricity that also powered TV sets, refrigerators and hot plates. The aroma of home-cooked food was everywhere. All the persons I met were exceptionally intelligent, nice and courteous.

I was in famous Mole City several stories below Manhattan. The rules for the community were strict. No drugs, weapons, fighting, alcohol or sex. Believe it or not, there were decent people with clean white sheets on their beds. They had chairs and tables that originally had been thrown away on the streets above and somehow transported to the city below.

The inhabitants of Mole City used the bathroom upstairs at Grand Central Station and took their showers at public baths. Some of the persons had lived in Mole City for several years. These persons were obviously not on the census rolls. However, some of them actually worked on Wall Street and left each weekday morning wearing appropriate clothing and carrying a briefcase.

I was happy to live there despite the fact that we had literally hundreds of neighbors living right beside us that we had to feed to keep them away from us. Some of the rats were easily recognizable and had been given names.

I stayed there for over a year and managed to stay clean from crack for the entire period. But I found myself becoming increasingly depressed, so I placed another ad in the *New York Times* seeking a superintendent's job again. I always had a telephone number placed in the ad to receive my calls that was managed from a mail and answering service.

Then one day I was sitting on a trash can at 50th Street and Broadway reading a newspaper. I was hungry and my clothing was homeless style. I paid no attention to a black limousine that was parked right beside me. Suddenly, the rear black-tinted window opened up part way and a black hand passed a huge cup of jumbo shrimp and a $20 bill to me. Later as I walked down the street I spotted the same vehicle stopping at the island in the middle of Times Square at 43rd Street and Broadway. There was a movie set on the island and the person who exited the limousine was Oprah Winfrey.

I got an answer to my superintendent ad in the *New York Times*. The owner of two buildings on 14th Street and Avenue B gave me a free apartment and $50 per week to oversee the two buildings, which had a beauty parlor on the ground floor of one and a Chinese restaurant on the ground floor of the other. The owner was a Muslim from Afghanistan who said he had converted to Judaism. There were about 48 tenants in both buildings, some of whom were very strange. Among these were two lesbians, one of whom was deaf. Both liked rough sex and every other day the police were called because they were slamming each other against the walls and floors. This was a near daily ritual. It never stopped. The police usually did nothing.

Another tenant called himself Bruce Lee and every night did his martial arts routine in his window, nude. He was 17 years old and Italian. Yet another tenant was a lady who was the local gossip. Her name was Helen. She could always be found sitting with her head out the window of her second floor apartment. She was a nice lady, but if she took a disliking to you she would call you what her name sounded like.

The owner of the building, whom I never did believe had converted to Judaism, one day told me when he had three empty apartments that he did not want to any "niggers or spics, only whites." He did not know how much he had offended me. So pursuant to his wishes I rented all three apartments out to upscale whites. As a matter of fact, I rented each apartment at the rate of $1000 per month when he actually wanted $2500 a month. The problem was that I rented each apartment to three different tenants, collecting $9000. I sent the tenants to pick up their apartment keys and their leases from the owner at his Long Island office, all on the same day. The day that I selected was his daughter's wedding day at his own restaurant.

Unfortunately I squandered all my new-found money on hotels and crack in Times Square. Yes, I was again hooked on crack. One day I went to Herald Square Park in front of Macy's to buy crack. I purchased 100 dimes of crack totaling $1000. I went to the subway station at Penn Station to go back to my hotel, which was the Hotel Carter at 43rd and Eighth Avenue. I had only $100 bills on me and I didn't want to break any of them so I jumped over the turnstill. I failed to notice two undercover detectives standing right there. They yelled for me to stop and asked why I jumped the turnstile. I did not answer them because I was scared shitless as I had $1000-worth of crack in my pocket. If they had found this on me I could have been sentenced to life in prison under the draconian Rockefeller drug laws. So I started acting crazy and scratching my butt, groin and head to make them think that I was a crazy homeless who had lice. They asked me again several times why I had jumped the turnstile and again I did not answer. Suddenly I saw a piece of dirty bread on the dirty concrete floor and picked it up and started eating it. The cops thought I was totally disgusting, which was what I wanted. They asked if I was homeless and I said yes and that I was sorry for jumping the turnstile but that I was cold and hungry and had bugs that wouldn't leave me alone. This caused the two cops to order me to get the hell out of there and not come back. They wouldn't come within five feet of me, so convinced were they that I was diseased with lice. If they had told me to empty my pockets this book would never have been written. Such are the twists and turns of life, which sometimes seems like a dream.

Not long afterwards I had a new place of residence and that was Madison Park. I lived there for several months and on a couple of occasions managed to get myself arrested for buying crack inside nearby hotels and delicatessens. The first arrest was on 25th Street and Madison Avenue. The police had observed me buying crack from a dealer in the Madison Hotel. I had two dime ($20) bags of crack. My wallet contained at least three different IDs, including one with my real name, date of birth and social security number. I was arrested by police officers Ron V. and Pedro S. from the 13th Precinct and was taken to the processing room right beside the holding cell. I was still in handcuffs, so I reached in my back pocket, pulled out my wallet, dropped it on the floor and kicked it into the holding cell. Luckily, no one saw me: if someone had I could have been sent back to Washington, D.C. as a fugitive from the law to face 13 years in prison for having "escaped" from the halfway house on Thanksgiving eve.

I gave the cops in the 13th Precinct my name as Tony Merritt, my date of birth as May 25, 1942 and my social security number as 142-34-5563. Fortunately, my thumbs and index fingers were burned to the second degree from the crack pipe. This meant I could not be fingerprinted. So the officer on duty was forced to calibrate my prints, which is illegal. He could have lost his job if it were known that he had fixed my prints and ID on the new high-tech laser fingerprint machine that was connected from the New York Police Department to the FBI in Washington. It was a machine that was meant not to be tampered with but, by a stroke of luck, this lazy officer was too impatient to fingerprint me. The result was that I now had a brand new ID. It was almost like being born again with a new birth certificate and social security number.

After the mug shots I was placed in the holding cell, where I retrieved my wallet and pushed my IDs into a crack in the wall that was made of cinder blocks. I had to sit in jail for the next 72 hours, eating dry bologna sandwiches, oranges and drinking kool-aid while waiting to see the judge whom, when I did see him, said "time served, case dismissed."

One day I walked by the Kenmore Hotel, which was only two blocks from my homeless shelter at Madison Square Park. I had just gotten welfare money for the first time and I decided to rent a room at the Kenmore to try to get my life together before I became a fatal victim from crack. I had a small room on the 15th floor, which had only a bed and chair. I bought a TV, a table and with some money left over got some clothes.

I soon discovered that the Kenmore Hotel was full of crack dealers, crack heads, prostitutes, thieves, murderers and every other type of criminal. What a perfect hideout for a fugitive from justice. I telephoned Carl Shoffler and told him where I was living, which made his day. He told me to stay there as he had an important assignment for me, one that had national security implications because it involved a possible double agent, one who had worked for the CIA and also for the North Vietnamese Communist Party. I asked him if it was bigger than the information I had given him on Watergate and he told me to forget about Watergate because that glory belong only to him. He tossed me a bone, however, by saying that I could take full credit for the new assignment if it were successfully carried out.

Carl began talking to me about a man named Tran Dinh Truong who was the owner of the Kenmore Hotel, Hotel Carter, Longacre Hotel and two other hotels, all of which were in New York City. Tran had been a defector from North Vietnam. When he and his wife defected, they brought with them over millions in gold bullion. My assignment was to get inside information about Tran and, hopefully, get to know him personally.

Not long after, I was walking down 23rd Street and saw a police officer who was at least six-and-a-half-feet tall. His height and uniform made him stand out. I walked up to him and asked him if his name was Stretch. He jokingly said that only bad guys called him by that moniker and that his real name was Scott Kimmins. I told him that I had experience in working with the police as a confidential informant and I was interested in cleaning up the Kenmore Hotel. His eyes lit up and he said he was happy about that, because the Kenmore had been on his beat for ten or more years and it was full of every type of criminal one can mention. He asked me for my name and I replied that I was Tony Merritt. He gave me a CI code number 0068, which happened to be the last four digits of his badge number, which was 10068. After that we entered into a long and friendly relationship.

I was on the verge of kicking my crack habit. In my bones I knew its end was near. One night I met two Dominican drug dealers, one by the name of José and the other I can't remember, at Park Avenue and 32nd Street and purchased two vials of crack from them. I failed to notice that I was being observed by police officer Ron V. and his partner, Pedro S. Fortunately before they stopped me I had already discarded the vials along the street where they could never be found. Ron did not get out of his squad car but talked to me through the car's rolled down window. He said that they had observed me buy the crack from the two Dominicans. Apparently it was the intent of the two officers to make me look like a snitch to make me get into trouble. The next night I again purchased crack from José and the other Dominican and they confronted me about why I had talked to the two police officers the night before. They said right after I left after talking to the police officers the two cops stopped and searched them, but failed to find anything. This was because they always hid their drugs by stashing them in the light in a public phone booth. I told them that I knew Ron and that he was a friend of mine. I added that Ron was a crack head and that he and I had smoked crack on many occasions. They asked me if Ron would take a bribe and whether I could arrange it. I replied that I would try to arrange it by talking to Ron, which I did.

Four weeks later Ron asked me to have José and his crack partner meet with him at a McDonald's on 23rd Street. Ron wanted me present also. José and his crack partner agreed. So on a Sunday afternoon I went to the McDonald's on the date scheduled. Ron intercepted me outside and pretended that the two drug dealers had made arrangements to meet him later and that he wanted to talk to me alone. Ron asked me what I thought he should do about the bribe, should he take it or not? I told him I thought he was crazy to do so because he had an excellent job as a police officer and the amount of bribe money involved wasn't worth it. He asked me what I wanted out of it and I told him I wanted nothing. I left him and went back to my room at the Kenmore. The next day I read in the *New York Post* that Ron had arrested two drug dealers from the Park Avenue area for drug dealing and attempting to bribe a police officer.

It was obvious to me that Ron had been trying to trick me the day before with his stupid conversation about whether or not he should take the bribe. Had I responded differently I would have been arrested, too. Sorry, Ron that I disappointed you. But to show how stupid Ron was he didn't realize that even though he had been secretly wired, and taping me, he failed to realize how crucial my testimony was to the case. As it turned out the prosecutor needed me to testify if any convictions were to be achieved. I refused, saying that I would not do so until I received a written apology from Ron, his partner and the prosecutor. I got it. So I testified and the two Dominican drug dealers each got seven year sentences.

After this incident I was arrested several more times but always managed to walk out as result of my new ID. One time I was arrested on 14th Street and Avenue D at a delicatessen that was already in the process of being raided by the police. Like an idiot and a dumb criminal I had a taxicab parked in front of the store while I attempted to enter it. The door was locked. I saw people in the back of the store and kept banging on the door and hollering about spending my $100 for crack. Finally, the cops got fed up with my banging and opened the door and told me I was under arrest.

After all these arrests I was thoroughly fed up with crack and with crack dealers.

I began to concentrate on the Kenmore Hotel where Tran Dinh Truong was allowing drugs and crime to run rampant. Police Officer Scott Kimmins had begun working diligently to correct the situation. He was in communication with U.S. Attorney Mary Jo White, New York FBI Agent Kenneth Weiss, the New York City Fire Department Chief, IRS, DEA and U.S. Marshall Service.

While plans were underway among these law enforcement entities, I had begun my own plan and strategy in cooperation with Carl Shoffler, which got a boost when I befriended Mrs. Tran, who was the second wife of Tran Dinh Truong. She asked me one night to come down to the lobby to talk to her about taking the position as chief of security for the Hotel Carter near Times Square, which was also owned by Tran. I accepted the offer and worked there for about a year. I received a free room with three meals a day and $50 a week. But I had to work seven days a week and sixteen hours a day.

The Hotel Carter had almost 1000 rooms. Besides being chief of security, I was delegated responsibility for paying off city inspectors.

I paid off dozens of inspectors with envelopes containing thousands of dollars in cash.

Tran and his first wife, Mrs. Sang, lived on the entire second floor of the Hotel Carter, which they had turned into a luxurious residence. The third floor was reserved for about 200 employees, all being Vietnamese with the exception of me. The employees, including me, were slaves to Tran. Everyday we would eat together in the employee lunch room, being given one piece of fish and a plate of rice. Tran's mother, who was in her 90's, hated her son for the way he treated his own people. She refused to eat with him and his family but instead chose to join the employees every day in our lunch room.

When an employee crossed or did something that displeased Tran, he would have his son, Boc Tran, beat the person severely, After Tran discovered that three employees had stolen from him, they were physically removed from their room early one morning at 3 A.M. I saw this happen as my room was next to theirs. I was using the bathroom the two rooms shared when I heard noise from the next room. I looked through a small hole in the wall and saw the three employees sitting on a bed with their hands tied behind their backs and duct tape over their mouths. I then saw two men march the employees out the room's door. I could have watched what happened next but was afraid I would be spotted. So I retreated to my bed. The three employees were never seen again.

Tran would advertise in a national Vietnamese newspaper for employees, promising a great career and future in hotel work. Many of his employees were from California. Once they arrived at the Hotel Carter he sent them to work at one of his five hotels in the city. These new arrivals had exhausted their money, so it was easy for Tran to pay them only $50 a week, a free room and three meals.

Tran hired a white manager to work at the Hotel Carter and to serve as general manager for the other four hotels. His job description, so to speak, was to take responsibility for the violations that the City levied upon the hotels and to go to jail if it were so required. After a while the white manager rebelled, openly declaring that he knew too much about Tran's hotel operation and said that he would not go to jail for failing to correct the violations levied by the City. He made a major mistake by trying to blackmail Tran. This man died mysteriously in his sleep at the Hotel Carter. Each year Tran would have a death anniversary party for him. I attended one of these and it was lavish.

Tran had a 16 year-old daughter that lived in the penthouse on the top floor of the Hotel Carter. She had a Black boyfriend that Tran did not approve of. One day his daughter and her boyfriend disappeared and were never heard from again. The rumor among the employees was that Tran had them killed or that they ran away together. On several occasions Tran had me accompany him to his daughter's penthouse suite, which had six locks on the door. Her living quarters remained untouched since the day she disappeared. Even her radio was still playing. Tran had bars of gold sitting around the walls in each room, which he would touch as he walked through the penthouse. He would then light some candles and we would leave, with Tran carefully locking each of the six locks.

Tran pretended to be a religious man and each day would go to the Holy Cross Catholic Church on 43rd and Eighth Avenue to put money in the donation box and light a candle at each statue. He even had a Vietnamese Catholic priest working for him at the Hotel Carter. The priest had his own room. I don't know how much money he received but his job was to stay in his room and pray all day for Tran. Even his meals were delivered to his room.

Tran claimed that he came to America on a small boat with little money. He also claimed that he and his family as Vietnamese refugees stayed with American sponsors in New Jersey upon their arrival in this country. He said it was the American sponsors who helped him purchase the five hotels, which he bought in one day.

Carl assigned me to monitor Tran because, as Carl told me, Tran and his family actually came to America on their own luxurious yacht. He and his wife had been bank managers in North Vietnam and had robbed their banks of millions of dollars in gold bullion. They arrived as instant millionaires and purchased the five hotels with a portion of the gold bullion.

The banks that Tran and his wife stole from belonged to the Communist Party in Vietnam. They had tracked Tran and his family to the Hotel Carter. One night when I was working as chief of security a telephone call came through the switchboard for Tran and the caller said he was a high official of the Vietnamese Communist Party. The person threatened Tran and his family. The employees at the hotel desk had always been warned never to put a call through to Tran or to give any information on the phone about his family. The young lady at the desk that night was new to the job and apparently had never been instructed about Tran's standing orders. That same night the young lady disappeared and was never seen again.

Carl told me that there was one major secret about Tran and his wife: In actuality, they were both spies for the CIA and U.S. military intelligence. That was why they were allowed to come into the country in their own yacht with all the gold bullion and immediately purchase five hotels. Tran and his family had received protection from the CIA until Tran started to allow crimes enter his life and profit from them and also after suspicions arose that maybe, he and his wife were double-agents, still working with the Vietnam Communist Party.

I did all the things on the Tran assignment that Carl instructed me to do. I submitted my information to him by Western Union and telephone. In return Carl paid me $500 a week for a full year while the assignment was active.

Pursuant to Carl's instructions, I stole documents from Tran, recorded conversations, and took photographs of vital records.

Finally my assignment came to an end. After all that I had gone through for one year, eating three bowls of fish and rice each day and working 16 hours a day for $50 a week and spying on Tran, nothing ever happened to him. Tran has never been arrested to this day.

It was time for me to go back to the Kenmore Hotel where I was asked to get all sorts of information and commit all sorts of acts for the multiple law enforcement agencies with which I was involved. Among the acts that I was directed to engage in were: tapping phone lines, planting wiretap bugs, breaking into rooms, planting drugs on persons and in rooms, spreading false rumors, purchasing narcotics for the police, setting fires as a pretext for rooms to be broken into, sabotaging telephone and electrical lines, filing false reports, and setting up innocent people to be arrested.

During the course of this activity I solved three rapes, three murders and one bank robbery, and I was instrumental in the arrests of several hundred persons for drugs and other crimes.

One day I was told that multiple law enforcement agencies were about to stage a raid on the Kenmore planned for June 9, 1994. All the work that Officer Scott Kimmons and I had done earlier was about to pay off. I was informed a raid would take place in two days. However, the raid was moved up by one day and took place the following morning without any advance notice to me. I was asleep and woke up about noon. It was summertime and the weather was hot. I had my room window wide open. I got up and turned on the TV. I ate some four or five bananas and mischievously tossed the peels out the open window. In a matter of a few minutes I heard banging on my room door and shouts of "Police, open up." I opened the door and there were two cops there who asked if I were throwing banana peels out the window. Of course, I denied doing so and told them that I had just got up and was watching TV. Fortunately, they believed me and went away. I couldn't understand how the hell they could figure out that of 621 rooms and 23 floors in the hotel the banana peels came from my window.

So out of curiosity I looked out the window and could not believe what I was seeing. There were some white shirts, that is police officials, with banana peels on top of the caps. But that was not the most amazing thing I saw. The street was completely closed for six or more blocks and there were over 1000 law enforcement officers massed in front of the building. Across the street at the Baruch College there were agents in every window with cameras taking pictures of the Kenmore Hotel and all the activity around it. I quickly got dressed and went to the elevator where I was met by FBI agents. They asked who I was and I gave them my alias ID, of course. They radioed to someone on the outside who told them to personally and privately escort me out of the hotel immediately to safety and to do so without being conspicuous.

I was later informed that the key law enforcement personnel all were aware that I was *the* informant who was responsible for the raid, which turned out to be the largest drug raid in U.S. history.

The next day, June 9, 1994, the *New York Times* published a lengthy article under a banner headline, "IN LARGEST DRUG-LAW TAKEOVER, U.S. SEIZES NEW YORK CITY HOTEL." The lead paragraphs read:

> Federal authorities seized a filthy, dilapidated residential hotel near Gramercy Park yesterday, saying that drug dealers used it to operate 'a virtual supermarket for crack cocaine.' The owner,

prosecutors said, did nothing about it. Roving bands of drug dealers and addicts took over whole floors at the Kenmore Hotel, the largest single-room occupancy hotel in New York City, regularly robbing and sometime killing elderly residents for a few dollars, prosecutors said. With unlighted stairwells, broken toilets in common bathrooms and prostitutes plying their trade in the hallways, the hotel 'was permeated with violence,' said the United States Attorney, Mary Jo White.

"In the late-morning raid, federal agents and the New York City police arrested 18 people and took control of the 22-story red-brick building at 145 East 23rd Street, where the writers Nathaniel West and Dashiell Hammett once lived. A private company will manage the hotel until a court rules on the seizure."

The article went on to state that the hotel's owner, Tran Dinh Truong, was not charged with any crime but that prosecutors maintained he was aware of the crimes taking place inside the building. Prosecutors pointed out that Tran received $2 million each year solely from tenants on public assistance. An Assistant District Attorney termed Tran's operation at the Kenmore to be a "cash cow." The U.S. Attorney said that security guards at the hotel were arrested for selling narcotics. Tran and his staff "deliberately left some rooms unlocked so that crack dealers could work there."

After the raid Officer Scott Kimmons was hailed as a hero. The hotel itself looked like a war zone long after the raid was over. Hundreds of doors were bashed in by the police and FBI. Rooms were stripped apart and in shreds. U.S. Marshals were stationed in the lobby. Hidden cameras were being installed.

Yet only a few weeks after the raid new drug dealers were slowly finding their way back into the hotel. They were like roaches.

Tran was very angry that he had lost his hotel. He put up a vigorous legal battle in the courts. He also recruited two tenants into a conspiracy to regain the hotel. These were Richard A. and Sal M. They made a money deal with Tran to cause as much havoc and chaos as possible to force the government out. Part of their plan was to let the drug dealers slip back into the hotel. Richard was in charge of the operation. He had a warrant outstanding that sought his arrest in Florida for molesting a little boy. The deal between Tran and Richard was if Richard succeeded in getting the hotel back for Tran, he and Sal would receive $250,000 in cash and be given the top floor of the hotel for the rest of their lives.

Their plan might have worked except that the government had a secret weapon called Tony Merritt.

Years later, the police raided the Kenmore again and some 40 persons were arrested, including me. I was handcuffed and arrested in the lobby in front of the persons there on the charge of suspicion of killing a cop. I was taken to the 13th Precinct with the rest of those arrested but was placed in a cell separate from them. My cell was full of prisoners unknown to me. I was still handcuffed. Officers would come by the cell and make smartass remarks directed at me and make threats to me about killing some cop. My cell was right next to the holding pen for the Kenmore arrestees, so they could hear and see everything that was going down. Soon I was removed from my cell and taken to a bathroom to be strip searched by a detective who had been involved in the raid at the Kenmore. I did not like him and refused to be strip searched. I started screaming so that everyone could hear me that the detective was trying to insert the toilet plunger in my butt. He became embarrassed when several police captains came running to see what was happening. The whole scene was a sensitive one because only a week earlier a prisoner at a different precinct in Brooklyn had been sodomized with a plunger, an event that quickly developed into a national scandal.

A captain ordered the dectective to get away from me and for my handcuffs to be removed and for me to be placed in a cell alone. A few minutes after being so placed about six undercover officers came to take me out of the cell and ordered me to go to the front lobby and get into an unmarked car. I refused to budge. They wanted to know why and I said that the handcuffs had been removed. What difference did that make, they asked? I responded that if I am not handcuffed, and am being held for killing a cop, then I feared I was being set up to be killed for an attempted escape. They assured me that was not the case. So I decided to walk out. I started to get into the back seat of the unmarked car but was ordered to sit in the front seat. Then a young officer by the name of Oquendo was ordered by Lt. Clarke to take me to the District Attorney's office immediately. Officer Oquendo turned on the siren and red light and we drove like a bat of hell at 80 miles per hour to the 100 block of Centre Street. Two other unmarked police cars followed us. When we arrived I waited inside the car until Office Oquendo opened it, half expecting to be handcuffed again. Instead he told me to open my door and to forget about the handcuffs. He said we were going upstairs to see an Assistant District Attorney to have me swear to an affidavit about narcotics at the Kenmore Hotel. I was outraged and asked whose idea was it to make me go through all the bullshit and he said that it was Lt. Clarke's plan.

I told Oquendo that I would go upstairs but I would tell the ADA about my being falsely arrested for killing a cop, and being put through the ringer as a result. He pleaded with me not to do that. So I calmed down and went upstairs and cooperated with Oquendo and the Assistant District Attorney. They were extremely pleased because I gave them such a detailed report that it provided more than sufficient evidence against some 40 bad guys, and implicated more than 50 persons altogether.

Oquendo and the ADA took me to the court house through a secret passageway where we met a judge in chambers to whom I gave a sworn statement regarding the arresting affidavit. After we left the court house Oquendo, who was known as the masked man because he always wore a ski mask during narcotic raids, returned to the Kenmore Hotel to arrest the 50-some people that I had named before the judge.

Here I was working with multi-law enforcement agencies – local, state and federal – and nobody knew I was a federal fugitive from justice. What a joke!

Still, my number one assignment was working for Carl Shoffler until he died on Saturday, July 13, 1996. My guess is that Carl is also laughing at just how clever I was in getting myself recruited by all these agencies, with everyone assuming I was vetted by another agency so that nobody bothered to get clearance on me. Carl told me on a number of occasions that the government was just as dumb as the people we worked for. Well, Carl was right.

Tran, Richard and Sal were losing the battle to regain the Kenmore Hotel. This still did not stop outrageous things from happening there. I kept smelling an odor that was most disgusting. Every day it would increase more and more. I called the police. The cop who came told me it was just dead rats and after all this was the Kenmore Hotel. After a week I couldn't take it anymore and I called the police again. This time two cops came and I met them at the elevator. As soon as they got off the elevator I asked them about the smell and they said it could be a dead body. The odor was overpowering. We went door to door trying to locate the source of the odor and couldn't find it. Finally the cops called someone for a special chemical used to locate dead bodies. It led the police to a room just three doors down from mine. They knocked and got no answer. No keys could be found that would open the door. The door was sealed tightly shut. But it did have a shaded glass panel in it that one of the officers smashed with his nightstick. Immediately there was a light explosion, like a balloon bursting, and then a heavy red dust came flying out of the room like a raging dust storm. The officers screamed and I got scared and slammed my door shut for the odor was unbearable. The two poor officers starting banging on my door, so I quickly let them in. They radioed for help and oxygen masks while they kept sheltered in my room.

It turned out that the dead man was an Asian who had recently had surgery. He had been robbed by a prostitute and stabbed in the same surgical incision that was trying to heal. His body had laid there in the room deteriorating for over two weeks.

It was becoming obvious to the inhabitants of the Kenmore Hotel that I was the government's secret weapon, and my name started popping up in the tenants' newsletter that was written by Richard and Sal. I was targeted as public enemy number one. Then photos of me, which apparently had been secretly taken, began appearing on a poster in various parts of the building. I refused to admit to the accusations, and continued to make fools out of Richard and Sal. Finally I got rid of Richard by letting authorities know about his outstanding warrant from Florida for molesting a little boy. Soon thereafter I was served with a RICO subpoena on a lawsuit filed by Richard and Sal that listed 80 defendants, including Vice President Al Gore, of all persons.

Since I knew in advance that the judge was Jewish, I showed up at the New York State Supreme Court wearing my yarmulke fort a hearing on the lawsuit. I had my own fan club there rooting for me which included representatives from most law enforcement agencies. Among these were FBI Special Agent Kenneth Weiss and people from the office of U.S. Attorney Mary Jo White. I was the first person to take the witness stand. I proceeded to destroy the lawsuit, which resulted in the immediate eviction from the Kenmore Hotel of Richard. This was done without due process of the law because he was forced to sign a deal to leave the hotel forthwith in exchange for criminal charges against him being dropped.

That pretty much ended the havoc and chaos at the Kenmore Hotel.

Almost immediately I was asked to take up residence at the Times Square Hotel and clear it of all drug activities, just as I had done at the Kenmore. This was done with the blessing of owner, Rosanne Haggerty. As part of the deal I got a free room.

I began working for NYPD Manhattan South Narcotics, where I was assigned to assist Detective Oquendo and another detective by the name of George. Thus, I had a new residence, a new assignment and a new confidential informant number, CI 15557-A-B. In less than six months I had furnished information and evidence that led to the arrests of 149 people. The Times Square Hotel was like Peyton Place. There were multiple personalities and diversified problems. Among these was the owner, Rosanne Haggerty.

I worked there for about two years. It would take another book to tell it all. Much of what happened was captured in an article that appeared in the *Village Voice* of September 7, 1999, titled "The User Who Got Used: For years, Tony Merritt did the dirty work for cops and landlords, helping them bust and evict drug dealers. So why is the Times Square Hotel, his latest home, showing him the door?"

After I was evicted from the Times Square Hotel in October 1999 I was homeless on the streets for about a month. Then I accepted an offer by a little angel named Debbie Man whom I had met at the Times Square Hotel just prior to my departure. Debbie was a public critic of Rosanne Haggerty and the latter's hypocritical campaign to clean up her hotel. Debbie lived in Brooklyn near Newkirk Avenue and 21st Street. She needed someone to share her apartment and help with the rent and electric bills.

I moved into Debbie's apartment on November 22, 1999. I had just weaned myself off of crack after being in its thrall for years. Even though Debbie served a vegetarian turkey on Thanksgiving,

I felt that I was beginning to rediscover what life was like before my binge on crack. I was also readjusting to life, having been out of reality or traditional living for ten years during which I had been on the run as a fugitive from the law and caught up in crack. It was almost like returning from outer space. I didn't even know the top shows on TV or even the latest hit songs. For those ten years I had been at rock bottom.

I had few clothes, mainly what I was wearing. My shoes were actually rubber sandals that were held together by duct tape. Debbie bought me a new pair of shoes. I was not accustomed to females buying me anything. I was raised with the understanding that women were not allowed to work and men were not allowed to be dependent on women. Not only was I becoming acclimated to civilization again but also to a new and fearful way of life.

After all I was 53 years old and Debbie was not even 24 years old. She was Chinese and a Buddhist. I was a mixed mutt. But despite our cultural and traditional differences, I was finding something new and strange in my life. I was beginning to have feelings for a female, Debbie.

I was a virgin to male-female sex until I met Debbie. I discovered a new found ecstasy in sex.

New Year's Eve 2000 was a special occasion. Debbie and I went to Times Square to see the ball drop at Midnight. The crowds were immense. We could only get as close as 34th Street, near Macy's and Herald Square. When the ball did drop, it was a new beginning for me. I could not believe that I had fallen in love with a beautiful Chinese girl named Debbie. We embraced as the new year arrived.

I had been working for NYPD Brooklyn South Narcotics as confidential informant CI number 15557 A-B-C, and became responsible for dozens of narcotics arrests in the borough. More important was my role in getting about a dozen cops busted on narcotics charges. This led to the inevitable newspaper headlines and media attention.

Debbie lived in a neighborhood around 600 East 21st Street in Brooklyn. This was the Flatbush area that was riddled with drugs and crime. It was mostly Jamaican. The locals, being racists, didn't like me and barely accepted Debbie. Everyone in the area was involved in some aspect of criminal activity. My assignment was to work with NYPD Brooklyn narcotics to start cleaning up the drug activity. There was a bunch of dirty cops. I worked with the allegedly top notch narcotics detectives in Brooklyn South but they turned out to be bigger crooks than those who roamed the streets. I ended up working with the Brooklyn District Attorney's office to get those corrupt cops busted.

In June 2000, I left Brooklyn and went into Manhattan to check my mail box at the U.S. post office next door to the Kenmore Hotel. I was arrested there on the old fugitive warrant issued out of Washington, D.C. and turned over to a U.S. Marshal who had been in the post office earlier that same morning flashing a wanted poster with my picture to the employees, most of whom knew me. I had been retrieving my mail from box 1271 at the Madison Square Post Office, New York City 10010 for ten years.

I thought a Puerto Rican named Juan, a post office employee, was behind my being arrested. He did not like me. He had good reason for it. Juan was heavily involved in drugs, money laundering and stealing mail, and he knew that I had turned him into the U.S. Postal Inspector and the U.S. Attorney's office. After the U.S. Marshall arrested me, another postal employee, Rhonda, who was a good friend, called Debbie to let her know what had happened.

I was taken to the Metropolitan Correctional Center (MCC) on Park Row in Manhattan. While en route I thought the entire world had fallen in on me. I could not believe that I had be tripped up by a 16 year old warrant. Carl Shoffler had always known where I was. He even knew about my post box in the post office next door to the Kenmore Hotel, because the Kenmore Hotel operation was the last assignment he had given me before he died. The thought quickly passed through my mind that perhaps Carl had left a letter to be found upon his death about where I was. But that did not make any sense.

Later I learned that my arrest stemmed from the FBI making computer warrant checks and searches against persons listed in the New York City Welfare Department.

I once again tried to adapt to the new harsh circumstances but after years on the run it was getting more and more difficult. I really contemplated suicide, because I was facing 14 years in prison. I was older, and my years of being the most popular guy around Dupont Circle was but just a faded memory. My health was bad. When I was arrested I was en route to Bellevue Hospital for oral surgery for my broken jaw from the incident in the Bronx when I was assaulted by the gang members. The federal judge who ordered me confined to MCC also ordered oral surgery for me forthwith, which was intentionally neglected by MCC.

My main reason for wanting to stay alive was because Debbie never gave up on me. She kept writing letters and sending money so I could purchase in the commissary small items that I needed. Each day for two months she accepted the charge for my phone calls even though prison calls are outrageously expensive. Her phone bills were over a thousand dollars for the two months, even though we only talked for five minutes on each occasion, and our calls were between Manhattan and Brooklyn.

It was from prison that I got up enough courage to ask Debbie to marry me, which she agreed to without hesitation.

I made several friends in MCC, but it was still the slammer. Strip searches were performed constantly. It was no secret that some inmates managed to smuggle drugs and weapons inside through mouth-to-mouth kissing with the visitors. Some inmates put these forbidden objects inside their rectum, in their hair, in their arm pits, under their testicles, inside the foreskin of uncircumcised penises, or even taped them to the bottom of their feet. Swallowing bags of drugs from visitors was a common practice, with the bags later being recovered when feces were passed. It was amazing what some inmates could get into MCC from the outside. On many occasions crooked guards were involved. You can buy almost anything when your locked up if you have the money.

The inmates cleverly transferred items from cell to cell by using a fishing line that would be thrown under the doors from one cell to another. This could even be done floor to floor by using a fishing line with a small weight attached to it, like a plastic spoon. The inmate in a cell above would attach an item wrapped in plastic and flush it down his toilet with the inmate below catching it through *his* toilet by snagging it in the sewer line.

I was in a cell block with several hundred inmates. About 90 percent were Hispanic, 2 percent Asian and the rest just about anything and everything. I was never once disrespected, harmed or molested. Incidents like these are common when the inmates serve long or life sentences. Of course, like most other prisoners I was filled with regret and remorse for wrongful things that I had done in life. But I came to the conclusion that there was nothing to regret because the charge against me was erroneous. So I also concluded that my being locked up was because of other wrongful things I had done in life that had gone unpunished. Maybe what was happening to me was a blessing in disguise. I had the opportunity to put my life in order. After all, I was in my mid-fifties. So I turned to God for guidance. I sometimes think prison is the wrong place and the wrong time to turn to God because many inmates claim they have become born-again Christians only to revert to a life of crime after they get out.

Nevertheless I decided to go this route and began attending Christian and Jewish religious services. I remember meeting a young Baptist pastor named Reverend Jason. Jason was in his last year in a seminary. He took a liking to me and we spent many hours talking about God and religion.

Near the sixtieth day at MCC, around August 22, 2000, I was told that I was to be extradited back to Washington, D.C. to answer to the arrest warrant. The U.S. Marshals placed me in a car that was to take me to a holding area for transport. Suddenly a radio message came that I was to be returned to MCC because my papers were not in order. This was a blessing because the plane on which I would have been transported developed serious mechanical problems. The next day I was told that I was being transported directly to Washington, D.C. A guard whispered to me that my trip would not be direct. I was driven to some undisclosed location in New York State: an airport far out in the woods. Inside the airport there were dozens of vans with hundreds of prisoners standing on the runway, all waiting for a federal military plane. I and the other prisoners stood chained together in the hot sun without food or water and unable to use the bathroom. Some prisoners were young and some old, some sane and some insane. Everyone had the same gauntly and empty look in their eyes and faces.

There were several hundred inmates in orange jump suits that were handcuffed to chains around their waists and shackled around their feet. When the planes arrived, the inmates found it difficult to walk up the plane steps because with their hands handcuffed there was nothing to hold onto. Each inmate had to hop and struggle to get up the steps.

When I finally managed to board the plane, I found an aisle seat and two inmates next to me. Behind me was an inmate who weighed at least 300 pounds. He was loud and boisterous. I quickly realized that he was a real nut, and when I looked around the plane I saw that about 100 mental prisoners were also being transported.

The air marshals attempted to feed us by placing a small tray on our laps that had a sandwich, a cookie and something to drink on it. The food was good but it was a struggle to eat because we were handcuffed at the waist, and going to the bathroom was out of the question because the marshals said that under no condition would they open the handcuffs. So it was quite the trip.

After about three hours in the air, we landed at our destination Oklahoma City. Once inside the federal facility we were finally uncuffed and placed in a large holding room where 300 prisoners had access to only one toilet.

Eventually we were moved to small holding areas that was partitioned, and underwent a strip search. We were given new clothing, which included brown pants, a white T-shirt and blue slippers. Then we were moved to a larger holding cell until all 300 prisoners had been processed. One by one we were called out and given a lunch bag and then underwent more processing. When I got to one processor I was told that I was identified on one page as being white with blond hair and green eyes and on the second page as a Black man with dark skin, nappy hair and six feet-four inches in height, with a violent criminal record to boot. It turned out that my records were mixed up with another prisoner because our inmate numbers were almost identical.

I was placed in a protective custody cell with another inmate who was a young white male with a record robbing gas stations on federal highways. He was facing incarceration for quite a few years and had adapted to the environment by falling in love with another inmate who was a transsexual.

Our cell was large and had bunk beds with a toilet, sink and shower. That way we never had to leave the cell. There was a window that was a foot wide and six feet in height. I used to gaze out the window but all I could see was flat land that stretched for miles and miles. The cell block was always dead silent, so much so that the silence was deafening. The guard in New York who had told me that I would not be going directly to Washington, D.C. had also told me that I would be held at the interim prison for only three days. When a week had passed, I started to get concerned. I had not been allowed to send out mail or make phone calls. However, I was armed with a court order signed by a federal judge that entitled me to oral surgery. So I began demanding that the prison authorities send me to a hospital so that the surgery could be performed. This caused quite a stir and suddenly the next day I was informed that I would be leaving for Washington, D.C.

So I soon found myself back on a plane, this time being lucky to get a window seat. The only drawback, and it was a big one, was that the inmate next to me had literally shit in his pants and smelled to high heaven. I looked out the window and saw how beautiful the land below was.

The plane landed at an airport outside Washington, D.C. We were placed in a bus and driven to the Washington, D.C. Jail. When we arrived at 9 P.M. I thought to myself, home, sweet home. We went through the mandatory strip searches and medical screening. I finished going through processing at 1 A.M. and was taken to a cell where I got a few hours of sleep. At 4 A.M. the guards awakened the inmates for breakfast, which consisted of slop. I gave my food away to other inmates, keeping only the milk and orange. At 6 A.M. we were en route to the District of Columbia Superior Court. Upon arrival at the courthouse we were placed in holding cells until our cases were called, and first met with our court-assigned attorney. The lawyer who came to see me was Ralph Robinson, he didn't appear to be aggressive. But what really scared me was when he disclosed that he had no criminal law experience, but was a tax attorney, and mine was his first big case.

One of the deputy U.S. Marshals who recognized me from prior years and worked directly under Judge Reggie Walton added to my panic when he told me that Judge Walton would probably send me to prison for the rest of my life. At this point I was in the holding cell behind Judge Walton's court room. I began looking for a way to hang myself using my T-shirt when this was interrupted by my case being called. When the U.S. marshal opened the cell door, instead of seeing him in his uniform I saw two beautiful angels holding some type of staff or swords in their hands, both of whom smiled gently at me.

When I walked into Judge Walton's court room I was in an orange jump suit that had big black letters emblazoned on the back of it that said, D.C. JAIL. I had a beard and my hair was wild and unkempt. The courtroom had been cleared out by the U.S. Marshals Service as I was supposed to be a high-risk prison escapee because of my early discharge on Thanksgiving Eve from a halfway house 18 years previously.

As I faced the judge I could not fail to notice that behind me in the cleared courtroom were three U.S. Deputy Marshals holding AK-47s. Even Judge Walton looked surprised at all the drama. In fact he smiled at me and I smiled back as if we both were amused at the way I was being held. Judge Walton greeted me by saying, "How are you, Mr. Merritt? Long time no see." I responded, "Not well, Your Honor, under the circumstances." This elicited another smile from the judge, who had a reputation for cutting to the chase and no time for nonsense. The judge asked me where I had been living and I said in New York City. He then asked me what I had been doing for the past 18 years and I told him I had been working for the New York Police Department, the FBI, the U.S. Marshals Service and the U.S. Attorney's Office. Judge Walton asked me if I was being serious and I replied that I was, and that there were dozens of persons in law enforcement who could vouch for me. The judge then noted that I was one of the most wanted fugitives in Washington, D.C., and observed that here I was in his courtroom telling him that for the past 18 years I had been working for law enforcement agencies. I told him it was all true. The judge responded, "Mr. Merritt, you are one of the most unusual and clever persons I have ever met. We have been looking for you all these years and you were working right under our noses and working with us."

With that, Judge Walton declared that he was releasing me under personal recognizance. Because the charge against me was for probation violation, he told me that I had to go forthwith to another courtroom to face the charge of prison breach. But Judge Walton quickly added that he was the senior judge in the D.C.

Superior Court, so that when I went to the other courtroom he was ordering that judge to release me on personal recognizance.

The three heavily armed U.S. Deputy Marshals, including Judge Walton's Deputy Marshall who had scared the hell out of me a few hours earlier, all gasped for breath. No one could believe what Judge Walton had just done.

I was escorted underground by Judge Walton's Deputy Marshal who told me en route that he was in a state of shock at what had just taken place. He said that I must know someone or that I had some type of juice or power to have commanded that respect from Judge Walton. I was then taken to the second judge for my arraignment for prison breach. This judge, whose name I cannot recall, struck me as a real bimbo. My tax attorney who had never handled a criminal case, was actually quivering in his shoes. With a look of amazement on his face, he asked me who the hell I really was.

The female judge who seemed to realize the celebrity of the case was smiling from ear to ear, so eager was she to swing down the gavel and declare my fate. But her demeanor slowing changed as she read my court file that contained Judge Walton's order that I be released immediately. She indicated for the record that she was upset but was compelled to obey Judge Walton's decree as he was senior judge. She then reluctantly signed my second release papers and I was taken back downstairs to be released by the U.S. Marshals' office, after I had been cleared through their computers to make certain that there were no other outstanding warrants. My court-appointed attorney appeared to congratulate me and then departed. But my ordeal was not over. The U.S. Marshal's office claimed it had lost my release papers. I was ordered to return to the D.C. Jail. I thought I was being tricked again, just as had occurred on Thanksgiving Eve 18 years before. I arrived at the D.C. Jail at 6:30 P.M. and I was the last prisoner left in the holding cell.

The jail officials were desperately trying to find my official release papers. I had a copy of these in my hand and took them to the bubble window and tried to push them through a slot to get the attention of the guards. However, one of the guards told me to go back and sit down because I might have generated the release papers on my own. I asked him to explain how I could have accomplished this while behind bars. The clock was nearing 7 P.M.,

"Count Time" for those incarcerated and the guards were frantic. Finally, at 6:58 P.M. a guard yelled out that he had found my release papers. It was now 6:59 P.M., one minute to Count Time, and I had to be out the door and through the gates and off the jail property in one minute. The guards yelled for me to go through the doors that were being electronically unlocked for me and to immediately get on the jail bus. I asked for some streets clothes but was denied these as the time was too short. So for the first time I was going through the doors without being handcuffed and restrained. I was told to pick up a heavy box of handcuffs and shackles and put it on the bus to be taken back to the courthouse for additional prisoners. The bus driver, a guard, raced to get me through the prison gates and we made it through exactly at 7 P.M.

Once outside the gates the driver told me I would have to get off the bus about two blocks from the jail. I pointed out to him that I was in an orange jump suit that had D.C. JAIL on its back. I said I could be shot by the D.C. police patrolling the area near the jail and that it was also the Capitol Hill neighborhood, known to be rich and prosperous. The guard opened the bus door and ordered me to depart or else he would push me out. I asked him for some street clothes and his only response was for me to get off the bus. I got off with a D.C. Police patrol car sitting one block away, watching the whole scene unfold. Luckily, I think they realized what was going on and they didn't bother me.

After I got off the bus, I pulled the top of my orange jump suit down to my waist and tied the sleeves around my waist so that only my white T-shirt was showing on my upper body. I realized that anyone in that particular neighborhood so close to the prison would still recognize that outfit. I walked about three blocks and saw a Black lady talking to her neighbor. I asked her politely for a quarter to use the pay telephone. She acted scared and asked me to leave the area. As I walked away she called back and asked me why I wanted the quarter and I told her I needed to make a phone call. She pulled a quarter out of her purse and tried to approach me but I said, "no thank you" and walked away. As I did so, she yelled that she was sorry for her initial reaction. I walked a few more blocks and night was approaching. I walked down a side street and saw furniture and a box of clothes sitting on the sidewalk where someone had been evicted. I was happy that I found clothes to change into but at the same time felt badly for whoever had been evicted and had their belonging tossed out. I put on pants, a shirt and a jacket, all of which were too small for me, but this did not bother me as I felt I looked at least half-way normal. My last meal was the orange and milk I had at breakfast at the D.C. Jail a few days previously. I found a half-eaten sandwich that had been thrown away and ate it. I walked a couple more blocks to the bus station. I remember while doing so that I saw an old man sitting on a bench alone and begged him for a cigarette. He did not appreciate my asking but gave me one anyway.

When I got to the bus station I found a telephone and managed to get an operator who placed a collect call to Debbie in New York City. By chance she had just walked into her apartment when my call came in, and after we spoke she went immediately to the Port Authority Bus Terminal to prepay a bus ticket for me to get home. I was able to catch a late bus and didn't arrive in New York City until 6 A.M. and I still had to get to Brooklyn from the Port Authority Bus Terminal but had no money. It was too far to walk. By a stroke of luck I had a friend named Karl who lived one block from the bus station. So I walked to his place and he gave me five dollars and also bought me breakfast. After I left Karl, I walked from Times Square to my post office box on East 23rd Street. This was where this problem had begun with my arrest. Guess who was the first person I saw inside the post office? The person, I thought had snitched me out, Juan. Upon seeing me, he turned tail and ran. My friend Rhonda gave me my mail and put $10 in my pocket. I then caught the subway train and went home. Debbie was surprised and happy to see me.

In October 2000 I returned to the District of Columbia Superior Court for a status hearing on whether I faced any further prosecution. I was ordered to return to the court in December. On December 13, 2000 (which happened to be the same day that five of the nine members of the U.S. Supreme Court voted to elect George W. Bush President) Debbie and I returned to the Superior Court. We waited all day in Judge Walton's courtroom for my case to be called. Finally, it was, and the prosecution announced that they wished to dismiss all charges against me due to the lack of cooperation they had received from their witness Madeline Furth. The prosecution also acknowledged that the some of the evidence had been lost and the remainder was stale. Judge Walton declared that he was pleased to hear the prosecution's decision because he was going to dismiss the case in any event. Judge Walton also said that, "I am dismissing all felony cases against you (Earl Robert Merritt, Jr.) that are underlying and overlying cases in the interest of justice." This had the effect of expunging my criminal record of any convictions.

After the hearing in Judge Walton's courtroom we went to a second courtroom before a paraplegic white female judge named Broderick for my case of prison breach. The prosecution asked for this case to be continued to the next morning for trial. Debbie and I left the courthouse with only $20 in our pockets and our two return bus tickets to New York City. We had no place to stay and it was raining. Again, by a stroke of luck, I got hold of a good friend, who allowed us to stay at his mother's house while his mother was away. During the evening my friend and his cousin brought us food and spent some time with us. Later my friend's brother and Edriss came by. Edriss was apparently living nearby in a halfway house and wanted to meet Debbie and see me. Our meeting was cordial, and I thank God we have not rekindle any friendship.

The next morning we went back to the courthouse to start the trial before Judge Broderick. However, my lawyer and tax attorney had done his homework the night before in researching his law book and challenged the prosecution on the evidence that had been stored over the 18 years. The prosecution could not offer a plea deal because no offers are permitted on escape charges. The case ended with the prosecution voluntarily dismissing the case and all charges against me. I couldn't believe my ordeal was finally over. Debbie and I spent the remainder of the day doing some sightseeing, including the Smithsonian Museum, the Capitol Building and the Washington Monument. We then caught the 7 P.M. bus back to New York City.

Thereafter our lives returned to a normal routine; that is until September 11, 2001.When Debbie and I heard the news of the planes crashing into the World Trade Center, and the collapse of the twin towers, our thought immediately went to concern for

Debbie's father who lived in Chinatown, only a short distance from the scene of the tragedy. Our fear was that her father and relatives might be inhaling deadly gases from the black smoke that covered lower Manhattan. Finally we managed to hear from her father who assured us that we need not worry.

The collapse of the South Tower affected me personally as I remembered the nights when I was homeless and found shelter from the rain, snow and cold in the subway area beneath it.

On December 18, 2001 Debbie and I moved from Brooklyn to Fordham Hill in the Bronx. I started working again for NYPD Bronx Narcotics. My confidential informant number was CI 1557-A-B-C-D. However, after a time this assignment began to sour as I got involved with NYPD Internal Affairs and the Bronx District Attorney's office over dirty cops in the Bronx who were on the take. It was the same old, same old that I had run into in Brooklyn but in this case the Internal Affairs investigators were so incompetent and inept that the dirty cops emerged victorious.

I suffered a personal loss on June 11, 2003 when my brother, Steve, was murdered. Steve was a confidential informant in West Virginia for the Drug Enforcement Administration. I have strong reasons to believe that certain relatives were behind the murder because of their involvement with narcotics distribution. Steve's diary, in which he methodically entered details of his work, went missing after his killing. As far as I can learn, nothing has been done by law enforcement to solve Steve's murder.

Steve's death caused me to return to West Virginia for a short period of time, try to solve the case and arouse interest in it in local and federal law enforcement. It was while I was there that Debbie and I decided to get married, which we did on Sunday, July 13, 2003 in the Kanawha Salines Presbyterian Church in Malden, West Virginia.

Today I look back at my life after I left West Virginia at age 18 and am amazed at what I see. I stumbled into one of the biggest and dirtiest conspiracies in American history called Watergate that brought down a President. The government has used, abused and exploited me. I had been trained to break the law and violate the constitutional rights of law abiding citizens. Afterwards, I was supposed to have been annihilated but the government found that was not so easily done. However, my life was forever scarred and I was pushed into a life style of crack and devastation from which, with the help of God, I managed eventually to escape. After being set up by the government I was able for 18 years to hide as a federal fugitive from justice by working right under the noses of the mightiest law enforcement agencies. Had I not been able to outwit the government and the professionals that were looking for me, and had I not met my wife, Debbie, I am convinced that I would have been dead years ago. As it is, I have survived and this book is my contribution to an important part of history that otherwise would never have been told if the government had its way.

Debbie Man in front of White House.

Chapter Eleven

Beyond Sorrow

In 1992, I was still a fugitive from justice and living in New York City. As usual, I was in constant contact with Carl Shoffler via telephone and I was still receiving instructions and assignments. Even though Carl had retired from the Washington, D.C. MPD, this meant nothing because Carl was still free-lancing or employed with federal intelligence agencies and continuing to extract information from me. After Carl retired in 1989 from the Washington, D.C. MPD, he volunteered for the Prince George's County Fire Department on February 22, 1990 as an investigator and he became the Chief Intelligence Investigator.

I started working for the Narcotics Division for the Washington, D.C. MPD in 1970 for Detectives Steve Finkleberg and Carl Shoffler. My work expanded to New York City Police Department in 1995 to 2005 (although I was again enrolled as a CI for NYPD in 2010, this time for its Intelligence Division.) During the 1995-2005 period I worked for the Manhattan South Narcotics and Brooklyn Narcotics. I was assigned a NYPD Confidential Informant Number 15557-A-B-C-D. My files are housed at 1 Police Plaza in New York City in the Confidential Informant's Office. They are kept in a safe under lock and key. These files are *supposedly* viewed only by the hierarchy of the police department. This is bull shit.

I was also signed up twice by the Bronx Narcotics Division, but never given any assignments. Bronx and Brooklyn Narcotics Divisions both became my assignments, that is, they were dirty cops and I started working for the Internal Affairs Division. As a result, dozens of dirty narcotics cops were busted in Brooklyn and dozens of narcotics cops were transferred out of the Bronx.

If I were asked to do a book on the subject of narcotics, it wouldn't be one book, but a dozen.

One of the best narcotics cops that I worked for with an impeccable record was Detective José Oquendo. To me he is NYPD finest.

I have witnessed and participated in crimes of all sorts with dozens of narcotics officers. The crimes that they committed and they asked me to do were unspeakable.

It is strictly for political reasons and purposes only that narcotics exist in the first place, whether it is local or national. Street dealers are being exploited and used by the politicians. It is nothing to go out, bust and corral hundreds of kids selling drugs on the streets on any given day. These kids are from poor families usually in the ghetto community. They know of no other way of life. To them selling drugs is the only future and career that they can look forward to in their life.

Believe it or not, in spite of all these strong social arguments that one can raise on this issue I am stating the fact that it is almost impossible for these kids to call anything other than selling drugs normal. Society offers them nothing except the welfare rolls.

The real drug dealers are the politicians on Capitol Hill, the Military and the Intelligence Agencies. Drugs come into this country by the tons everyday. The war on drugs must be stopped in the very backyards of those who started the drug war in the first place.

I was taught by the Metropolitan Police Department Intelligence Division and the Washington Field Office of the FBI to profile and to identify subjects of investigation.

One of the main methods that seemed to be very effective was to use astrology. It was very easy to engage in a conversation with almost anyone by bringing up "What is your sign?" No one ever made a connection or was suspicious to the fact that the person asking this question was a CI.

Almost everyone loves to talk about their astrological sign and the horoscope.

It never failed. I always got the answer that I was looking for and that was their date of birth. After getting the date of birth then, the subject was identified. And it was easy to get almost any other information regarding the subject like their place of birth and even their place of employment. And if they were promised an astrological chart then, they gave up their home address to me, again without any suspicion.

However, the police intelligence agencies and the FBI both used astrology to actually profile their subjects by knowing their signs. The police and the FBI both used astrology, mediums and fortune tellers to their advantage to orchestrate their subjects by staging their sessions, in other words it was all scripted. Sometimes the fortune tellers were actually intelligence agents.

Secret courts exist in this country. These courts are not conducted in the normal courtroom settings. These courts can convene in a supply room or in the sub-basement of a garage of an apartment house, like the one I was taken to in the Georgetown section of Washington, D.C. on two occasions. These courts serve many purposes. They are used on so that a confidential informant in a highly sensitive case can tell a judge what he knows and then sign an affidavit without his identity being exposed to the public. Both local and federal law enforcement agencies use these courts to obtain a search warrant or an order or writ that would not commonly be granted in a normal public court room setting.

The judge in these courts almost invariably accedes to the wishes of the prosecutor as no defense attorneys are ever present. Warrants and other unusual and sometime questionable requests are almost routinely granted.

The United States has more persons in prison than any other country in the world. Over one million inmates are incarcerated in prisons that in many cases are worst than gulags due to the inhuman conditions that exist there. The prisoners who are incarcerated because they committed heinous crimes are in the minority. Many inmates are serving length sentences for minor drug offenses. It is long past time for the prison system in our country to be revamped. I have been inside our prisons and can attest to the need for reform.

I wish to make it perfectly clear that I do not hate cops or any officers or agents of law enforcement. This book is not against the police, FBI, CIA, or NSA. It is against the powerful and many times controlling rogue elements within these agencies.

I want it known that I am deeply sorry and remorseful to all persons that I have caused injury to in my life. I cannot express enough sorrow that I have caused so much serious and personal harm.

E. Howard Hunt

EPILOGUE

By Douglas Caddy

"From there I drove to the White House Annex – the Old Executive Office Building, in bygone years the War Department and later the Department of State.

"Carrying three heavy attaché cases, I entered the Pennsylvania Avenue door, showed my blue-and-white White House pass to the uniformed guards, and took the elevator to the third floor. I unlocked the door of 338 and went in. I opened my two-drawer safe, took out my operational handbook, found a telephone number and dialed it.

"The time was 3:13 in the morning of June 17, 1972, and five of my companions had been arrested and taken to the maximum-security block of the District of Columbia jail. I had recruited four of them and it was my responsibility to get them out. That was the sole focus of my thoughts as I began talking on the telephone.

"But with those five arrests the Watergate affair had begun....

"After several rings the call was answered and I heard the sleepy voice of Douglas Caddy. 'Yes?'

"'Doug? This is Howard. I hate to wake you up, but I've got a tough situation and I need to talk to you. Can I come over?'

"'Sure. I'll tell the desk clerk you're expected.'

"'I'll be there in about 20 minutes,' I told him, and hung up.

"From the safe I took a small money box and removed the $10,000 Liddy had given me for emergency use. I put $1,500 in my wallet and the remaining $8,500 in my coat pocket. The black attaché case containing McCord's electronic equipment I placed in a safe drawer that held my operational notebook. Then I closed and locked the safe, turning the dial several times. The other two cases I left beside the safe, turned out the light and left my office, locking the door."

— E. Howard Hunt, *Undercover: Memoirs of an American Secret Agent* (Berkley, 1974).

WATERGATE ATTORNEY

Beginning with Hunt's phone call, I served as the original attorney for the seven defendants – Hunt, Gordon Liddy, James McCord and the four Cuban-Americans. Subsequently, as the result of my being the first witness pulled before the Watergate grand jury, I was forced to withdraw representation of my clients as my role involuntarily changed – from attorney for the defense to witness for the prosecution. As will be shown shortly, the net effect of this was that the seven defendants were denied a fair trial from the inception of the case.

About half an hour after he telephoned me, Hunt arrived at my Washington apartment located in the Georgetown House at 2121 P St., N.W., about a five-minute drive from the both the White House and Watergate. He informed me of what had occurred.

Hunt then telephoned Liddy from my apartment and they both requested that I represent them as their attorney in the case as well as the five arrested individuals – McCord and the four Cuban-Americans.

On June 28 – 11 days later – I was served with a subpoena to appear "Forthwith" before the grand jury. The subpoena was served on me by Assistant U.S. Attorney Donald Campbell while I was in the federal court house, who grabbed me by my arm and pulled me into the grand jury room.

The prosecutors asked me hundred of questions over the next two weeks and subpoenaed my personal bank records. Ultimately I refused to answer 38 questions that I and the five attorneys representing me believed were protected by the attorney client privilege. For example, one question was: "At what time did you receive a telephone call in the early morning hours of June 17, 1972?" By answering this question, I could ultimately be forced to identify Hunt and thus incriminate him. The 38 questions are reproduced in an appendix to this book.

Principal Assistant U.S. Attorney Earl Silbert argued in court that my refusal to answer the grand jury questions on the grounds of the attorney-client privilege was "specious, dilatory and....an obstruction of justice."

Judge John Sirica, who assigned himself Watergate case, saw a golden opportunity to inflate his ego and ambition at the expense of the best interests of justice and the country. At a hearing on July 12, 1972 – less than a month after the case broke – Sirica rejected outright my and my attorneys' argument that the attorney-client privilege was being egregiously violated by the 38 questions. Declared Sirica to a courtroom packed with lawyers, the press and spectators:

> You see, to put the matter perfectly bluntly, if the government is trying to get enough evidence to indict Mr. Caddy as one of the principals in this case even though he might not have been present at the time of the alleged entry in this place, I don't know what the evidence is except what has been disclosed here, if the government is trying to get an indictment against Mr. Caddy and he feels that way and you feel it and the rest of you attorneys feel it, all he has to say is 'I refuse to answer on the grounds what I say would tend to incriminate me.' That ends it. I can't compel him to say he know Mr. Hunt under the circumstances. He doesn't do that, understand? He takes the other road. He says there is a confidential communication. Who is he to be the sole judge or not it is confidential or not? That is what I am here for.

Sirica, a homophobic jurist cut from the same cloth as the FBI and the Washington, D.C. police whose actions against me in early days of the case have previously been chronicled, used his position to try to frame me. He was to fail but at a severe cost to the defendants and the nation.

The next day, after I refused to answer the 38 questions before the grand jury on the grounds that doing so would violate the attorney-client privilege, Sirica convened a court hearing to hold me in contempt.

Robert Scott, one of my attorneys who later was to be named to the bench, asked Sirica to honor professional courtesy by not ordering me incarcerated while an appeal was filed with the U.S. Court of Appeals, by stating:

"If Your Honor please, there is nothing malicious in this refusal. It is done in good faith, good conscience, it is done because we believe it is the proper course. I would respectfully suggest this is very harsh treatment – not the finding of contempt, I don't say that. I disagree that he should be found in contempt, but I think it is very harsh treatment that your honor would commit him when it is perfectly clear that these positions are being put forth in the utmost good faith and utmost of sincerity. This is a young man, I just think it would be as harsh as it could be to commit him at this time."

Of course, this plea fell upon the deaf ears of a bully who took delight in destroying the careers and lives and the innocent as well as the guilty. Sirica ordered the U.S. Marshal to take me into custody to be jailed.

On July 18, 1972 the U.S. Court of Appeals affirmed Sirica's contempt citation of me. It did so in by employing gratuitously insulting language, declaring that "Even if such a relationship does exist, certain communications, such as in furtherance of a crime, are not within the [attorney-client] privilege."

The day after the decision of the Court of Appeals, I appeared again before the grand jury and pursuant to the threat posed by the Court's decision answered all the questions posed to me by the prosecutors.

The actions of Sirica and the Court of Appeals did not go unnoticed by the White House. In an Oval Office tape of July 19, 1972, an incredulous President Nixon asked John Ehrlichman, "Do you mean the circuit court ordered an attorney to testify?" to which Ehrlichman responded, "It [unintelligible] to me, except that this damn circuit we've got here with [Judge David] Bazelon and so on, it surprises me every time they do something."

Nixon then asked, "Why didn't he appeal to the Supreme Court?"

What Nixon and Ehrlichman did not realize was that I and my attorneys firmly believed that we had created a strong legal record of the rights of the defendants and me as their attorney being violated so that if Hunt, Liddy and the five arrested defendants were found guilty, their convictions could be overturned as a result of the abusive actions of Sirica and the Court of Appeals.

However, Sirica's vitriolic courtroom antics, aided and abetted by a biased Court of Appeals, had the effect of encouraging the defendants to embark on a "hush money" cover-up after they realized early on that the courts were not going to give them a fair trial. Hunt later wrote that "If Sirica was treating Caddy – an Officer of the Court – so summarily, and Caddy was completely uninvolved in Watergate – then those of us who were involved could expect neither fairness nor understanding from him. As events unfolded, this conclusion became tragically accurate." Bear in mind all the above described courtroom events occurred in the first 33 days of the case. The dye was cast then by the prosecutors and the courts for denying the seven defendants a fair trial.

Soon after indictments were handed down against all seven defendants in September 1972, the prosecutors informed me that I would be a government witness at their trial and that I should review my grand jury transcripts in their office in preparation of so testifying.

William Bittman, a former Justice Department prosecutor who succeeded me in representing Hunt, advised me that because the prosecutors had gone too far in their persecution of me, they had jeopardized their case and were worried about that fact. No evidence had been uncovered that I had engaged in any criminal activity. One of the prosecutors even disclosed that an examination of my bank records, obtained by subpoena, revealed that I was "scrupulously honest." Bittman asked me when I reviewed my grand jury transcripts to check to determine if any alternations had been made in them. His fear was that the prosecutors had rewritten my testimony so as to weaken the attorney-client privilege. He said that if I found any of my transcripts had been altered, he planned to call Principal Assistant U.S. Attorney Earl Silbert to the witness stand at the trial to question him about the alteration. He declared, "Hunt deserves a fair trial and I am going to see that he gets one."

When I did review the grand jury transcripts, I determined that a key alteration had been made by the prosecutors. This alteration dealt with my attempt to tell the grand jury on July 19, 1972 that I had been approached in early July to act as conduit for "hush money" to be distributed to the defendants.

The overture was made by Anthony Ulasewicz, a former New York City police detective, acting upon the instructions of Herbert Kalmbach, President Nixon's personal attorney. Here is the testimony of Kalmback subsequently before the Senate Watergate Committee:

> Mr. **Dash:** Now, what was the first instruction you received to give the money?
>
> Mr. **Kalmbach:** Again, as I have tried to reconstruct this, Mr. Dash, the first instruction that I received, which I passed to

Mr. Ulasewicz was to have Mr. Ulasewicz give $25,000 to Mr. Caddy. I don't know too much of Mr. Caddy, I understand that he is an attorney here in Washington. And, as I recall it, this was probably from approximately July 1 through July 6 or 7. There were a number of calls. I would either talk to Mr. Dean or Mr. LaRue. I would then call Mr. Ulasewicz who, in turn, would call Mr. Caddy. He would have some response from Mr. Caddy, and I would call back up either Mr. Dean or Mr. LaRue.

Mr. Dash: What was the response from Mr. Caddy?

Mr. Kalmbach: Well, the sum and gist of it was that Mr. Caddy refused to accept the funds.

Mr. Dash: In that manner?

Mr. Kalmbach: That is correct. That was the end-all. There were several phone calls, but the final wrap-up won it was that he refused the funds."

My grand jury testimony was not the only one altered by the prosecutors. Alfred Baldwin, a key figure in the case, later charged that his grand jury testimony also had been altered by the prosecutors.

At the first Watergate trial, Hunt and the four Cuban-Americans pleaded guilty at its beginning. This came about because about a month previously Dorothy Hunt had died in a mysterious plane crash in Chicago. For Hunt a trial following on the heels of his wife's tragic death was more than he could bear. The four Cuban-Americans, loyal to a fault to Hunt, followed his lead. Liddy and McCord stood trial and were found guilty. Liddy appealed his conviction. The same Court of Appeals that had forced me to testify before the grand jury in its gratuitously insulting decision opined as to the defendant Liddy being denied Sixth Amendment counsel because of what the courts had done to me as his attorney: "The evidence against appellant... was so overwhelming that even if there were constitutional error in the comment of the prosecutor and the instruction of the judge, there is no reasonable possibility it contributed to the conviction."

Neither Judge Sirica, who later was named "Man of the Year" by *Time* magazine, nor the U.S. Court of Appeals ever acknowledged that their abusive actions and decisions in the first month of the case as relating to me and the attorney-client privilege were a principal cause of the cover-up that ensued.

Sirica later wrote a book, fatuously titled, *To Set the Record Straight,* for which he pocketed one million dollars. James Jackson

Kilpatrick, a nationally syndicated columnist, wrote at the time: "It would be pleasant if someone would set the record straight about this tin pot tyrant. Sirica is a vainglorious pooh-bah, an ill-tempered and autocratic as any judge since Samuel Chase of Maryland 180 years ago. When the Watergate criminal trials were assigned to him in the fall of 1972, he set out to enjoin the whole countryside with an encompassing gag order that perfectly reflected his lust for power. The order was patently absurd – it embraced even 'potential witnesses' and 'alleged victims' and had to be watered down."

Despite the homophobic efforts of Sirica and the Court of Appeals to set me up, I was never indicted, named as an unindicted co-conspirator, disciplined by the Bar or even contacted by the Senate Watergate Committee.

[The homophobia that I was subjected to in Watergate can still be found in certain quarters even today. *The Huffington Post*, quoting from the Associated Press, reported on May 3, 2010, that Tennessee Republican congressional candidate Ron Kirkland had recently boasted that when he served in the military during the Vietnam War, gay service members "were taken care of." Kirkland's candid remarks came at a Tea Party forum when the GOP hopeful criticized the Obama administration's support for overturning the "Don't Ask, Don't Tell" policy. Kirkland, a Vietnam veteran, said of his time in the military: "I can tell you if there were any homosexuals in that group, they were taken care of in ways I can't describe to you." Conservative House candidate Randy Smith, who served in the first Iraqi war, added: "I definitely wouldn't want to share a shower with a homosexual. We took care of that kind of stuff, just like (Kirkland) said." Based on anti-gay incidents in the military, it can be assumed that Kirkland and Smith were referring to the shooting gays in the back while engaged in active combat against the enemy, throwing gays overboard at night from Navy ships, and attacking gays while they slept in their barrack's bunk bed.]

Watergate, as Senator Sam Ervin, Chairman of the Senate Watergate Committee said at the time, was the most publicized event in American political history. It certainly was the country's biggest criminal case of the 20th century. As can be deduced from Robert Merritt's revelations about the role played by Officer Carl Shoffler in the origin of the case and my abbreviated account about the roles played by the Judge Sirica and the U.S. Court of Appeals, it is clear that a fraud has been perpetrated upon the American people and upon history as to what really happened in Watergate.

Shoffler, as usual, may have had the final word as to what really occurred. When Shoffler told Merritt in 1986 on the occasion of the court hearing on the Lenny Bias death case in Upper Marlboro, Maryland that Merritt would have died if he has taken the blue pills offered to him as part of the conspiracy in 1972 to assassinate me, he elaborated further upon questioning by Merritt. Merritt asked him, "What were the real reasons why the government wanted Douglas Caddy dead?" Shoffler replied that "I think he knew too much." Merritt then asked him, "What do you mean?" to which Shoffler replied, "You really wouldn't understand." Shoffler went on to say, "I think they were dumb because how do you set-up someone to be set-up when they are already set-up?" Merritt asked him to explain and Shoffler again replied, "You wouldn't really understand." adding "Maybe some day history will have to be rewritten and only through time may history reveal the true facts – maybe."

The implication of Shoffler statements, as understood by Merritt, is that Watergate was a set-up, a charade from the beginning orchestrated by military intelligence, the NSA and the CIA. Behind the curtain, as in the Wizard of Oz, these three intelligence agencies, once they learned of the planned break-in via Merritt's source, Rita Reed, knew precisely how the saga would ultimately go down. Rather than aborting the break-in using their prior knowledge, they let it take place knowing that a cover-up would inevitably follow. From the time they learned of the planned break-in, they had all the actors wiretapped using the latest techniques devised by NSA's Vint Hill Farm Station in Virginia. So when Ulasewicz telephoned me at my law firm about being the first conduit for "hush money" to the defendants and heard my refusal to do so, they merely had to follow the trail, which led next to attorney William Bittman, who succeeded me in representing Hunt, agreeing to pass the cover-up funds to the defendants.

The intelligence agencies orchestrating the set-up were aided and abetted, wittingly and unwittingly, by key figures. Carl Shoffler, who had telephoned the *Washington Post* shortly after the arrests at Watergate, continued anonymously to supply the paper with information gleaned from his wire-taps. Bob Woodward, himself a former Naval Intelligence Officer who had Nixon White House contacts before the *Washington Post* employed him as a reporter, took these tips and followed the money trail. Woodward and Bernstein, far from being heroes of Watergate, faithfully played out the roles assigned to them by military intelligence, the NSA and the CIA. The *Washington Post* and these two reporters perpetrated one of history's greatest frauds in their reporting of the Watergate case, relying on information provided by the *real deep throat.* When Merritt attempted to communicate with them about what he knew, they refused to listen. Bernstein even denied knowing Merritt although the latter had seen and talked to him on the occasions when Bernstein visited Riggin's porn shop.

Len Colodny and Robert Gettlin in their authoritative book, *Silent Coup: The Removal of a President* (St. Martin's Press, 1991), revealed how the Pentagon had infiltrated the White House before Watergate and established a fifth column that spied on the President Nixon.

There are some who would say that the burglars and those involved in the cover-up got what they deserved. What is overlooked in such a view is that the break-in planned for June 18, 1972 could have been cancelled. The burglars themselves or a higher-up such as Jeb Magruder could have come to the realization that such a criminal enterprise was stupid and reckless. However, once Shoffler entered the picture and through triangulation and wire-tapping enticed the burglars to change the date of the break-in and to go after a non-existent package of supposedly extremely valuable documents, there was no longer any question but that the break-in plan had to go forward.

There is no evidence that President Nixon had any knowledge of the planned break-in. What about the cover-up that ensued after the case broke? There would have been no cover-up if soon after the burglars' arrests it became known that Shoffler as the arresting officer had prior knowledge of the planned break-in and as a result developed his plan to set-up and entrap the burglars. The attention of law enforcement and the media would then have focused upon Shoffler and the CIA and Military Agents in the intelligence community who assisted him in the set-up operation. Had Shoffler and Merritt subsequently been served with subpoenas to testify before the federal grand jury, the whole story would have come out, including that Shoffler telephoned the *Washington Post* shortly after the arrests to report what had transpired. FBI agents Tucker and O'Connor would also have been called to testify before the grand jury and they would have had to disclose who in the Bureau had ordered them to interrogate Merritt about the planned break-in two weeks before it occurred and two days after the arrests. As a result President Nixon would have served out his full term and the history of Watergate, indeed of the world, would be far different from the accepted version of today.

Based on the lingering questions about what really happened in Watergate as revealed by Robert Merritt, I wrote the following letter on March 20, 2010, to Senator Christopher Bond, the ranking minority member of the Senate Select Committee on Intelligence:

Senator Christopher S. (Kit) Bond
274 Russell Senate Office Building
Washington, D.C. 20510

Dear Senator Bond:

I am writing you in your capacity as a member of the Senate Intelligence Committee to provide you with information about illegal and unconstitutional activities of the Intelligence Community as disclosed in a new book of which I am co-author. The book is "Watergate Exposed: A Confidential Informant Tells How the Watergate Burglars Were Set-Up and Reveals Other Government Dirty Secrets, by Robert Merritt as told to Douglas Caddy, Original Attorney for the Watergate Seven."

The primary purpose of this public letter is to request that the Senate Intelligence Committee open an investigation into the heretofore undisclosed role of Intelligence Agencies and their Agents in the origins of Watergate. It is also to request that based upon the information that would be gathered by the Committee pursuant the inquiry that the investigation be expanded to include the numerous illegal and unconstitutional activities engaged in by these Agencies today that infringe upon the basic liberties of the American public.

By way of background, in 1970 Washington, D.C. Metropolitan Police Detective Carl Shoffler enrolled Merritt as a Confidential Informant for the police. Shoffler was a Military Intelligence Agent assigned to the Washington Police Department. On June 3, 1972, Merritt provided information gained from a highly unusual source to Shoffler about the planned Watergate break-in two weeks before event, which occurred on June 17, 1972. That same evening, June 3, 1972, Shoffler brought two Intelligence Agents to Merritt's apartment so that he could brief them on what he had learned about the planned break-in at Watergate. Shoffler later made the arrests on June 17, 1972, and became famous for doing so, when in fact, based on the advance information provided him by Merritt, he set up the burglars by means of wiretap triangulation.

Upon Shoffler's recommendation, the FBI in 1971 enrolled Merritt as a CI. He worked principally with two FBI agents: Bill Tucker and Terry O'Connor. Agents Tucker and O'Connor, upon the instruction of FBI Associate Director Mark Felt, visited Merritt on June 4, 1972, to inquire about rumors they had heard that Merritt knew of a planned break-in at Watergate. They visited him two days after the scandal broke on June 17, 1972, to inquire again what he knew.

I am enclosing documents with this letter that support the allegations made above and those that follow.

Under the direction of Officer Shoffler and FBI Agents Tucker and O'Connor, Merritt as a CI engaged in activities that blatantly violated the law and the rights of individual citizens. A partial list of these actions includes:

1. Planting drugs on innocent persons and having them arrested

2. Planting wiretap bugs in the offices and vehicles of targeted individuals

3. Breaking into the offices of targeted individuals and organizations to steal files

4. Having sex with 70 targeted individuals and five targeted Washington, D.C. police officers

5. Stealing mail and signed petitions from targeted organizations

6. Cutting the wires to loud speakers at public rallies

7. Spreading false rumors

8. Targeting Members of Congress based on gossip

9. Distributing blue-striped capsules that caused nausea to demonstrators

What makes Merritt's disclosures so unusual is that this is the first time a Confidential Informant has revealed publicly the grossly unconstitutional activities that he engaged in under the direction of government agencies.

The U.S. Department of Justice recently distributed a memorandum to Intelligence Agencies directing that all efforts be made to hinder publication of "Watergate Exposed." The reason the Department did this is because it is gravely concerned that Merritt's revelations about the illegal activities of Intelligence Agencies in the period immediately before and after Watergate would open the window onto the illegal and unconstitutional activities engaged in by the Intelligence Community today, which are even more serious than those in the 1970's. Were the American people fully aware of these present illegal activities they would be outraged at the wholesale shredding of the Bill of Rights. An important aspect of what is going on at the present time is the cost to the American taxpayer and its impact on the budget's deficit. What are the legal and budgetary justifications for these agencies conducting domestic intelligence?

Robert Merritt and I are willing to provide the Committee a copy of our book manuscript, "Watergate Exposed," for use by the Committee in determining whether it wishes to pursue an investigation into the abuses by the Intelligence Community. We only ask that the Committee provide us a Confidentiality Agreement governing use of the manuscript so as not to undercut sales of the book upon its publication. Also, both Robert Merritt and I stand ready to provide testimony to the Committee if that is desired.

I am enclosing with this letter a few of the hundreds of relevant documents in our possession. These include my preface to "Watergate Exposed", a chapter from the book titled, "A Series of Missed Opportunities: There Would Have Been No Watergate", a section from the book titled, "Who Was Mark Felt?", the book's Table of Contents, Jack Anderson's column of Oct. 23, 1975, *The Daily Rag* of October 5-12, 1973, a Watergate Special Prosecution Force report on Merritt dated Nov. 20, 1973, an article from the *New York Times* of July 14, 1972 titled "Lawyer Held in Contempt in Democratic Raid Inquiry" and an op-ed article by me titled "What if Judge Sirica Were With Us Today?" from the *Wall Street Journal* of March 24, 1998.

Please contact me or Robert Merritt should you need additional information to reach a decision whether to pursue this matter.

Sincerely yours,

Douglas Caddy

Attorney

Americans like to believe they live in a constitutional republic, governed by the three branches of government – the Executive, Legislative and Judiciary. In reality Americans live in a country ruled by three other branches of government – "Military Intelligence," the NSA and the CIA – that possess the power and means to destroy anyone, including a President of the United States, who poses a threat to their supremacy. Today the American people serve as unwitting stage props in an ongoing charade orchestrated by these intelligence agencies. America has been reduced, in the words of Reagan administration official Paul Craig Roberts, to a country of serfs.

Scholar and historian Howard Zinn, who died in January 2010, offered his thoughts on the plight we face when he reflected on President Obama's first year in office: "I thought that in the area of constitutional rights he would have been better than he has been. That's the greatest disappointment, because Obama went to Harvard Law School and is presumably dedicated to constitutional rights."

Could it be that President Obama has come to fear that should he attempt to restore the eroded constitutional rights of Americans, which include freedom from domestic surveillance and from illegal activity by these intelligence agencies, that he could suffer the fates of President Kennedy who was assassinated, or of President Nixon who was set-up, or even something beyond our current President's contemplation upon reaching for the Presidency, such as harm being inflicted upon a member of his family?

Article II, Section 1 of the U.S. Constitution declares "The executive power shall be vested in a President of the United States of America." This means whoever occupies of the Office of the Presidency should do so with full confidence that he is the nation's chief executive responsible for the security and well being of all those who live in the land. In turn, citizens should be able to rest with full knowledge that the President can carry out his vested duty without fear that enemies of the nation's best interests, whatever may be the basis of their motivation, cannot devise a means or plan that would cripple Office of the President so as to put the entire country in harm's way.

SUGGESTED FURTHER READING ABOUT WATERGATE

Secret Agenda: Watergate, Deep Throat and the CIA by Jim Hougan (Random House: 1984)

Silent Coup: The Removal of a President by Len Colodny and Robert Gettlin (St. Martin's Press: 1991)

The Strong Man: John Mitchell and the Secrets of Watergate by James Rosen (Doubleday: 2008)

Blind Ambition: The End of the Story by John Dean (Polimedia: 2009)

Will: The Autobiography of G. Gordon Liddy by G. Gordon Liddy (St. Martin's Press: 1996)

Family of Secrets: The Bush Dynasty, America's Invisible Government, and the Hidden History of the Last Fifty Years by Russ Baker (Bloomsbury Press: 2009)

The American Police State: The Government Against the People by David Wise (Random House, 1976)

The Great Heroin Coup by Henrik Kruger (South End Press: 1980)

APPENDICES

OPTIONAL FORM NO. 10
MAY 1962 EDITION
GSA FPMR (41 CFR) 101-11.6

UNITED STATES GOVERNMENT

Memorandum

TO : SAC, WFO (157-2396) (P)   DATE: 11/1/71

FROM : SA _____

SUBJECT: _____ aka,
EM-NYA

      On 10/29/71, _____ telephonically contacted
the writer. Source stated that a friend, _____ had
offered to sell him some incendiary devices. The source had
previously had an opportunity to purchase two of these
devices while the source was employed by the MPD Intelligence
Division and had photographed the devices at that time. Source
advised he will provide these photographs. The source described
the devices as tubular in shape and about 2½" to 3" in length.
_____ told the source that he could also obtain dynamite,
dynamite caps, fragmentation and smoke grenades, stink bombs
and another small type of incendiary device. The incendiary
devices were priced at $7.50 apiece and the fragmentation
grenades at $25.00. The source advised that he would attempt
to determine the prices of the various items which he was
offered.

      The source was told by _____ that the incendiary
devices and explosives are obtained from a _____ (LNU), who
works with _____ at _____ Virginia
Avenue, N.W. WDC. According to _____ obtains these
items from _____ former member of the NSWPP, who
operates _____ in WDC. The source was
also told that there is an unidentified chemist involved who
may be the person manufacturing the incendiary devices (which
are not marked in any way).

      _____ has told the source that _____ is a former
member of the NSWPP who quit that party because he believed
that its members were not true Nazis. _____ is involved in
assisting _____ with National Youth Alliance activities
and works at _____ occasionally. _____

b2
b6
b7c

7-WFO
  (1-157-1) (NSWPP)   (1-157-NEW)   (NU)
  (1-157-   ) (NYA)   (1
  (1-157-NEW)   (1

Buy U.S. Savings Bonds Regularly on the Payroll Savings Plan

FBI reports on Merritt's CI activities

157-2396

was supposed to have been arrested for assaulting a demon-
strator during the May, 1971, demonstrations near the Capitol
in WDC. He has also told [____] that he had set off stink
bombs in several WDC theatres in the past.

The source understood that [____] was one of the
persons who had made Nazi Party telephone recordings and
that [____] had recently been arrested for stealing a
mailing list.

The source described [____] as a white male,
about 24 years old, long brown hair which turns up at the
ends and brown eyes. [____] who is originally from West
Virginia, is a female impersonator. He works as [____]
[____] at [____] The source described [____] as anti-police and
anti-government but not affiliated with any particular
group.

[____] [____] resides at [____]

b6
b7C

The source emphasized that his information concerning the source of the explosives and incendiary devices
comes by way of [____] who source believes has no reason
to deceive him.

Special Investigator [____] ATF Unit,
Treasury Department, was advised of this information on
10/29/71.

On 10/27/71, the source telephonically contacted
the writer and advised that he had met an individual named
[____] who claimed to have lived with [____]
a person arrested by the MPD for placing firebombs at financial institutions in the WDC area. [____] claimed to have lived
with [____] whose true name is [____] at the
time of the latter's arrest. (On 10/29/71, the source advised
that [____] also uses the name [____] and claims to have lived
with [____] at [____]

2

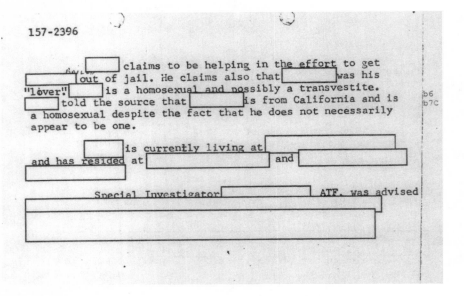

157-2396

_____ claims to be helping in the effort to get _____ out of jail. He claims also that _____ was his "lover". _____ is a homosexual and possibly a transvestite. _____ told the source that _____ is from California and is a homosexual despite the fact that he does not necessarily appear to be one.

b6
b7C

_____ is currently living at _____ and has resided at _____ and _____

Special Investigator _____ ATF, was advised _____

OPTIONAL FORM NO. 10
MAY 1962 EDITION
GSA FPMR (41 CFR) 101-11.6

UNITED STATES GOVERNMENT

Memorandum

TO : SAC, WFO (157-2396) (P)   DATE: 11/17/71

FROM : SA ████████████████

SUBJECT: ████████████████

████████████ advised this date that he had gone
to the Columbia Plaza Apartments on the evening of 11/16/71
to visit a friend. While in the apartment building the
source saw ████████████ who introduced him to ████ (LNU),
the person from whom ████████ was supposed to have obtained
incendiary devices which he sold to the source. The source
stated that ████ resembled the photograph of ████████
████████ except that ████ has a moustache and a "Van Dyke"
beard which he is supposed to have had for only a short time.
The source believes that ████████ is probably identical with
████████████████. The source described ████ as a white male,
6'1" tall, relatively thin build, brown hair and appearing
to be in his mid-twenties. He further described ████ as
seemingly intelligent and pleasant. The source got the
impression from ████████ and from talking with ████ that
████ is looking for friends.

The source was told by ████ that ████ had
worked as ████████████████████████████████ before
coming to work at ████████████████████████

The source told ████ that he is not interested
in purchasing incendiaries or explosives at this time because the source's buyer doesn't need any and the source
is not making money on the deals. The source told ████
this story to insure that he will not be expected to buy
any more of the materials at this time. ████ told the source
that if the source was interested he would be happy to
take him sometime to see the incendiary devices constructed.

On the evening of 11/16/71, the source also talked

8-WFO
(1-157-2278) (NYA)
(1-████████████
(1-████████████ (LNU)
(1-████████████

(1-100-NEW) ████████
(1-████████████
(1-

157-2396

with ⬚ aka ⬚ and ⬚ who had
previously told the source that he knew ⬚
aka ⬚ who has been arrested by the MPD for
the firebombing of financial institutions in the NW section
of WDC. This matter is also being investigated by the ATFB.
⬚ told the source that he had helped construct the
firebombs placed by ⬚ He told the source that these
devices had been constructed in the residence of ⬚
aka ⬚ on M Street, N.W., WDC. The source talked with
⬚ for some time but ⬚ elaborated very little on the
matter of the firebombs. The source determined that at this
time ⬚ can be found at ⬚ is active
in the Gay Liberation Front in WDC according to the source.

It should be kept in mind that in disseminating any
of the above information to the MPD or the ATFD that every
precaution should be taken to protect the source of the information.

b6
b7C

Cover Sheet for Informant Report or Material
FD-306 (Rev. 9-30-69)

Date prepared

3/22/72

Date received

3/17/72

Received from (name or symbol number)

Received by

SA

Method of delivery (check appropriate blocks)

☒ in person ☐ by telephone ☐ by mail ☐ orally ☐ recording device ☐ written by Informant

If orally furnished and reduced to writing by Agent:
Date

Dictated _____ to _____

Transcribed _____

Authenticated
by Informant _____

Date of Report

Date(s) of activity

Febuary, 1972

b2
b6
b7C

Brief description of activity or material

copy of "the furies" Febuary 1972

issue

File where original is located if not attached

100-55290-1A-3

* INDIVIDUALS DESIGNATED BY AN ASTERISK (*) ONLY ATTENDED A MEETING AND DID NOT ACTIVELY PARTICIPATE.
VIOLENCE OR REVOLUTIONARY ACTIVITIES WERE NOT DISCUSSED.

☐ Information recorded on a card index by _____ on date _____.

Remarks: This source has provided reliable information in the past.
Below named individuals listed as [   ] Some have
16-WFO   written articles in this issue.
        100-55290 (the furies)
        100-55290-1A

Block Stamp

163

SEARCHED _____ INDEXED _____
SERIALIZED _____ FILED _____
MAR 27 1972
FBI — WASH. FIELD OFFICE

DIRECTOR, FBI   2/4/72

SAC, WFO [   ] (P)

[   ]

Re WFO letter to the Bureau, dated 12/7/71.

An extra copy of this letter is being furnished
for the Domestic Intelligence Division, because the informant
furnishes information of value in the security field.

RECOMMENDATION

The purpose of this letter is to recommend authority be given
to expend an additional [   ] in payments to the informant
under provisions of Section 108-J, 2, Manual of Instructions.

During the period the informant has been contacted,
he has shown no signs of emotional instability or unreliability.
He has maintained very regular contact and there has been no
indication that he has furnished any false information.

This informant has been paid a total of [   ] under
SAC authority during the period 12/10/71 to 1/28/72. Author-
ization to pay the informant on additional [   ] under SAC
authority was granted per Bureau letter dated 12/9/71.

The following payments were made during the above
mentioned period:

Date	Amount
12/10/71	
12/17/71	

b2
b6
b7C
b7E

-119

3 - Bureau
① - WFO
TJO: sup
(4)

sent by courier

Searched ____
Serialized ____
Indexed ____
Filed ____

DIRECTOR, FBI ⬚   3/22/72

SAC, WFO ⬚ (P)

⬚

Re WFO letter to the Bureau, 2/4/72.

An extra copy of this letter is being furnished
for the Domestic Intelligence Division because the informant furnishes information of value in the security field.

Recommendation

The purpose of this letter is to recommend
authority be given to expend an additional ⬚ in payments to the informant under provisions of Section 108-J,
2, Manual of Instructions.

During the period the informant has been contacted,
he has shown no signs of emotional instability or unreliability. He has maintained very regular contact and there
has been no indication that he has furnished any false
information.

This informant has been paid a total of ⬚
under SAC authority during the period 2/8/72 - 3/17/72.
Authority to pay the informant an additional ⬚ under
SAC authority was granted per Bureau letter dated 2/8/72.

The following payments were made during the
above-mentioned period:

Date   Amount   ⬚ -159

2/8/72   Searched _____
2/11/72   Serialized _____
2/18/72   Indexed _____
                                        Filed _____

3 - Bureau
(1) - WFO
TTO:kmz
(4)

b2
b7E

WFO [redacted]

2/24/72
3/6/72
3/13/72
3/17/72

[redacted box]

CASES WHICH INFORMATION HAS BEEN FURNISHED

[redacted box]

CAPSOM
(CO: WFO)
Bufile 174-1091
WFOfile 174-318

WEATHFUG
(CO: CG)
Bufile 176-1594
WFOfile 176-265

b2
b6
b7C
b7E

The informant has been targeted against [redacted] and an admitted associate of WEATHFUG subjects. The informant has been attempting to further develop his association with [redacted] and has furnished information of value concerning [redacted] activities and associates. The source is, of course, constantly alert for indications of any contact on [redacted] part with WEATHFUG subjects or other New Left fugitives as well as any implication of knowledge on [redacted] part regarding CAPSOM.

On 2/6/72, the source provided information concerning a recent conversation he had had with [redacted] He

WFO ▢

further recalled that sometime during April, 1971, ▢
had made a statement to an attorney who is a mutual friend
of ▢ and the source and who was providing legal advice
to both, that he had been told by an individual that that
individual had been involved in the bombing of the U.S.
Capitol, 3/1/71. The attorney, ▢ told ▢
that he would talk to this unnamed individual for ▢ to
determine whether this person had actually been involved
in the bombing. The source had been making an effort to
recall as best he could what had been said during this
conversation and reported it only when he was sure that he
recalled enough for the information to be of value.

On 2/13/72, the source advised that he had
spoken with ▢ on that same date and furnished information regarding ▢ activities and proposed activities
at that time.

On 2/16/72, the source provided information regarding a trip he had taken to New York City with ▢
during April, 1971, believing that the information might
be of value to the Bureau.

On 2/18,20,25, and 26/72, the source provided
information regarding recent contacts he had had with ▢

On 2/29/72, the source provided information regarding a conversation with ▢ on 2/28/72. During this
conversation ▢ told the source about being interviewed
by an FBI Agent ▢

▢ and that he would have nothing further to do
with the FBI. ▢ also told the source that he intended
to travel to New York City after work that night to visit
"Weather fugitives" and other unnamed persons.

b2
b6
b7

- 3 -

215

UFO [ ]

On 3/4/72, the source furnished information concerning [ ] associates.

On 3/6/72, the source furnished information concerning conversations he had had with [ ] on 3/5-6/72.

On 3/10/72, the source provided information concerning a conversation he had with [ ] on 3/9/72. During this conversation [ ] asked the source to rent an apartment under an assumed name to be used by [ ] the source and others whom [ ] would not name as a meeting place.

On 3/13, 15, and 16/72, the source provided additional information concerning [ ]

[ ]

On 3/4/72, the source furnished information regarding the possible location of [ ]

[ ] The source had previously furnished considerable information of value concerning this individual and remains alert regarding his activities and location.

[ ]

b2
b6
b7C

WFO [redacted]

On 2/9/72, the source furnished information concerning an individual known to the source as [redacted] who apparently works as [redacted] at [redacted] in Washington, D.C. (WDC), and who has told the source that he is involved in thefts from [redacted]

> THE DEFENSE COMMITTEE, aka;
> IS - NEW LEFT
> (OO: PH)
> Bufile 100-457862
> WFOfile 100-53301

On 2/8/72, and 3/10/72, the source furnished literature received from the Harrisburg Defense Committee. This literature was of value in regard to this case.

> DEMONSTRATION SPONSORED BY D.C. CITIZENS
> CONCERNED FOR PEACE IN INDO-CHINA AT THE
> WHITE HOUSE,
> WASHINGTON, D.C.
> 2/17/72
> IS - NEW LEFT
> VIDEM;
> PREVIT
> (OO:WFO)

On 2/16/72, the source advised that captioned demonstration was to take place and appropriate agencies were advised re this matter. This demonstration did take place on 2/16/72.

MISCELLANEOUS

The source has provided to this office information of value to the Metropolitan Police Department (MPD) concerning narcotics activity in WDC.

- 5 -

WFO ▭

On 2/25/72, provided information concerning
marijuana dealings on the part of persons at ▭
▭ and possible heroin dealings on the
part of persons at ▭ and
on the part of an individual who frequents the Dupont
Circle area of WDC. The source later furnished additional
information regarding narcotics activity at ▭
▭ All of this information has been furnished to
appropriate officers of the MPD who advised that this
information is of value to the MPD.

b2
b6
b7C

EVALUATION

The informant has been making every effort to
further develop his relationship with ▭
and has succeeded in doing so. Further development of
this association will hopefully enable the source to
obtain information of value concerning the WEATHFUG and
CAPEOM investigations. The source continues to furnish
to this office information of value to both the Bureau
and other law enforcement agencies concerning criminal
activity in WDC and particularly in the Dupont Circle, N.W.
area of the city. Additionally, the source has provided
information of value to the Bureau in the New Left security
field and is in a position to continue to do so.

- 6 -

218

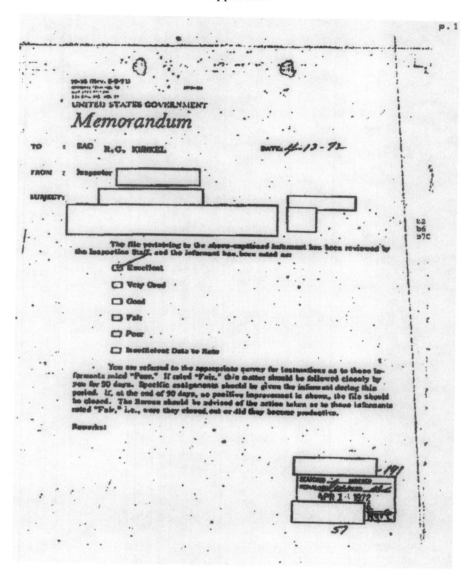

UNITED STATES GOVERNMENT

Memorandum

TO : SAC R.C. KUNKEL   DATE: 4-13-72

FROM : Inspector

SUBJECT:

The file pertaining to the above-captioned informant has been reviewed by
the Inspection Staff, and the informant has been rated as:

- [x] Excellent
- [ ] Very Good
- [ ] Good
- [ ] Fair
- [ ] Poor
- [ ] Insufficient Data to Rate

You are referred to the appropriate survey for instructions as to those informants rated "Poor." If rated "Fair," this matter should be followed closely by you for 90 days. Specific assignments should be given the informant during this period. If, at the end of 90 days, no positive improvement is shown, the file should be closed. The Bureau should be advised of the action taken as to those informants rated "Fair," i.e., were they closed out or did they become productive.

Remarks:

SEARCHED
APR 1 1972

57

Abbott. Sammie

Abernathy, Ralph

Alliance to End Repression

American Communism

American Friends Service Committee

American Jewish Committee

American Jewish Congress

American Legion

American National Socialist Party

American Nazi Party

American University

Anarchy Party

Anti-war union

Asian Americans for the Peace

Barry, Marion

Black Liberation

Black Panther

Black Power movement

Black Social Workers' union

Black United Front

Catholic Peace Fellowship

Common Cause

Communist Party

Communist Workers' Party

Congress of Racial Equality

Daily Worker

Davis, Angela

Davis, Rennie

Davis, Jack

D.C. Statehood Party

Democratic Party National Policy

Democratic Socialist Organizing

Dohrn, Bernadine

Drug culture (hippies-yippies)

Fauntroy, Walter

Federal City College

Fonda, Jane

Friends of the Black Panthers

Friends of Peace Committee

Gay Activists Alliance

Gay Community Services Center

George Washington University

Hearst, Patty

Hobson, Julius

Hobson, Tina

Hoffman, Abbie

Howard University

Institute for Policy Studies (IPS)

Jackson, Jesse

Jewish Defense League (JDL)

Kennedy, Ethel

Kennedy, Robert F

King, Coretta Scott

King, Martin Luther Jr.

Ku Klux Klan

Kunstler, William

Legal Aid Foundation

Legal Aid Society

Markin, Richard

Middle East Resource and Information Project

National Association for the Advancement of Colored People

National Catholic Conference for Inter-Racial Justice

National Council of Churches

National Lawyers' Guild

National Organization for Women (NOW)

National Rifle Association

National Socialist White People's Party

National Student Association (NSA)

Nazis

New Mobilization Committee to End the War in Vietnam

Off our Backs

People's Coalition for Peace and Justice

People United to Save Humanity

Quakers

Red Squads

Revolutionary Action Movement

Rubin, Jerry

Socialist Party

Socialist Workers' Party (SWP)

Southern Christian Leadership Conference

Student Nonviolent Coordinating

Students for a Democratic Society

Tenants' Rights Workshop

Tucker, Sterling

United Church of Christ

United Farm Workers of America (UFW)

United Presbyterian Church

Veterans and Reservists against the War (V and R)

Veterans for Peace

Veterans of Foreign Wars (VFW)

Vietnam Moratorium Committee (VMC)

Vietnam Veterans' Association

Washington Area Peace Action Committee (WAPAC)

Washington Peace Council

Weather Underground

Welfare Rights Organization

Women International League for Peace and Freedom

Women's Strike for Peace (WSP)

World Peace Council

X, Malcolm

Yippies

Young Communists

Young Socialist Alliance (YAS)

Superior Court of the District of Columbia
Washington, D.C. 20001

Robert I. Richter
Judge

July 7, 2005

Commissioner Jo Anne B. Barnhart
Social Security Administration
6401 Security Boulevard
Baltimore, MD 21235-0001

      Re: *United States v. Robert Merritt*
            Criminal Case No. F-643-84

Dear Commissioner Barnhart:

    This is to notify you that on April 22, 2005, the Superior Court of the District of Columbia quashed the November 9, 2004, bench warrant issued by the Superior Court of the District of Columbia against Robert Merritt in the above-captioned case, terminated Mr. Merritt's probation, and closed the above-captioned case.

                Sincerely,

                Robert I. Richter

cc: Robert Merritt
        P.O. Box 697
        Bronx, NY 10468
        [FAX 646-670-9518]

DATE: 4-22-05	COUNT(S)	PLEA OF NOT GUILTY WITHDRAWN JURY DEMAND WITHDRAWN PLEA GUILTY, JUDGMENT GUILTY	COUNT(S)	CONTINUED DATE	Continued for:	In Courtroom Nbr.
COURT REPORTER TAPE ☒ C. FRANKLIN	COUNT(S)	Bench Warrant Ordered and issued Forthwith Bench Warrant Bond $	COUNT(S)	Preliminary Hearing [ ] Held [ ] Held for G.J. Action [ ] Waived [ ] No Probable Cause		☐ Remaining counts to be dismissed at sentencing
☒ IS PRESENT Counsel: ☐ IS NOT PRESENT		☒ IS PRESENT Defendant: ☐ IS NOT PRESENT	BOND $		☐ CASH ☐ SURETY %	☐ P.R.

ATTY F. D'ANTUONO ENTERS APPEARANCE AS PRO BONO COUNSEL.
B/W IS QUASHED. THE SHOW CAUSE ORDER IS DISCHARGED BY THE COURT.
PROBATION IS TERMINATED.

Count(s)		Nolle Prosequi Prosecutor		Defendant released and warned ☐ of Penalties for failure to return
☐ New Commitment Executed	☐ Back To Jail O.C.	☐ Release Executed	☑ Not In Custody
BG DISPOSED	PENDING	B/W	CLERK	JUDGE/COMM. RICHTER
CLOSED Held G.J. CONT. PAY Show Cause	B/W Status Jury Non Jury Sent.	Others Updated By		

DATE:	COUNT(S)	PLEA OF NOT GUILTY WITHDRAWN JURY DEMAND WITHDRAWN PLEA GUILTY, JUDGMENT GUILTY	COUNT(S)	CONTINUED DATE	Continued for:	In Courtroom Nbr.
COURT REPORTER TAPE ☐	COUNT(S)	Bench Warrant Ordered and issued Forthwith Bench Warrant Bond $	COUNT(S)	Preliminary Hearing ☐ Held ☐ Held for G.J. Action ☐ Waived ☐ No Probable Cause		☐ Remaining counts to be dismissed at sentencing
☐ IS PRESENT Counsel: ☐ IS NOT PRESENT		☐ IS PRESENT Defendant: ☐ IS NOT PRESENT	BOND $		☐ CASH ☐ SURETY %	☐ P.R.

Count(s)		Nolle Prosequi Prosecutor		Defendant released and warned ☐ of Penalties for failure to return
☐ New Commitment Executed	☐ Back To Jail O.C.	☐ Release Executed	☐ Not In Custody
DISPOSED	PENDING		CLERK	JUDGE/COMM.
CLOSED Held G.J. CONT. PAY Show Cause	B/W Status Jury Non Jury Sent.	Others Updated By		

DATE:	COUNT(S)	PLEA OF NOT GUILTY WITHDRAWN JURY DEMAND WITHDRAWN PLEA GUILTY, JUDGMENT GUILTY	COUNT(S)	CONTINUED DATE	Continued for:	In Courtroom Nbr.
COURT REPORTER TAPE ☐	COUNT(S)	Bench Warrant Ordered and issued Forthwith Bench Warrant Bond $	COUNT(S)	Preliminary Hearing ☐ Held ☐ Held for G.J. Action ☐ Waived ☐ No Probable Cause		☐ Remaining counts to be dismissed at sentencing
☐ IS PRESENT Counsel: ☐ IS NOT PRESENT		☐ IS PRESENT Defendant: ☐ IS NOT PRESENT	BOND $		☐ CASH ☐ SURETY %	☐ P.R.

A TRUE COPY
TEST: MAY 3 1 2005

Clerk, Superior Court of the
District of Columbia
By: _____

Count(s)		Nolle Prosequi Prosecutor		Defendant released and warned ☐ of Penalties for failure to return
☐ New Commitment Executed	☐ Back To Jail O.C.	☐ Release Executed	☐ Not In Custody
DISPOSED	PENDING		CLERK	JUDGE/COMM.
CLOSED Held G.J. CONT. PAY Show Cause	B/W Status Jury Non Jury Sent.	Others Updated By		

Name: E. ROBERT MERRITT	Docket No.: F 643-84

Form CD-103B/JUNE 90   PAGE   6-9854 ed239

Appendix D

No Papers Count(s)		Court File Date		LOCK UP	PDID	376-468			
Charges Filed		8-22-00		L-60	DOB	6-22-1944			
Felony	A	☐ CITATION	☐ BOND	☐ Collateral $	CCR			Page	

THE UNITED STATES
Versus
EARL R. MERRITT
EARL R. MERRITT, JR.
AKA
ROBERT MERRITT

		Defense Counsel ☐ PRO SE			CODE	S	C	A	R	DATE WITHDRAWN
Misdemeaner		1. Ralph Robinson 441797				☐	☒	☐	☐	
Traffic		2.				☐	☐	☐	☐	
D.C.										

A	Brian Brook	PROSECUTOR		CODE	ASSIGNED TO JUDGE
B	Prison Breach	1.			
C		2.			Cal. Number F2-4
D		☐ Defendant Informed of rights to pursuant to Superior Court Rule 5 (b) including the right to counsel.			☐ LINEUP ORDER FILED
E					☐ Sworn Statement Filed
F		Count(s) a PLEA: ☐ Not Guilty ☐ Guilty, JUDGMENT Guilty			Rule 5(c) Determination ☐ Made ☐ Waived

G		CONTINUED DATE		BOND CONDITIONS	
H	☐	PREL. HEARING	9-25-00	BOND AMOUNT $	
I		STATUS HEARING		☐ CASH _____ % ☐ SURETY	
		JURY TRIAL		☒ PERSONAL RECOGNIZANCE	
PROBATION ☐ DOMESTIC VIOL. ☐ 163 FILED		NON-JURY		☐ Third Party Custodian	
Sentence Date				☐ Collateral Remains	
Report Due Date		☒ Defendant Advised of Penalties for Failure to Appear.			
Date Jacket Ready For Probation		See Entry in F 643-84			
Date Received in Probation					
By		Count(s) Nolle Prosequi Prosecutor			
Date Jacket Returned to Crim. Div.		COURT REPORTER TAPE ☐ CLERK SB		JUDGE/COMM. Garrett	
Diversion		☐ NEW COMMITMENT ☐ BACK TO JAIL O.C.		☐ RELEASE EXECUTED ☐ NOT IN CUSTODY	
Date Admitted		DISPOSED		PENDING	
		CLOSED CONT. HRG Show Cause B/W Status Jury Non-Jury Sent. Others Updated By			

DATE: 12/13/00	FINAL DISPOSITION ONLY
	Dismissed by the Govt.

Count(s)	Nolle Prosequi Prosecutor Y. Lee		
COURT REPORTER	TAPE ☒ CLERK SB	JUDGE/COMM. Broderick	
☐ NEW COMMITMENT EXECUTED 1/7	☒ BACK TO JAIL O.C.	☐ RELEASE EXECUTED ☒ NOT IN CUSTODY	

All Accounts Closed							
JACKET MAY GO TO CLOSED FILES	Updated by	☐ CLOSED Held G.J.	CONT. HRG	Show Cause	B/W	Others	Updated by

Superior Court of the District of Columbia

CRIMINAL DIVISION

FELONY

INDICTMENT FILED 09-20-00
GRAND JURY NO
ARRAIGNMENT SET 09-25-00
ASSIGNED TO
CAL-IV

F 5098 '00

ADDITIONAL INFORMATION FOR
NEW YORK CITY CHAPTER

TOTAL ARRESTS FOR NYC & DC
IN CAREER AS A CI

CITY	MURDERS	ROBBERIES	NARCOTICS
WASHINGTON DC	4	27	243
NEW YORK CITY			
MANHATTAN			
KENMORE HOTEL	3	18	239
TIMES SQUARE HOTEL	2	9	149
TIME SQUARE AREA	0	3	42
HARLEM	8	17	79
MADISON SQUARE HOTEL	0	2	11
MADISON SQUARE VICINITY	3	22	39
UNION SQUARE PARK	0	0	32
STUYVESANT PARK	0	0	49
TRIBECA	1	1	9
SOHO	0	0	17
NOHO	0	0	8
BOWERY	1	0	17
WASHINGTON SQUARE PARK	0	0	27
EAST VILLAGE	2	1	29
WEST VILLAGE	2	1	29
PROJECTS			
20TH STREET & 8 AVENUE	2	8	18
NATHAN STRAUSS HOUSE	1	8	49
TOTAL AMOUNT	**27**	**119**	**1075**

- **ONLY 12 PEOPLE SERVING TIME IN PRISONS FOR MURDERS AND NARCOTICS.**

- **ONE PIT BULL SHOT AND KILLED**

- **TWO DRUG DEALERS (HUSBAND & WIFE) WERE DEATH**

- **ONE DRUG DEALER WAS BLIND**

- **CASH AND DRUG VALUE CONFISCATED UNKNOWN**

STATE OF NEW YORK)
COUNTY OF NEW YORK) ss.:

14/10 71

AFFIDAVIT OF ROBERT N. WALL

I, Robert N. Wall, being duly sworn, depose and say on the basis of my own knowledge:

1. I am currently a resident of Buffalo, New York.

2. During the period 1965-1970, I was a Special Agent for the Federal Bureau of Investigation, and during the period 1967-1970, I was assigned to the Washington, D. C. Field Office of the F.B.I. During that time, it came to my attention that records of banks in the Washington, D. C. area could be obtained for the purposes of our investigation. My understanding is that these records were obtained by a special agent in the Washington, D. C. Field Office who had developed relations with various officers and employees of ban in this area. These banking records were not obtained through any legal procedures (eg. Grand Jury subpoenas or otherwise), but as an accommodation to the F. B. I.

3. I, as well as other agents investigating the so-called "new left" and "black" organizations, were able to obtain the banking records we were intere in by requesting them from the agent on this detail. It was in this context I saw the banking records of the Institute for Policy Studies, during the per 1968-1970.

4. By banking records of the Institute for Policy Studies, I mean a list of checks issued by IPS showing check number, date of issuance, maker, payee and endorser, if any, with respect to the Institute for Policy Studies accou in the Riggs National Bank in Washington, D. C.

.obert N. Wall - 2

5. While the checks written by the Institute for Policy Studies were routinely obtained, the F.B.I. was also able, on special request, to obtain comparable information with respect to IPS account of deposits made in Riggs National Bank.

6. In addition to the financial records of IPS, the F.B.I. was able to secure in similar fashion the financial records of The New School for Afro-American Thought, The Drum and Spear Bookstore, the Center for Black Education, and those of selected individuals, including Stokely Carmichael and Jean Hughes.

Then personally appeared before me the above-named ROBERT N. WALL and made oath that the foregoing statements subscribed by him are true.

Robert N. Wall
Robert N. Wall

12/16/71
Date

Bella Greene
Notary Public

My Commission expires:

BELLA GREENE
Notary Public, State of New York
No. 24-1154843
Qualified in Kings County
Commission Expires March 30, 1973

Appendix G

GRAND JURY

United States District Court

For the District of Columbia

THE UNITED STATES

vs.

Pos. Vio. 18 U.S.C. §371, et al.

REPORT TO UNITED STATES DISTRICT
COURT HOUSE
Between 3d Street and John Marshall Place
and on Constitution Avenue NW.
ROOM 3600-K, EJS #26
Washington, D.C.

To: Douglas Caddy, Esq., 1250 Connecticut Avenue, N.W., Washington, D. C.

RECEIVED JUN 28 12 53 PH '72 PROCESS CONTROL CENTER

You are hereby commanded to attend before the Grand Jury of said Court on ...FORTHWITH

the .... day of ...., 19......, at .... o'clock ......M., to testify
on behalf of the United States, and not depart the Court without leave of the Court or District Attorney.

WITNESS: The Honorable John J. Sirica, Chief Judge of said Court, this

28th day of June, 19 72.

JAMES F. DAVEY, Clerk.

By Ruby H. Kelly, Deputy Clerk.

Attorney for ....

Form No. USA-91-184 (Rev. 7-1-71)

231

UNITED STATES DISTRICT COURT
FOR THE DISTRICT OF COLUMBIA

In Re:)
)
        MICHAEL DOUGLAS CADDY)   Misc. No. 60-72

ORDER

This matter having come before the Court on the
oral motion of the United States Attorney for the District
of Columbia on behalf of the Grand Jury for an order finding Michael Douglas Caddy in contempt of this Court for
his refusal to answer certain questions before the grand
jury on July 13, 1972; and

The witness Michael Douglas Caddy being present
before this Court and represented by counsel;

The Court, after hearing argument and being advised
in the premises, finds

That the witness Michael Douglas Caddy was duly
subpoenaed to appear before the Grand Jury;

That he did appear before the Grand Jury on June 30,
1972, July 5, 1972, and July 7, 1972;

That he refused to answer certain questions pro-
pounded to him before the Grand Jury;

That on July 12, 1972, this Court, after having
received written memoranda and heard oral argument at
a hearing at which Michael Douglas Caddy was present
and represented by counsel, ordered Michael Douglas
Caddy to appear before the Grand Jury on July 13, 1972,
at 10:00 a.m. and answer the questions contained in the
Appendix to the written motion, filed in this Court by

COMMITMENT TO JAIL

-2-

the United States Attorney on July 10, 1972, to compel
the testimony of Michael Douglas Caddy;

That Michael Douglas Caddy did appear before the
Grand Jury as ordered but refused to answer any of the
questions as ordered by this Court;

That Michael Douglas Caddy having failed to show
why he should not be held in contempt of this Court and
his contempt having tended to defeat, impair, and impede
the lawful function of the Grand Jury and this Court;

-The witness Michael Douglas Caddy is hereby found
in direct contempt of the order of this Court; and,
therefore,

It is by the Court this 13th day of July, 1972,
ORDERED, ADJUDGED and DECREED that Michael Douglas Caddy
is in direct contempt of this Court for his failure to
obey a lawful order of this Court to answer certain
questions before the Grand Jury and he is hereby committed to the custody of the United States Marshal for
the District of Columbia and the Attorney-General of
the United States or his authorized representative,
for the life of the June 1972 No. 1 Grand Jury sworn in
on June 5, 1972, or unless and until he complies with
the order of the court and purges himself of this
contempt.

/S/ JOHN J. SIRICA
CHIEF JUDGE

A TRUE COPY
JAMES F. DAVEY, CLERK
BY James P Capitano

APPENDIX ONE

Nine

On July 10, 1972 Harold H. Titus, Jr., U.S. Attorney for the District of Columbia; Earl J. Silbert, Principal Assistant U.S. Attorney; Donald E. Campbell, Assistant U.S. Attorney; and Seymour Glanzer, Assistant U.S. Attorney filed a "Motion to Compel Testimony of Grand Jury Witness Michael Douglas Caddy." The Motion stated, "The United States of America, therefore, seeks the following relief from this Court:

"An order that the witness Mr. Caddy be directed on pain of contempt to respond before the grand jury to the questions specified in the Appendix attached to this motion, all questions which he without justification refused to answer on Friday, June 30, 1972, Wednesday, July 5, 1972 and Friday, July 7, 1972."

The following is the Appendix attached to the motion listing the 38 key questions.

1. The question was, when was the last time that you saw Mr. Hunt?
2. When, that is the approximate date, was the attorney-client relationship established on the current matter in which you represent Mr. Hunt?
3. All right, do you represent Mr. Hunt with respect to the matters being investigated by this grand jury?
4. When was the last time you spoke to your client... Mr. Hunt?
5. Other than legal fees, have you received any money, or any pecuniary, or financial benefits from Mr. Hunt in any manner, shape, or form during the entire period you have known him?
6. All right, I believe the first question that we asked you, at which point you indicated a desire to consult with counsel, was the date on which Mr. X. became your client.
7. When was the last time you saw Mr. X?
8. When was the last time you spoke to Mr. X?
9. Did you see Mr. Hunt within one-quarter mile of the Watergate Hotel on June 16 or June 17 of this year?
10. Now again, just for the record, what was the subject matter, the general field of law, in which you represented Mr. X prior to July 7th, 1972?
11. I believe the question was prior to Thursday, July 6th of this year, when you represented Mr. X., what fee arrangement or retainer agreement did you have with Mr. X relevant to the subject matter in which you represented him as an attorney.
12. The question is prior to July 6th of this year -- that is yesterday -- have you ever -- has Mr. X. ever paid you a fee for representing him as an attorney?
13. At what time did you receive a telephone call in the early morning hours of Saturday, June 17, 1972?

14. From whom did you receive a telephone call in the early morning hours of June 17, 1972?

15. Did you receive a telephone call from Mrs. Barker, the wife of Bernard L. Barker?

16. Did you receive a telephone call from Everett Howard Hunt in the early morning hours of Saturday, June 17, 1972?

17. Did you receive a telephone call from Mr. X in the early morning hours of Saturday, June 17, 1972, and just so the record is clear, I will confine the time from 12 A.M., in the morning, until 6:00 A.M. in the morning?

18. From whom were the half dozen phone calls you received between midnight, Friday, June 16th and 8:30 A.M., Saturday, June 17th?

19. Now, as to those half a dozen phone calls in which you have now invoked the attorney-client privilege as to the identity of the person, were they from men or from women?

20. I believe the question that was asked you...was whether or not any of the half a dozen phone calls that you received were from clients of yours in the attorney-client sense of the word?

21. During the hours of midnight, June 16th, Friday, through 8:30 Saturday morning, that is 8:30 A.M., Saturday, June 17th, to whom did you make telephone calls?

22. Were any of the persons to whom you made telephone calls clients of yours in the attorney-client sense of the relationship?

23. I believe the question was between the hours of midnight, Friday, June 16th, and 8:30 A.M., Saturday, June 17th, did you receive or have any visitors at your apartment?

24. Whether or not any of the about half a dozen telephone calls that you have indicated that you made while in your apartment between the hours of midnight, June 16th, and 8:30 A.M. Saturday, June 17th, were any of those long distance telephone calls?

25. Between the hours of Friday, June 16th and Saturday, 8:30 A.M., June 17th did you receive -- were any of the half a dozen phone calls that you received long distance?

26. Between the hours of Friday at midnight, June 16th, and 8:30 A.M. Saturday, June 17th, did you receive a visit from Mr. Everett Howard Hunt?

27. Did you receive a visit during that same period of time, that is midnight, June 16th, to 8:30 A.M., June 17th, from Mr. X?

28. When did Mrs. Dorothy Hunt first become a client of yours?

29. Outside of occasions to which Mr. Everett Howard Hunt has used his -- a different pen name under which he authored a number of books, to which you have referred in your previous answer, has Mr. Everett Howard Hunt used any names other than his own?

30. To your knowledge has Mr. X ever used any names other than his own name of Mr. X?

31. At the central cellblock, did you speak to anyone there, or what did you do there, sir?

32. Now, with respect to Mr. Bernard L. Barker, what fee arrangement or retainer agreement did you make with him at that time with respect to his representation?

33. With respect to Mr. (Rolando) Martinez what fee arrangement did you make to represent him?

34. With respect to Virgilio Gonzalez?

35. With respect to James W. McCord, Jr.?

36. With respect to Mr. Frank Fiorini or Frank Sturgis?

37. Prior to your going to 23rd and L Streets, Northwest, that morning, Saturday, June 17th, 1972, had you been asked by anybody to represent those, any, or all or some of those five individuals?

38. Who, if anyone, asked you to represent those five individuals who were in the jail at 23rd and L Streets, Northwest, that morning?

Appendix J

E. Howard Hunt - Testament

to

His Son, Saint John Hunt
Recorded January 2004

(Transcribed from original audio recording in his own words & voice.)

I heard from Frank, that LBJ had designated Cord Meyer, Jr. to undertake a larger organization, while keeping it totally secret.

Cord Meyer, himself was a rather favored member of the eastern aristocracy. He was a graduate of Yale University and had joined the Marine Corps during the war, and lost an eye in the Pacific fighting.

I think that L.B.J. settled on Meyer as an opportunist / paren (like himself) a paren and a man who had very little left to him in life, ever since J.F.K. had taken Cord's wife as one of his mistresses.

I would suggest that Cord Meyer welcomed the approach from L.B.J., who was after all, only the Vice-President at that time, and of course could not number Cord Meyer among J.F.K.'s admirers. Quite the contrary.

As for Dave Phillips, I knew him pretty well at one time. He worked for me during the Guatemala project. He had made himself useful to the Agency in Santiago, Chile, where he was an American businessman. In any case his actions, whatever they were, came to the attention of the Santiago Station Chief, and when his resume became known to people in the Western Hemisphere Division, he was brought in to work on Guatemalan operations.

Sturgis and Morales, and people of that ilk, stayed in apartment houses during preparations for the big event. Their addresses were very subject to change. So that where a fella like Morales had been one day, you'd not necessarily associate him with that same address the following day. In short it was a very mobile experience.

Let me point out at this point, that if I had wanted to fictionalize what went on in Miami and elsewhere during the run up for the big event, I would have done so.

But I don't want any unreality to tinge this particular story—or the information, I should say. I was a 'benchwarmer' on it and I had a reputation for honesty.

I think it's essential to refocus on what this information that I have been providing you—and you alone, by the way—consists of. What is important in the story is that we've backtracked the chain-of-command up through Cord Meyer, and laying the doings at doorstep of L.B.J.

He, in my opinion, had an almost maniacal urge to become President. He regarded J.F.K. as—as he was in fact—an obstacle to achieving that. He could have waited for J.F.K. to finish out his term and then undoubtedly a second term.

So that would have put L.B.J. at the head of a long list of people who were waiting for some change in the Executive Branch.

To replay the audio clip, simply refresh your browser.

_____ Click Here for E. Howard Hunt's Eulogy _____

236

THE SECRET KEY TO THE WATERGATE BREAK-IN

When Carl Shoffler arrested the five Watergate burglars on June 17, 1972 at 2:30 AM, he claimed that he found one key on the person of the burglar known as Eugenio Martinez. He asserted that the key was taped on the front of a notebook found on Martinez and that he subsequently inscribed his own notes in his detective's pad about what he had found relating to the arrests. Martinez' notebook, bearing Shoffler's initials with the key taped on it, was later placed in the U.S. National Archives, where it sat for almost two decades before being noticed.

This key was the subject of an A&E Investigative Report broadcast in 1992 with the title of "Key to Watergate." Officer Shoffler was interviewed in the program. Here is the link to the A&E Investigative Report: http://www.nixonera.com/library/watergate.asp

Shoffler lied in his official police report on the burglars' arrest. In actuality there were two keys involved and he removed both keys, not just one, from Eugenio Martinez. The key that he removed and disclosed was a key to the desk of a secretary at the Democratic National Committee. The key that he failed to disclose was a blank safe deposit box key that he had arranged to be placed in the secretary's desk prior to the break-in as part of his plan to set up the burglars.

I have personal knowledge about the second key. About a week before the arrests took place Carl asked me to go to a local locksmith and purchase a blank safe deposit key, which I did. When I returned to our apartment Carl produced a one-page document that had encrypted writing on it. He explained to me that the writing was gibberish. He handed the one page document to me using only his fingernails. After I took the document he asked that I fold it so that it would fit inside a white no. 10 business envelope, which he also provided to me using only his fingernails. He directed me to place the document and the key inside the envelope. As I did so I purposely pressed my thumb down hard on the document so that if it later became an issue my thumbprint could be traced, as well as all my other fingerprints on the paper, key and envelope. I licked the envelope and sealed it with the encrypted document and key inside. Shoffler then directed me to insert the envelope into an inside pocket of the jacket he was wearing.

Why did I purposely leave my fingerprints? Because I began not to trust Shoffler fully after the sudden disappearance of my close friend, Rita Reed, if something had happened to Rita because she knew too much, then I figured something could happen to me. My fingerprints on the key, document and envelope were a form of insurance for me, or so I thought.

When he employed his triangulation wiretapping after June 3 he led the burglars to believe that a safe deposit key and paper inside an envelope in the secretary's desk would lead them to a treasure trove of vitally important documents. Possession of the documents would ensure the victory of President Nixon in his re-election campaign and bestow other political benefits.

Shoffler, using his wiretap triangulation, also managed to persuade the burglars to move the planned break-in date from June 18 to June 17, which was his birthday. He did so without the burglars being aware that the conversation that they had monitored detailing the safe deposit key in the secretary's desk and June 17 date was a set up conversation orchestrated by him and had no connection to the offices of the Democratic National Committee. In the orchestrated conversation Shoffler indicated that the key to open the secretary's desk was under her telephone on top of her desk.

There is a question even today whether the object of the burglars' wiretap operation was the Democratic National Committee. It may be that the wiretap operation was instead after the prostitution ring being operated from an apartment in the Columbia Plaza Apartments across the street from the Watergate complex. The prostitution ring allegedly serviced referrals by telephone from someone inside the Democratic National Committee. The man having the most knowledge about the Watergate wiretap operation was burglar, James McCord.

After Shoffler returned to my apartment at 7 A.M. on June 17, he roused me from sleep and embraced me and kissed me. He was obviously elated. He said to me, "Thanks to you my operation was a total success. I arrested five burglars. But you must promise me never to tell what you know." He then showed me the blank safe deposit key that he had withheld from the arrest record, which he had arranged to be planted before hand in the secretary's desk. He told me that Martinez was hiding both keys – the first one to open the desk and the second the safe deposit key – in one of his hands at the time of the arrests and that he physically forced Martinez to surrender both keys. He also showed me the envelope that I had sealed earlier with the key and encrypted writing inside. It had been opened. He told me that he was going to destroy the envelope, encrypted document and key. He then left my apartment, telling me that he was going to grab breakfast at the nearby Hartnett Hall restaurant and then proceed to the courthouse to assist in the arraignment of the burglars.

As the A&E video clearly shows, the investigation of the actual break-in on June 17 was given sparse attention in contrast to the thorough investigation given the cover-up that followed, whose aim was to remove Nixon from office. Howard Liebengood, Counsel to the Senate Watergate Committee, asserts in the video that "I must tell you that I am disturbed about the Watergate break-in and that I am convinced that what we don't know about the Watergate break-in may well be more important than what we do know twenty years after."

In the months that followed the arrests, Shoffler in conversations with me would repeatedly refer to the team of burglars of Liddy, Hunt, McCord and the four Cuban-Americans as his "little duckies." He was especially contemptuous of Liddy and chortled when Liddy, after he was found guilty, boasted that he planned to remain quiet. In reality Shoffler was fearful that if Liddy did talk, he would provide sufficient information and clues that would lead to discovery of Shoffler's role in setting up the burglars, a role that Liddy was unaware of. Liddy's plan to remain quiet fit in perfectly with Shoffler's own plan, which had duped the burglars from its beginning.

He later expanded his "little duckies" pejorative category to everyone involved in the Watergate saga – President Nixon, the Senate Watergate Committee, the Watergate Special Prosecution Force, the media, etc. – as being his "duckies." He said, "It is like shooting ducks sitting in a pond with a blindfold on." Since he held the ace card in clandestinely setting up the burglars, Shoffler could direct its ultimate outcome from behind the scenes. In fact shortly after he made the arrests Shoffler telephoned the Washington Post and reported what had occurred. This inaugurated a relationship with the Post. Shoffler was the primary Deep Throat, out rivaling Mark Felt in his disclosures to the Post.

I believe that Mark Felt had knowledge that a planned break-in of some sort was in the works. It was he who directed FBI Agents Tucker and O'Connor to visit and quiz me about the rumor they had picked up that I knew something about a planned break-in. Their visit came a day or two after I informed Shoffler and his two associates on June 3 of what Rita Reed had told me.

Why did Felt and the FBI agents never acknowledge their prior knowledge that a break-in had been in the offing? I strongly suspect they felt that their doing so would lead directly to me and once I became a central figure in Watergate I would be forced to disclose to the investigative authorities the numerous crimes that I had committed under the FBI's COINTELPRO. Disclosure of these crimes might have meant Felt, Tucker and O'Connor would have faced prosecution for directing these crimes be done. (As it turned out, Felt was later indicted in 1978 and stood trial for certain activities that he had engaged in as part of COINTELPRO.) So it was in the interest of the FBI that I remain silent and out of the public spotlight after the break-in case broke on June 7.

In viewing the video, special attention should be given to Shoffler's eye movements, facial expressions, body language, and oral statements. He boasted to me on numerous occasions that, as a military intelligence agent, he had been trained to lie without being detected. However, a careful watching of him being interviewed shows that he was not a total master at doing this.

Was he under secret orders or was it a simple burning desire to become celebrated as the most famous policeman in the world, that drove Shoffler to design a plan that ended-up forcing a sitting president from office, thereby immeasurably destroying the faith of the American people in their system of government, and launching a bitter political partisanship that has divided this country ever since? It boggles the mind that a single individual could have so changed the course of history, but this is what was accomplished.

Index

Since 1954, the world's most powerful people have met in secret once a year ... until now!

The True Story of The Bilderberg Group

29 BESTSELLER

Daniel Estulin

3RD U.S. PRINTING • OVER 1,500,000 COPIES SOLD WORLDWIDE

The True Story of the Bilderberg Group
BY DANIEL ESTULIN
NORTH AMERICAN UNION EDITION

More than a center of influence, the Bilderberg Group is a shadow world government, hatching plans of domination at annual meetings ... and under a cone of media silence.

THE TRUE STORY OF THE BILDERBERG GROUP goes inside the secret meetings and sheds light on why a group of politicians, businessmen, bankers and other mighty individuals formed the world's most powerful society. As Benjamin Disraeli, one of England's greatest Prime Ministers, noted, "The world is governed by very different personages from what is imagined by those who are not behind the scenes."

Included are unpublished and never-before-seen photographs and other documentation of meetings, as this riveting account exposes the past, present and future plans of the Bilderberg elite.

Softcover: **$24.95** (ISBN: 9780979988622) • 432 pages • Size: 6 x 9

ShadowMasters
BY DANIEL ESTULIN

AN INTERNATIONAL NETWORK OF GOVERNMENTS AND SECRET-SERVICE AGENCIES WORKING TOGETHER WITH DRUG DEALERS AND TERRORISTS FOR MUTUAL BENEFIT AND PROFIT

THIS INVESTIGATION EXAMINES HOW behind-the-scenes collaboration between governments, intelligence services and drug traffickers has lined the pockets of big business and Western banks. Beginning with a last-minute request from ex-governor Jesse Ventura, the narrative winds between the author's own story of covering "deep politics" and the facts he has uncovered. The ongoing campaign against Victor Bout, the "Merchant of Death," is revealed as "move/countermove" in a game of geopolitics, set against the background of a crumbling Soviet Union, a nascent Russia, bizarre assassinations, wars and smuggling. DANIEL ESTULIN is an award-winning investigative journalist and author of *The True Story of the Bilderberg Group*.

Softcover: **$24.95** (ISBN: 9780979988615) • 432 pages • Size: 6 x 9

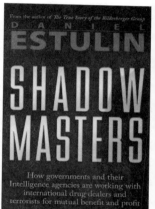

From the author of *The True Story of the Bilderberg Group*

DANIEL ESTULIN

SHADOW MASTERS

How governments and their Intelligence agencies are working with international drug dealers and terrorists for mutual benefit and profit

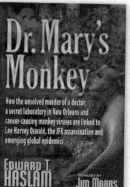

Dr. Mary's Monkey

How the unsolved murder of a doctor, a secret laboratory in New Orleans and cancer-causing monkey viruses are linked to Lee Harvey Oswald, the JFK assassination and emerging global epidemics

EDWARD T. HASLAM
FORWARD BY JIM MARRS

Dr. Mary's Monkey
How the Unsolved Murder of a Doctor, a Secret Laboratory in New Orleans and Cancer-Causing Monkey Viruses are Linked to Lee Harvey Oswald, the JFK Assassination and Emerging Global Epidemics
BY EDWARD T. HASLAM, FOREWORD BY JIM MARRS

Evidence of top-secret medical experiments and cover-ups of clinical blunders
The 1964 murder of a nationally known cancer researcher sets the stage for this gripping exposé of medical professionals enmeshed in covert government operations over the course of three decades. Following a trail of police records, FBI files, cancer statistics, and medical journals, this revealing book presents evidence of a web of medical secret-keeping that began with the handling of evidence in the JFK assassination and continued apace, sweeping doctors into cover-ups of cancer outbreaks, contaminated polio vaccine, the genesis of the AIDS virus, and biological weapon research using infected monkeys.

Softcover: **$19.95** (ISBN: 0977795306) • 320 pages • Size: 5 1/2 x 8 1/2

The Oil Card
Global Economic Warfare in the 21st Century
BY JAMES NORMAN

Challenging the conventional wisdom surrounding high oil prices, this compelling argument sheds an entirely new light on free-market industry fundamentals.
By deciphering past, present, and future geopolitical events, it makes the case that oil pricing and availability have a long history of being employed as economic weapons by the United States. Softcover **$14.95** (ISBN 0977795390) • 288 Pages

The Oil Card
GLOBAL ECONOMIC WARFARE IN THE 21ST CENTURY

James R. Norman

THE 9/11 MYSTERY PLANE
AND THE VANISHING OF AMERICA

BY **MARK GAFFNEY**

FOREWORD BY

DR. DAVID RAY GRIFFIN

Unlike other accounts of the historic attacks on 9/11, this discussion surveys the role of the world's most advanced military command and control plane, the E-4B, in the day's events and proposes that the horrific incidents were the work of a covert operation staged within elements of the U.S. military and the intelligence community. Presenting hard evidence, the account places the world's most advanced electronics platform circling over the White House at approximately the time of the Pentagon attack. The argument offers an analysis of the new evidence within the context of the events and shows that it is irreconcilable with the official 9/11 narrative.

Mark H. Gaffney is an environmentalist, a peace activist, a researcher, and the author of *Dimona, the Third Temple?*; and *Gnostic Secrets of the Naassenes*. He lives in Chiloquin, Oregon. Dr. David Ray Griffin is a professor emeritus at the Claremont School of Theology, and the author of *The 9/11 Commission Report: Omissions and Distortions*, and *The New Pearl Harbor*. He lives in Santa Barbara, California.

Softcoverr • **$19.95** • 9780979988608 • 336 Pages

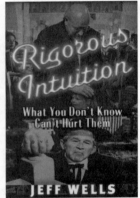

Rigorous Intuition
What You Don't Know, Can't Hurt Them
BY *JEFF WELLS*

"In Jeff's hands, tinfoil hats become crowns and helmets of the purest gold. I strongly suggest that you all pay attention to what he has to say."
—Arthur Gilroy, Booman Tribune

A welcome source of analysis and commentary for those prepared to go deeper—and darker—than even most alternative media permit, this collection from one of the most popular conspiracy theory arguments on the internet will assist readers in clarifying their own arguments and recognizing disinformation. Tackling many of the most difficult subjects that define our time—including 9/11, the JonBenet Ramsey case, and "High Weirdness"—these studies, containing the best of the Rigorous Intuition blog as well as original content, make connections that both describe the current, alarming predicament and suggest a strategy for taking back the world. Following the maxim "What you don't know can't hurt them," this assortment of essays and tools, including the updated and expanded "Coincidence Theorists' Guide to 9/11," guides the intellectually curious down further avenues of study and scrutiny and helps readers feel empowered rather than vulnerable.

Jeff Wells is the author of the novel *Anxious Gravity*. He lives in Toronto, Ontario.

Softcover • **$19.95** • 978-0-9777953-2-1 • 505 Pages

PERFECTIBILISTS
The 18th Century Bavarian Illuminati
BY *TERRY MELANSON*

The shadowy Illuminati grace many pages of fiction as the sinister all-powerful group pulling the strings behind the scenes, but very little has been printed in English about the actual Enlightenment-era secret society, its activities, its members, and its legacy … until now.

First choosing the name Perfectibilists, their enigmatic leader Adam Weishaupt soon thought that sounded too bizarre and changed it to the Order of the Illuminati.

Presenting an authoritative perspective, this definitive study chronicles the rise and fall of the fabled Illuminati, revealing their methods of infiltrating governments and education systems, and their blueprint for a successful cabal, which echoes directly forward through groups like the Order of Skull & Bones to our own era.

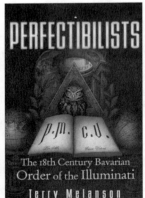

Featuring biographies of more than 400 confirmed members and copiously illustrated, this book brings light to a 200-year-old mystery.

Softcover: **$19.95** • 9780977795381 • 530 pages • Size: 6 x 9

The King of Nepal
Life Before the Drug Wars
BY JOSEPH PIETRI

From the halcyon days of easily accessible drugs to years of government intervention and a surging black market, this tale chronicles a former drug smuggler's 50-year career in the drug trade, its evolution into a multibillion-dollar business, and the characters he met along the way. The journey begins with the infamous Hippie Hash trail that led from London and Amsterdam overland to Nepal where, prior to the early 1970s, hashish was legal and smoked freely; marijuana and opium were sold openly in Hindu temples in India and much of Asia; and cannabis was widely cultivated for use in food, medicine, and cloth. In documenting the stark contrasts of the ensuing years, the narrative examines the impact of the financial incentives awarded by international institutions such as the U.S. government to outlaw the cultivation of cannabis in Nepal and Afghanistan and to make hashish and opium illegal in Turkey—the demise of the U.S. "good old boy" dope network, the eruption of a violent criminal society, and the birth of a global black market for hard drugs—as well as the schemes smugglers employed to get around customs agents and various regulations.

Softcoverr • **$19.95** • 9780979988660 • 240 Pages

Expendable Elite
One Soldier's Journey into Covert Warfare
BY DANIEL MARVIN , FOREWORD BY MARTHA RAYE

A special operations perspective on the Viet Nam War and the truth about a White House concerned with popular opinion

This true story of a special forces officer in Viet Nam in the mid-1960s exposes the unique nature of the elite fighting force and how covert operations are developed and often masked to permit — and even sponsor — assassination, outright purposeful killing of innocents, illegal use of force, and bizarre methods in combat operations. *Expendable Elite* reveals the fear that these warriors share with no other military person: not fear of the enemy they have been trained to fight in battle, but fear of the wrath of the US government should they find themselves classified as "expendable." This book centers on the CIA mission to assassinate Cambodian Crown Prince Nordum Sihanouk, the author's unilateral aborting of the mission, the CIA's dispatch of an ARVN regiment to attack and destroy the camp and kill every person in it as retribution for defying the agency, and the dramatic rescue of eight American Green Berets and hundreds of South Viet Namese.

DANIEL MARVIN is a retired Lieutenant Colonel in the US Army Special Forces and former Green Beret.

Softcover: **$19.95** (ISBN 0977795314) • 420 pages • 150+ photos & maps

Fighting For G.O.D.
(Gold, Oil, Drugs)
BY JEREMY BEGIN, ART BY LAUREEN SALK

This racehorse tour of American history and current affairs scrutinizes key events transcending the commonly accepted liberal/conservative political ideologies — in a large-size comic-book format.

This analysis delves into aspects of the larger framework into which 9/11 fits and scrutinizes the ancestry of the players who transcend commonly accepted liberal/conservative political ideologies. This comic-book format analysis examines the Neo Con agenda and its relationship to "The New World Order. This book discusses key issues confronting America's citizenry and steps the populace can take to not only halt but reverse the march towards totalitarianism.

Jeremy Begin is a long-time activist/organizer currently residing in California's Bay Area. Lauren Salk is an illustrator living in Boston.

Softcover: **$9.95**, (ISBN 0977795330) 64 Pages, 8.5 x 11

Me & Lee
HOW I CAME TO KNOW, LOVE AND LOSE
LEE HARVEY OSWALD
BY JUDYTH VARY BAKER
FOREWORD BY
EDWARD T. HASLAM

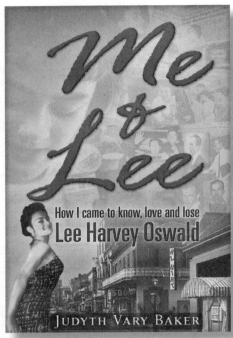

JUDYTH VARY WAS ONCE A PROMISING science student who dreamed of finding a cure for cancer; this exposé is her account of how she strayed from a path of mainstream scholarship at the University of Florida to a life of espionage in New Orleans with Lee Harvey Oswald. In her narrative she offers extensive documentation on how she came to be a cancer expert at such a young age, the personalities who urged her to relocate to New Orleans, and what lead to her involvement in the development of a biological weapon that Oswald was to smuggle into Cuba to eliminate Fidel Castro. Details on what she knew of Kennedy's impending assassination, her conversations with Oswald as late as two days before the killing, and her belief that Oswald was a deep-cover intelligence agent who was framed for an assassination he was actually trying to prevent, are also revealed.

JUDYTH VARY BAKER is a teacher, and artist. Edward T. Haslam is the author of *Dr. Mary's Monkey*.
Hardcover • **$24.95** • ISBN 9780979988677 • 580 Pages

America's Nazi Secret
AN UNCENSORED HISTORY OF THE US JUSTICE DEPARTMENT'S OBSTRUCTION OF CONGRESSIONAL INVESTIGATIONS INTO AMERICANS WHO FUNDED HITLER, POSTWAR IMMIGRATION OF EASTERN EUROPEAN WAR CRIMINALS TO THE US, AND THE EVOLUTION OF THE ARAB NAZI MOVEMENT INTO MODERN MIDDLE EASTERN TERRORISTS
BY JOHN LOFTUS

Fully revised and expanded, this stirring account reveals how the U.S. government permitted the illegal entry of Nazis into North America in the years following World War II. This extraordinary investigation exposes the secret section of the State Department that began, starting in 1948 and unbeknownst to Congress and the public until recently, to hire members of the puppet wartime government of Byelorussia—a region of the Soviet Union occupied by Nazi Germany. A former Justice Department investigator uncovered this stunning story in the files of several government agencies, and it is now available with a chapter previously banned from release by authorities and a foreword and afterword with recently declassified materials.

John Loftus is a former U.S. government prosecutor, a former Army intelligence officer, and the author of numerous books, including *The Belarus Secret, The Secret War Against the Jews, Unholy Trinity: How the Vatican's Nazi Networks Betrayed Western Intelligence to the Soviets*, and *Unholy Trinity: The Vatican, the Nazis, and the Swiss Banks*. He has appeared regularly as a media commentator on ABC National Radio and Fox News. He lives in St. Petersburg, Florida.

Softcover • **$24.95** • ISBN 978-1-936296-04-0 • 288 Pages

The Hunt for Kuhn Sa
Drug Lord of the Golden Triangle
by Ron Felder

For TWO DECADES, the Burmese warlord Khun Sa controlled nearly 70 percent of the world's heroin supply, yet there has been little written about the legend the U.S. State Department branded the "most evil man in the world"—until now. Through exhaustive investigative journalism, this examination of one of the world's major drug lords from the 1970s to the 1990s goes behind the scenes into the lives of the DEA specialists assigned the seemingly impossible task of capturing or killing him. Known as Group 41, these men would fight for years in order to stop a man who, in fact, had the CIA to thank for his rise to power. Featuring interviews with DEA, CIA, Mafia, and Asian gang members, this meticulously researched and well-documented investigation reaches far beyond the expected and delves into the thrilling and shocking world of the CIA-backed heroin trade.

Ron Felber is the CEO of Chemetell, North America, and the author of eight books, including *Il Dottore: The Double Life of a Mafia Doctor*, *Presidential Lessons in Leadership*, and *Searchers: A True Story of Alien Abduction*. He lives in New Jersey.

Softover • **$19.95** • ISBN 9781936296156 • 240 Pages

1-800-556-2012

Mary's Mosaic
Mary Pinchot Meyer & John F. Kennedy and their Vision for World Peace

by Peter Janney
Foreword by Dick Russell

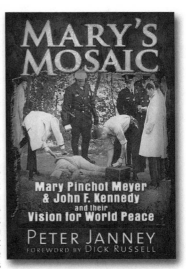

Challenging the conventional wisdom surrounding the murder of Mary Pinchot Meyer, this exposé offers new information and evidence that individuals within the upper echelons of the CIA were not only involved in the assassination of President John F. Kennedy, but her demise as well. Written by the son of a CIA lifer and a college classmate of Mary Pinchot Meyer, this insider's story examines how Mary used events and circumstances in her personal life to become an acolyte for world peace. The most famous convert to her philosophy was reportedly President John F. Kennedy, with whom she was said to have begun a serious love relationship in January 1962. Offering an insightful look into the era and its culture, the narrative sheds light on how in the wake of the Cuban Missile Crisis, she helped the president realize that a Cold War mentality was of no use and that the province of world peace was the only worthwhile calling. Details on her experiences with LSD, its influences on her and Kennedy's thinking, his attempts to negotiate a limited nuclear test ban treaty with Soviet Premier Nikita Khrushchev, and to find lasting peace with Fidel Castro are also included.

Peter Janney is a former psychologist and naturopathic healer and a cofounder of the American Mental Health Alliance. He was one of the first graduates of the MIT Sloan School of Management's Entrepreneurship Skills Transfer Program. He lives in Beverly, Massachusetts. Dick Russell is the author of *Black Genius: And the American Experience*, *Eye of the Whale*, *The Man Who Knew Too Much*, and *Striper Wars: An American Fish Story*. He is a former staff writer for *TV Guide* magazine, a staff reporter for *Sports Illustrated*, and has contributed numerous articles to publications ranging from *Family Health* to the *Village Voice*. He lives in Boston, Massachusetts and Los Angeles.

Hardcover • **$29.95** • ISBN 978-1-936296-49-1 • 576 Pages

Radical Peace
BY WILLIAM HATHAWAY
REFUSING WAR

THIS SYMPHONY OF VOICES — a loosely united network of war resisters, deserters, and peace activists in Afghanistan, Europe, Iraq, and North America — vividly recounts the actions they have personally taken to end war and create a peaceful society. Frustrated, angered, and even saddened by the juggernaut of aggression that creates more counter-violence at every turn, this assortment of contributors has moved beyond demonstrations and petitions into direct, often radical actions in defiance of the government's laws to impede its capacity to wage war. Among the stories cited are those of a European peace group that assisted a soldier in escaping from military detention and then deserting; a U.S.-educated Iraqi who now works in Iran developing cheaper and smaller heat-seeking missiles to shoot down U.S. aircraft after U.S. soldiers brutalized his family; a granny for peace who found young allies in her struggle against military recruiting; a seminary student who, having been roughed up by U.S. military at a peace demonstration, became a military chaplain and subverts from within; and a man who expresses his resistance through the destruction of government property — most often by burning military vehicles.

WILLIAM T. HATHAWAY is a political journalist and a former Special Forces soldier turned peace activist whose articles have appeared in more than 40 publications, including *Humanist*, the *Los Angeles Times, Midstream Magazine*, and *Synthesis/Regeneration*. He is an adjunct professor of American studies at the University of Oldenburg in Germany, and the author of *A World of Hurt, CD-Ring*, and *Summer Snow*.

Softcover: **$14.95** (ISBN: 9780979988691) •240 pages • Size: 5.5 x 8.5

Fixing America
Breaking the Stranglehold of Corporate Rule, Big Media, and the Religious Right
BY JOHN BUCHANAN, FOREWORD BY JOHN MCCONNELL

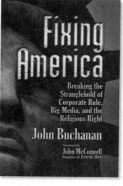

An explosive analysis of what ails the United States
An award-winning investigative reporter provides a clear, honest diagnosis of corporate rule, big media, and the religious right in this damning analysis. Exposing the darker side of capitalism, this critique raises alarms about the security of democracy in today's society, including the rise of the corporate state, the insidious role of professional lobbyists, the emergence of religion and theocracy as a right-wing political tactic, the failure of the mass media, and the sinister presence of an Orwellian neo-fascism.

Softcover: **$19.95**, (ISBN 0-975290681) 216 Pages, 5.5 x 8.5

Fleshing Out Skull & Bones
Investigations into America's Most Powerful Secret Society
EDITED BY KRIS MILLEGAN

"From original 19th-century rosters and nearly forgotten archives right up to recent aerial photos of the Bonesmen's 'Tomb,' no stone is left unturned in this must-read book for anyone desiring to know the truth behind this mysterious organization which has produced an unnatural number of national leaders. Names are named— including President George W. Bush—and the group's affiliation with a German Illuminati cell revealed, all in one well-documented volume." —Jim Marrs, journalist and author, *Rule by Secrecy* and *The War on Freedom*

This chronicle of espionage, drug smuggling, and elitism in Yale University's Skull & Bones society offers rare glimpses into this secret world with previously unpublished documents, photographs, and articles that delve into issues such as racism, financial ties to the Nazi party, and illegal corporate dealings. Contributors include Anthony Sutton, author of America's Secret Establishment; Dr. Ralph Bunch, professor emeritus of political science at Portland State University; Webster Griffin Tarpley and Anton Chaitkin, authors and historians. A complete list of members, including George Bush, George W. Bush, and John F. Kerry, and reprints of rare magazine articles are included.

Kris Millegan is the son of a CIA intelligence official. He has written articles for *High Times* and *Paranoia Magazine*. He lives in Oregon.

Softcover: **$24.95**, (ISBN 0-975290681) 216 Pages, 5.5 x 8.5

The Franklin Scandal
A Story of Powerbrokers, Child Abuse & Betrayal
BY NICK BRYANT

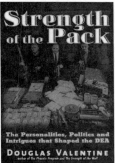

A chilling exposé of corporate corruption and government cover-ups, this account of a nationwide child-trafficking and pedophilia ring tells a sordid tale of corruption in high places. The scandal originally surfaced during an investigation into Omaha, Nebraska's failed Franklin Federal Credit Union and took the author beyond the Midwest and ultimately to Washington, D.C.. Implicating businessmen, senators, major media corporations, the CIA, and even the venerable Boys Town organization, this extensively researched report includes firsthand interviews with key witnesses and explores a controversy that has received scant media attention.

The Franklin Scandal is the story of a underground ring that pandered children to a cabal of the rich and powerful. The ring's pimps were a pair of Republican powerbrokers who used Boys Town as a pedophiliac reservoir, and had access to the highest levels of our government and connections to the CIA.

Nick Bryant is a journalist whose work largely focuses on the plight of disadvantaged children in the United States. His mainstream and investigative journalism has been featured in Gear, Playboy, The Reader, and on Salon.com. He is the coauthor of America's Children: Triumph of Tragedy. He lives in New York City.

Hardcover: **$24.95** (ISBN: 0977795357) • 480 pages • Size: 6 x 9

Strength of the Pack
The Personalities, Politics and Intrigues that Shaped the DEA
BY DOUG VALENTINE

Through interviews with former narcotics agents, politicians, and bureaucrats, this exposé documents previously unknown aspects of the history of federal drug law enforcement from the formation of the Bureau of Narcotics and Dangerous Drugs and the creation of the Drug Enforcement Administration (DEA) up until the present day. Written in an easily accessible style, the narrative examines how successive administrations expanded federal drug law enforcement operations at home and abroad; investigates how the CIA comprised the war on drugs; analyzes the Reagan, Bush, and Clinton administrations' failed attempts to alter the DEA's course; and traces the agency's evolution into its final and current stage of "narco-terrorism."

Douglas Valentine is a former private investigator and consultant and the author of The Hotel Tacloban, The Phoenix Program, The Strength of the Wolf, and TDY.

Hardcover: **$24.95** (ISBN: 9780979988653) Softcover **$19.95** (ISBN 9781936296095) • 480 pages • Size: 6 x 9

A TERRIBLE MISTAKE
THE MURDER OF FRANK OLSON AND THE CIA'S SECRET COLD WAR EXPERIMENTS
BY H.P. ALBARELLI JR.

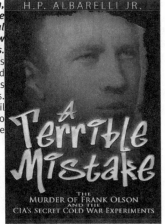

In his nearly 10 years of research into the death of Dr. Frank Olson, writer and investigative journalist H.P. Albarelli Jr. gained unique and unprecedented access to many former CIA, FBI, and Federal Narcotics Bureau officials, including several who actually oversaw the CIA's mind- control programs from the 1950s to the early 1970s.

A Terrible Mistake takes readers into a frequently bizarre and always frightening world, colored and dominated by Cold War concerns and fears. For the past 30 years the death of biochemist Frank Olson has ranked high on the nation's list of unsolved and perplexing mysteries. A Terrible Mistake solves the mystery and reveals in shocking detail the identities of Olson's murderers. The book also takes readers into the strange world of government mind-control programs and close collaboration with the Mafia.

H. P. Albarelli Jr. is an investigative journalist whose work has appeared in numerous publications and newspapers across the nation and is the author of the novel The Heap. He lives in Tampa, Florida.

Hardcover **$34.95** (ISBN 978-0977795376) • 852 pages • Size: 6 x 9
Softcover **$29.95** (ISBN 978-1936296088)

America's Secret Establishment
An Introduction to the Order of Skull & Bones
BY ANTONY C. SUTTON

The book that first exposed the story behind America's most powerful secret society

For 170 years they have met in secret. From out of their initiates come presidents, senators, judges, cabinet secretaries, and plenty of spooks. This intriguing behind-the-scenes look documents Yale's secretive society, the Order of the Skull and Bones, and its prominent members, numbering among them Tafts, Rockefellers, Pillsburys, and Bushes. Far from being a campus fraternity, the society is more concerned with the success of its members in the post-collegiate world.

Softcover: **$19.95** (ISBN 0972020748) 335 pages

Sinister Forces
A Grimoire of American Political Witchcraft
Book One: The Nine
BY PETER LEVENDA, FOREWORD BY JIM HOUGAN

A shocking alternative to the conventional views of American history.

The roots of coincidence and conspiracy in American politics, crime, and culture are examined in this book, exposing new connections between religion, political conspiracy, and occultism. Readers are taken from ancient American civilization and the mysterious mound builder culture to the Salem witch trials, the birth of Mormonism during a ritual of ceremonial magic by Joseph Smith, Jr., and Operations Paperclip and Bluebird. Not a work of speculative history, this exposé is founded on primary source material and historical documents. Fascinating details are revealed, including the bizarre world of "wandering bishops" who appear throughout the Kennedy assassinations; a CIA mind control program run amok in the United States and Canada; a famous American spiritual leader who had ties to Lee Harvey Oswald in the weeks and months leading up to the assassination of President Kennedy; and the "Manson secret.

Hardcover: **$29.95** (ISBN 0975290622) • 396 pages • Size: 6 x 9

Book Two: A Warm Gun
The roots of coincidence and conspiracy in American politics, crime, and culture are investigated in this analysis that exposes new connections between religion, political conspiracy, terrorism, and occultism. Readers are provided with strange parallels between supernatural forces such as shamanism, ritual magic, and cult practices, and contemporary interrogation techniques such as those used by the CIA under the general rubric of MK-ULTRA. Not a work of speculative history, this exposé is founded on primary source material and historical documents. Fascinating details on Nixon and the "Dark Tower," the Assassin cult and more recent Islamic terrorism, and the bizarre themes that run through American history from its discovery by Columbus to the political assassinations of the 1960s are revealed.

Hardcover: **$29.95** (ISBN 0975290630) • 392 pages • Size: 6 x 9

Book Three: The Manson Secret
The Stanislavski Method as mind control and initiation. Filmmaker Kenneth Anger and Aleister Crowley, Marianne Faithfull, Anita Pallenberg, and the Rolling Stones. Filmmaker Donald Cammell (Performance) and his father, CJ Cammell (the first biographer of Aleister Crowley), and his suicide. Jane Fonda and Bluebird. The assassination of Marilyn Monroe. Fidel Castro's Hollywood career. Jim Morrison and witchcraft. David Lynch and spiritual transformation. The technology of sociopaths. How to create an assassin. The CIA, MK-ULTRA and programmed killers.

Softcover **$24.95** (ISBN 9780984185832) • 422 pages • Size: 6 x 9